PENGUIN BOOKS

NEFERTITI

Joyce Ann Tyldesley was born in Bolton, Lancashire. She gained a first-class honours degree in archaeology from Liverpool University in 1981 and a doctorate from Oxford University in 1986. She is now Honorary Research Fellow at the School of Archaeology, Classics and Oriental Studies at Liverpool University, and a freelance writer and lecturer on Egyptian archaeology. Her previous books include *Daughters of Isis*, *Hatchepsut*, *Ramesses*, *The Private Lives of the Pharaohs*, *Egypt's Golden Empire*, *Judgement of the Pharaoh*, *The Mummy*, *Pyramids* and *Tales from Ancient Egypt*.

NEFERTITI

EGYPT'S SUN QUEEN

JOYCE TYLDESLEY

Revised edition

PENGUIN BOOKS

PENGUIN BOOKS

Published by the Penguin Group
Penguin Books Ltd, 80 Strand, London WC2R ORL, England
Penguin Group (USA) Inc., 375 Hudson Street, New York, New York 10014, USA
Penguin Group (Canada), 10 Alcorn Avenue, Toronto, Ontario, Canada M4V 3B2
(a division of Pearson Penguin Canada Inc.)
Penguin Ireland, 25 St Stephen's Green, Dublin 2, Ireland
(a division of Penguin Books Ltd)
Penguin Group (Australia), 250 Camberwell Road,
Camberwell, Victoria 3124, Australia (a division of Pearson Australia Group Pty Ltd)
Penguin Books India Pvt Ltd, 11 Community Centre,
Panchsheel Park, New Delhi – 110 017, India
Penguin Group (NZ), cnr Airborne and Rosedale Roads, Albany,
Auckland 1310, New Zealand (a division of Pearson New Zealand Ltd)
Penguin Books (South Africa) (Pty) Ltd, 24 Sturdee Avenue,
Rosebank 2196, South Africa

Penguin Books Ltd, Registered Offices: 80 Strand, London WC2R ORL, England

www.penguin.com

First published in Viking 1998
Published in Penguin Books 2003
This edition with revisions published in Penguin Books 2005

2

Copyright © Joyce Tyldesley, 1998, 2005
All rights reserved

The moral right of the author has been asserted

Set by Rowland Phototypesetting Ltd, Bury St Edmunds, Suffolk
Printed in England by Clays Ltd, St Ives plc

For Frank and Su,
who in the past eight years
have been joined by
Louisa and Phoebe.

Contents

Plates

replica of the Berlin head reproduced on the cover, in Bolton
Museum & Art Gallery, Bolton)

Photographic Acknowledgements

AKG London: 9, 13
Author collection: 19
Bildarchiv Preußischer Kulturbesitz, Berlin: 3, 14, 16, 17
British Museum, London: 4
Bulloz, Paris: 15
The Cleveland Museum of Art, Ohio: 12
C M Dixon, Canterbury: 1, 11
E T Archive, London: 5, 7
Giraudon, Paris: 2
National Museum, Cairo: 6, 8, 10
Werner Forman Archive, London: 18

Figures

Chapter 1

Chapter 2

Chapter 3

Map and Chronologies

The Amarna Royal Family

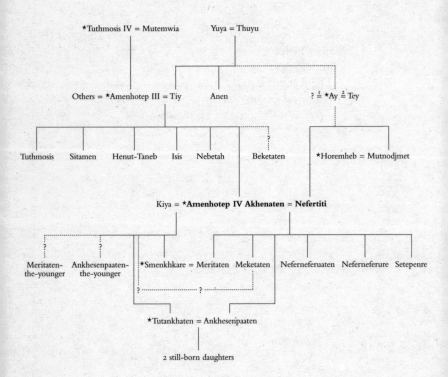

*Tuthmosis IV = Mutemwia   Yuya = Thuyu

Others = *Amenhotep III = Tiy   Anen   ? $\underline{1}$ *Ay $\underline{2}$ Tey

Tuthmosis Sitamen Henut-Taneb Isis Nebetah Beketaten   *Horemheb = Mutnodjmet

Kiya = **Amenhotep IV Akhenaten = Nefertiti**

Meritaten-the-younger Ankhesenpaaten-the-younger *Smenkhkare = Meritaten Meketaten   Neferneferuaten Neferneferure Setepenre

*Tutankhaten = Ankhesenpaaten

2 still-born daughters

*King of Egypt

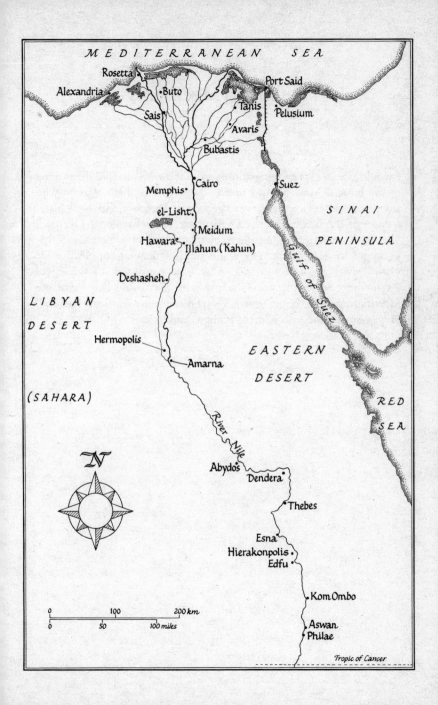

Acknowledgements

I would like to express my gratitude to all those involved in the writing of this book. Thanks are due to Eleo Gordon and Sheila Watson who gave practical advice whenever needed, to Professor Elizabeth Slater for use of the facilities of the Department of Archaeology, Liverpool University, and to the members of the Liverpool University S.E.S. photography department. The wonderful line drawings of Norman de Garis Davies are here reproduced by kind permission of the Egypt Exploration Society. Joyce Filer provided invaluable help with the identification of the bones from KV 55. Finally I must thank my husband, Steven Snape, and my children, Philippa and Jack.

Preface

In 1997 I wrote a book telling the story of Nefertiti's life. A year later that book was published as *Nefertiti: Egypt's Sun Queen*. Not exactly a biography – we lack too many of the major details and all of the minutiae and trivia of daily life to be able to write a full and unbiased history of any character from ancient Egypt – the book nevertheless included all the known archaeological and textual evidence concerning the life and death of Egypt's most famous queen.

Egyptology books can quickly become dated. Since my original book was published there has been a steady stream of scholarly publications concerning Nefertiti and her husband, the unorthodox pharaoh Akhenaten, plus a flurry of more speculative books, each claiming to reveal their own particular 'truth' about Nefertiti. In addition, there have been important developments in the field of mummy studies. While our understanding of Nefertiti's life remains fundamentally unchanged, our understanding of her death, or rather the treatment of her body beyond death, has been challenged by recent re-discoveries in the Valley of the Kings. The Amarna period, never simple, has grown alarmingly complex. We now have, in KV 55, a once-female mummy definitely reclassified as a young royal male, while in nearby KV 35 there rests a once-male mummy reclassified as a female – and a queen of Egypt, too – who may perhaps be male after all.

The intervening seven years – seven years of reading and of discussions with colleagues, students and friends – have also brought changes in my own understanding of the complexities of the Amarna age, and in particular the complexities of Amarna art. This therefore seems a good time to revise my original book. To eliminate the few factual errors and emotive assumptions that crept into the original text, to delete some of the endnotes which are not strictly necessary to my argument and which seem to annoy some readers, to revise the bibliography, and to expand chapters six and seven to take account of recent fieldwork. I have taken

a fresh look at all the evidence for the life and times of Nefertiti, and
have built on this to provide my own explanation of events at the end
of the Amarna age.

Introduction

The Hereditary Princess, Great in Favour, Lady of Grace, Endowed with Gladness. The Aten rises to shed favour on her and sets to multiply her love. The great and beloved wife of the King, Mistress of South and North, Lady of the Two Lands Nefertiti, may she live for ever.[1]

For just over a decade Queen Nefertiti was the most influential woman in the ancient world. Standing proud beside her husband Akhenaten, Nefertiti was the envy of all; a beautiful, fertile woman blessed by the sun-god, adored by her six daughters and worshipped by her people. Her image and her name were celebrated throughout Egypt and her future seemed golden. Suddenly Nefertiti disappeared from the heart of the royal family. No record survives to detail her death, no monument serves to mark her passing, and to this day her end remains an enigma. Nefertiti's body has never been recovered.

Soon after Nefertiti's disappearance her husband's unorthodox reign was erased from Egypt's official record. With history successfully re-written, king and queen were conveniently forgotten. It was as if Nefertiti and Akhenaten had never been. The decoding of the hieroglyphic script at the beginning of the nineteenth century restored Nefertiti's name to scholars, but she remained a shadowy figure, merely one amongst the many faceless queens of Egypt. It was left to archaeology to return her to her unique position in Egyptian history. A succession of egyptologists excavating at the Middle Egyptian site of Amarna did much to reconstruct her story, but it was not until 1924, when a painted limestone bust was put on display in Berlin Museum, that the general public became aware of Nefertiti's existence (plate 19). This was perfect timing. Western Europe, already experiencing a bout of Egypto-mania following the 1922 discovery of Tutankhamen, immediately hailed Nefertiti as one of the most beautiful and fascinating women of all time.

Ever since, this image of Nefertiti has stood alongside the death mask of Tutankhamen, the pyramids of Giza and the sphinx as a universally recognized symbol of Egypt's history. Nefertiti now gazes out from a wide variety of tourist-orientated bric-à-brac. Anything which could feasibly be embellished with her head has been, and the hapless holidaymaker looking for a suitable souvenir is presented with a tempting display ranging from Nefertiti earrings to key-rings, postcards, playing cards, tea-towels, tablecloths and of course 'ancient' papyri. Even the carrier bags from Cairo airport's duty-free shop display Nefertiti's image, and many of the tourists carefully selecting their Nefertiti-enhanced T-shirts seem completely unaware that the original bust is actually housed almost two thousand miles away in Berlin.

Nefertiti lived during the late 18th Dynasty, an idyllic period of unprecedented luxury tinged with more than a hint of decadence. Egypt had always been a wealthy country blessed with abundant natural resources and a plentiful supply of water but now, with an empire stretching unchallenged from Nubia to Syria, tribute and gifts poured in until the royal coffers were full as they had never been before. The Egyptian court was the sophisticated centre of the civilized world, and everyone bowed down before its king. Scribes, artists and craftsmen, stimulated by this new internationalism and, of course, by increased funding, started to produce some of their finest work; this was the age of lyric love poetry, sensual sculpture and brightly painted tombs. At the same time monumental architecture flourished and massive stone temples dedicated to a variety of gods started to dominate the skylines of towns and cities up and down the Nile.

The New Kingdom élite decorated their tombs with images of the idyllic life that they fully expected to enjoy beyond death. Theirs was an afterlife heavily based on their earlier Egyptian experiences. Here we can see the deceased dressed in robes of finest white linen as they enjoy a leisurely sail on the river or dawdle in a field of gleaming corn. Evenings are times of feasting and fun, when vast amounts of food can be washed down with endless cups of wine while listening to an all-female orchestra or watching an exciting troupe of semi-naked dancers. Even allowing for a certain amount of wishful thinking, the Egyptian upper classes had never had it so good. The middle classes, benefiting from the necessary expansion of the state bureaucracy, flourished in a more muted manner, while the labourers employed on the royal building projects were kept busy as they had never been before. Meanwhile the peasant farmers, the vast majority of the population, remained largely untouched by Egypt's new prosperity and continued to live the life led by their parents and grandparents before them.

The women of the 18th Dynasty enjoyed a freedom that made them unique in the ancient world. They had the same legal rights as men, and were permitted to own property, to work outside the home, and to live alone and raise their children without the protection of a male guardian. Nevertheless, few women received a formal education and, in a country where maybe between two and ten per cent of the population was literate, few women could read or write. Women were not expected to train for careers. They were expected to marry and produce children, and mothers enjoyed a position of great respect within the home and the wider community. Nefertiti was no exception. Born a non-royal member of Egypt's élite, she was married as a young girl to the most enigmatic individual in Egyptian history. By the age of thirty Nefertiti had borne at least six children and had transformed herself into a semi-divine human being. Meanwhile her husband, Akhenaten, had instigated a religious revolution and founded a capital city.

Akhenaten dominates Nefertiti's story making it impossible to entirely separate the two. I make no apology for including him as a major character throughout Nefertiti's tale. It is through his eyes – his sculptures, his monuments, his city and the unique demands of his religion – that we are allowed to look at his queen. We see only what he sanctioned, only what he wanted us to see, and Akhenaten appears, directly or indirectly, in every chapter of Nefertiti's life, subtly directing the way that we view his wife. Perhaps this is why so many writers have been keen to grant Nefertiti a life beyond the stifling confinement of Amarna, beyond her husband's overwhelming influence.

Akhenaten, the so-called heretic king formerly known as Amenhotep IV, had either the courage or the folly to challenge a religious tradition that stretched back over one and a half thousand years to Egypt's pre-historic past. Discarding many of the long-established gods, he replaced them with a single religious icon, the sun-disc or Aten. But who was Akhenaten? He has been famously described as: 'not only the world's

first idealist and the world's first *individual*, but also the earliest mono-
theist, and the first prophet of internationalism'.[2] His religious convic-
tions and distinctive, almost mystical, appearance have allowed him to
evolve beyond death, carrying him far beyond the narrow world of
Egyptian history into the realm of the occult. He now has his own
mythology celebrated by a diverse band of modern-day disciples who
range from the most scholarly of students of egyptology through those
interested in wider issues of religion to those who have been described,
with perhaps more accuracy than tact, as 'cranks'. Akhenaten has inspired
poets, artists, authors, composers, designers, theologians, Afrocentrists,
psychotherapists and fascists. The history of his cultural life beyond death
is now an academic subject in its own right.[3]

Nefertiti, too, has developed a cultural life beyond death. But unlike
Akhenaten, who is respected/hated for his thoughts and beliefs, Nefertiti
is celebrated worldwide first and foremost for her beauty. The Berlin
bust shows us an aloof, remote being, seemingly attractive to every
race, every generation and every gender of every age. It is a powerful,
compelling, and curiously modern image which allows Nefertiti's name
and face to sell beauty products to women born three thousand years
after her death. Nefertiti has joined that select band of beautiful, blessed
women – typified by Princess Diana and Princess Grace of Monaco –
whose perceived goodness masks the fact that they are real, thinking,
flesh and blood women. It is hard to accept the sudden disappearance of
these icons. This may explain why there are so many theories concerning
Nefertiti's final years, why so many archaeologists are intent on finding
her body.

Akhenaten has generally been recognized as a more complex character. He, more than any other ancient Egyptian, has been interpreted via
the cultural conditioning of his modern observers. Early egyptologists,
many of whom came to their subject as committed Christians intent on
expanding their knowledge of the Bible, generally respected Akhenaten
as the inspired founder of a pre-Christian monotheistic religion. Today
he is more widely regarded as an oddity whose ill-considered attempt
to impose a comfortless religion on his people was always doomed to
failure. His detractors have generally seen him as either an ineffectual
intellectual or a blinkered zealot, while his admirers have variously
recognized a pacifist theologian, the world's first openly gay man (a

charge also levied against him by his detractors), a brave king coping with a debilitating illness, or simply 'one of the most attractive characters in Egyptian history'.[4] Many have attempted to delve into Akhenaten's psyche with perhaps the most devastating, and in my view inaccurate, analysis being suggested by Velikovsky, a great admirer of the work of Freud:

Were it possible for King Akhnaton (sic) to cross the time barrier and lie down on an analyst's couch, the analysis would at an early stage reveal autistic or narcissistic traits, a homosexual tendency, with sadism suppressed and feminine traits coming to the fore, and a strong unsuppressed Oedipus complex.[5]

In a remarkable flouting of centuries of tradition Akhenaten allowed Nefertiti to play a major role in his new religion. The queen was now to be regarded as the female element of the new state god, and as such was permitted to perform rituals hitherto restricted to the king. The late 17th and earlier 18th Dynasties had already yielded a series of powerful queen regents and queen consorts, with Tiy, wife of Amenhotep III and mother of Akhenaten, one of the most prominent. Tiy, conspicuously featured in many inscriptions and statues, abandoned traditional queenly reticence and stood alongside rather than behind her husband, providing the female complement to his kingly role. Weigall was not the only historian to believe that Tiy was effectively the power behind two thrones, not only ruling on behalf of her lazy, effeminate husband, but exerting a strong, almost unwholesome, influence over her young son:

... there is every reason to suppose that queen Tiy possessed the ability to impress the claims of new thought upon her husband's mind, and gradually to turn his eyes, and those of the court, away from the sombre worship of Amon (sic) into the direction of the brilliant cult of the sun ... By the time that Amenophis III had reigned for thirty years or so, he had ceased to give much attention to state affairs, and the power had almost entirely passed into the capable hands of Tiy.[6]

Mother was therefore to be blamed, or praised, for Akhenaten's all-consuming absorption in the sun-cult. Freud, neatly classifying Akhenaten as one of the earliest examples of the Oedipus complex, very much enjoyed Weigall's writings. Weigall was, however, drawing his conclusions at a time when the archaeological record was profoundly biased. Many of Tiy's monuments were known but few of Nefertiti's had yet been recovered or identified. This selective recovery naturally led to the distortion of each woman's relative importance so that Tiy was for a long time assumed to be the dominant queen – indeed almost the dominant royal – of the Amarna epoch. Tiy therefore overshadows Nefertiti in almost all early accounts of Akhenaten's reign, and Janet Buttles when writing the history of the Queens of Egypt in 1908 was only able to accord Nefertiti a meagre six pages.[7] More recent restoration work at Karnak and Amarna has done much to redress this imbalance of evidence, and today the relative importance of the two can be more accurately assessed, as can the long-overlooked influence of Amenhotep III in his son's life. Although the assumption that Tiy was pharaoh in all but name must now be discarded and there is no evidence at all to indicate that she was the mastermind behind Akhenaten's religious reforms, it cannot be denied that Tiy set a useful precedent. By the time Nefertiti became queen the active consort was an accepted phenomenon and it was natural for Akhenaten and Nefertiti to develop this role one step further.

The distortion of the archaeological record in respect of the relative importance of Tiy and Nefertiti is a sobering reminder of the problems that can beset an author attempting to reconstruct the life of a person who lived over three thousand years ago. Our knowledge of all dynastic Egyptians has to be gleaned from a random assortment of archaeological remains supplemented by a small collection of historical documents plus a great deal of religious and mortuary art and architecture. The Amarna period in particular has suffered from ancient and modern vandalism, and from a deliberate attempt to erase all memory of Akhenaten and Nefertiti from Egypt's history. The evidence that remains is in many respects infuriatingly vague. We simply do not have the information to write the definitive 'warts and all' biography which we have come to expect of more modern subjects. Anyone who claims to be able to reveal the true story of the Amarna age is wrong. Every aspect of Nefertiti's life has to be pieced together from meagre shreds of evidence which are often capable of a variety of interpretations, while there is at all times the possibility that a single archaeological find may overturn decades of scholarly reasoning. Egyptologists have argued long and hard, and indeed are still arguing, over many aspects of Nefertiti's queenship. As a result, Nefertiti's story has evolved into a fascinating tale of archaeological detection, and her life has become inextricably entangled with the thoughts and deeds of those who have sought to re-discover her.

The New Kingdom Egyptians, always highly practical, built their temples and tombs of stone or cut them into living rock so that they might last for ever. Meanwhile palaces, towns and villages were built of mud-brick, a plentiful and inexpensive material eminently suited to the climate. The ease with which pharaohs were able to raise and occupy new palaces and, indeed, entire cities (Akhenaten at Amarna, Ramesses II at Pi-Ramesses to give just two examples) never ceases to amaze observers accustomed to modern building procedures. But the elaborately decorated palaces, plastered, painted and tiled so that they sparkled in the ever-present sunlight, were temporary structures, doomed in some cases to last for less than one reign. Almost all the domestic sites of Egypt have now crumbled away and many have been flattened and built over so that they lie under many centuries of domestic architecture. Others have been ruthlessly pillaged by local peasants seeking *sebakh*, a highly fertile soil formed by the decomposed mud-brick.

We are therefore extremely lucky to have two relatively well-preserved sites surviving from the reign of Akhenaten and his father Amenhotep III. The Malkata Palace, an extensive and rambling complex of buildings situated on the west bank of the River Nile at Thebes, was occupied by both father and son and, although now reduced to the level of a ground-plan, has proved a mine of information for archaeologists. Of even greater importance is Akhenaten's new city of Akhetaten – now known as Amarna – which was built, occupied and abandoned all within the space of thirty years and which in consequence is able to provide us with a snapshot of late 18th Dynasty daily life. Amarna can never be regarded as a typical Egyptian city, but is of crucial importance to those studying events during Akhenaten's reign.

Amarna was deserted a short time after the death of Akhenaten when the court returned to Thebes. Soon after, the persecution of Akhenaten's memory began. In a determined attempt to remove all trace of the heretic and his religion from the historical record monuments were dismantled, Akhenaten's image was defaced and his name was removed from the list of kings of Egypt. Nefertiti, as both queen and coworshipper, suffered a similar fate. It is therefore ironic that, in spite of this deliberate vandalism, the atypical Akhenaten is now one of the most famous kings of Egypt while Nefertiti's name is recognized by millions. The excavation of the Amarna studio of the sculptor Tuthmosis has yielded some breathtaking pieces abandoned in the move to Thebes, including the famous Berlin bust of Nefertiti, and the women of Amarna are now far better known to us than the women of any other dynastic court. We may have no contemporary unbiased description of the queen and her actions, but we have more engravings and sculptures of Nefertiti than of any other Egyptian queen.

One Amarna treasure, however, was never properly excavated. In 1887 a peasant woman digging for *sebakh* at Amarna stumbled across hundreds of sun-dried clay tablets inscribed with odd signs. Her attempts to sell the tablets were frustrated by the 'experts' who declared them to be forgeries. By the time they were recognized as genuine antiquities, fewer than four hundred tablets and fragments remained. We now know that the tablets, inscribed in cuneiform and written in the language of ancient Babylon, are the remains of the correspondence between Egypt and her neighbours and vassals in the Near East. Most of the letters are addressed to the king of Egypt, but a few represent copies of his responses. The collection is both incomplete and presents difficulties of translation, with many of the letters being undated and therefore difficult to sort into chronological order. Nevertheless, the so-called Amarna Letters have provided scholars with tantalizing glimpses of New Kingdom diplomacy, and of the characters who ruled the great Bronze Age states of the Near East.

Throughout this book I have avoided the use of calendar dates, preferring to use dynasties and regnal years to pinpoint specific events. The Egyptians themselves dated events by reference to the reign of the current king, and this dating of necessity started afresh with every new monarch. Thus we have a hieratic docket from Amarna which, originally dated to Year 17 – the final year of Akhenaten's rule – was, on the death of the king, re-labelled to Year 1 of his successor's reign. By modern convention the various reigns are grouped into families or dynasties, and further sub-divided into successive 'Kingdoms' and 'Intermediate Periods'. Akhenaten's rule therefore belongs to the latter part of the 18th Dynasty, which is itself a part of the New Kingdom. In order to keep track of their country's history the ancient scribes were forced to maintain lengthy lists of successive kings and their reign lengths. The accuracy of these lists was distorted by inadvertent errors, by co-regencies and by the deliberate omission of kings such as Akhenaten who were excluded because of their unacceptable behaviour. Although several king lists have survived it has not proved possible to tie them in exactly with our modern dating system so that precise calendar dates for Akhenaten's rule are a matter of some debate, although he is most likely to have reigned for seventeen years from approximately 1353 to 1336 BC (BC being the direct equivalent of the more modern BCE).

Hieroglyphs preserve only the consonants within Egyptian words. As we are lacking all vowels, it is often impossible to decide the original pronunciation of a particular word and, because of this, Egyptian names may be found with many different modern spellings. The personal names used in this book have all been chosen to reflect the names most familiar to modern readers, although any errors of translation have been corrected. Thus Nefertiti remains Nefertiti throughout, even though for many years she was more formally known as Neferneferuaten-Nefertiti. Her husband started his reign as Amenhotep IV and then changed his name to Akhenaten; to avoid confusion I refer to him as Amenhotep in Chapters 1 and 2, Akhenaten thereafter. Queen Tiy, and the Lady Tey wife of Ay, shared a name. However I have used variant spellings to differentiate between the two women. Akhenaten's capital city, Akhetaten, is consistently referred to as Amarna even though this is an entirely modern, made-up name, a contraction of Tell-Amarna which is itself derived from the nearby villages of el-Till and Beni Amran. Amarna is not in fact an archaeological *tell* (a high mound formed by the compacted remains of mud-brick buildings). It is a flat site with relatively little stratigraphy. Akhenaten would never have referred to himself as a pharaoh as this is a modern metonymy derived from the Egyptian term *per a'a* (literally 'great house'). However I use the words king and pharaoh interchangeably in order to avoid stylistic monotony. These inconsistencies seem to me to be justified on the grounds of clarity; I can only apologize if they offend any egyptological purists.

1

The Imperial Family

*Words to be spoken by Amen, Lord of the Thrones of the Two Lands
in front of her majesty . . . 'Amenhotep III, ruler of Thebes, is the name
of this child whom I have planted in your womb . . . His shall be an
excellent kingship throughout the entire land. My soul is his, my honour
is his, my crown is his. It is he who shall rule the Two Lands like Re
for ever.'[1]*

Once upon a time, a long time ago in a far-away land, the king of the
gods, Amen-Re, fell in love with a fair maiden who dwelt in the
southern Egyptian city of Thebes. Thoth, his ibis-headed messenger, was
dispatched to Egypt where he discovered that the maiden, Mutemwia,
was indeed fair, easily the most beautiful woman in the land, but that she
was a married lady, a wife of King Tuthmosis IV. Amen-Re found
himself haunted by thoughts of Mutemwia's charms. He very much
wanted to sleep with her, but knew that she would always be faithful to
her husband. So Amen-Re hatched a cunning plan to seduce his beloved,
and to make her the mother of his child. When night fell, the great god
disguised himself as Tuthmosis and crept into the bedchamber where
Mutemwia lay dreaming:

There he found her as she slept in the innermost part of her palace. His divine
fragrance awoke her. Amen went to her immediately, he lusted after her.
When he had appeared before her he allowed her to see him in the form of a
god; the sight of his beauty made her rejoice. Amen's love entered her body,
and the palace was filled with the fragrance of the god, as sweet as the scents
from Punt . . .[2]

Nine months later Mutemwia bore a son whom Amen-Re decreed
should be named Amenhotep after her husband's father. That son was

destined to become Nebmaatre Amenhotep III, Ruler of Thebes, the
Good God, Lord of the Two Lands, Son of Re, Lord of Appearances,
and Beloved of Amen.

Amenhotep III acceded to the throne of the world's only acknowledged
superpower in his early teens, his father, Tuthmosis IV, having ruled
for only nine years. During his brief reign Tuthmosis had raised an
obelisk at the Karnak Temple, campaigned successfully in Nubia and
established good diplomatic relations with the Syrian kingdom of Mitanni by marrying the daughter of King Artatama I. His main claim to fame
was, however, that he had instigated the world's first rescue archaeology
by freeing the great sphinx at Giza from the sand which threatened to
overwhelm it completely. A stela set between the paws of the sphinx tells
us how, as a young prince hunting in the Giza desert, Tuthmosis had fallen
asleep in the shadow of the monument. The sun god, Re-Harakhty, had
spoken to him in a dream and had asked that the sphinx be saved from his
sandy grave.[3] As a reward, the grateful god granted Tuthmosis the throne
of Egypt, even though he was only a younger son of Amenhotep II.
The body of Tuthmosis IV, now housed in Cairo Museum, shows that
the king died an emaciated young man whose long, narrow face was,
in the opinion of the anatomist G. Elliot Smith, 'very effeminate [in]
appearance'.[4]

   Thanks to the military expertise and administrative skills of his 18th
Dynasty forebears who had ruled Egypt for almost 200 years, the young

Fig. 1.1   The royal names of Amenhotep III

Amenhotep III inherited an empire whose borders stretched from the fourth Nile cataract in Nubia to northern Syria, and whose sphere of influence extended much further afield. Following Egyptian tradition the widowed Mutemwia ruled as regent during the first few years of her young son's reign, and under her guidance Amenhotep grew into the archetypal New Kingdom monarch, healthy, vigorous and brave. His courage in the hunting field was unprecedented; by his own account he shot 102 savage lions in the first ten years of his reign, while in a single day's hunting in the Faiyum he killed no fewer than fifty-six wild bulls. His bravery on the field of battle was less easy to prove. The well-trained Egyptian army was second to none in the ancient world, and a severe shortage of enemies willing to face inevitable defeat made it virtually impossible for Amenhotep to enjoy the sort of victorious campaign which had enhanced the reputations of earlier 18th Dynasty kings. This difficulty was eventually overcome by elevating a minor Nubian scuffle in Year 5 into the status of a full-blown war. Amenhotep's victory against the vile Ibhat, which yielded a meagre 740 living captives and 312 hands cut from the bodies of the dead, was commemorated by a series of stelae erected at strategic points in Nubia, while monumental carvings along Egypt's southern border at Aswan showed Amenhotep in the traditional role of pharaoh as defender of Egypt, smiting his enemies in the presence of the gods.

The predictable behaviour of the River Nile made Amenhotep's own country the most prosperous and fertile in the ancient world. The annual inundation, or flooding, ensured that the Egyptian farmers could, with relatively little effort, grow crops which were the envy of their neighbours and, while the agricultural land was under water, provided a vast labour force available for work on state projects. If the Nile failed to flood, or if the waters rose too high, there could be grave problems, but Amenhotep was truly blessed by Amen, and the Nile behaved impeccably throughout his lengthy reign. Grain was grown in vast quantities; it was used to pay the wages and to make the bread and beer which were staples of the Egyptian diet, while any surplus was stored in vast warehouses to provide against future lean times. Amenhotep's highly efficient civil service, which included a band of tax collectors who visited the primary producers on a regular basis to extract payment in kind, ensured that the warehouses were constantly topped-up.

Life was good for those who dwelt along the Nile. A wide range of vegetables, fruit, fish, fowl, small game and meat was available to supplement the basic diet of bread and beer. The thick Nile mud, sun-dried into bricks, made an excellent and very cheap building material, while both limestone and sandstone were available for the more permanent construction of temples and tombs. Flax was grown to spin into linen cloth, papyrus was grown for paper, and the deserts which bounded the Nile Valley were exploited for their precious metals and minerals which included gold, turquoise, amethyst and jasper. Only good quality timber was missing; this had to be imported from Lebanon. This superabundance of natural bounty had been boosted during the earlier part of the 18th Dynasty by the booty brought back from successful foreign campaigns. As the Egyptian empire grew, the royal coffers were further supplemented by the taxes and tribute extracted from Asian and African vassals eager to remain on good terms with their overlord. Egypt now held control over Nubia's mineral riches, and a steady stream of gold flowed into the treasury. At the same time there was an expansion in merchant shipping and an increase in foreign trade which was accompanied by an influx of exotic visitors who introduced new ideas and new skills so that Aegean, Asian and African influences started to creep into the hitherto rather insular Egyptian arts and crafts. Egypt was now truly cosmopolitan in a way that she had never been before.

Exaggerated rumours of Amenhotep's fabulous wealth spread throughout the Near East. His brother kings were envious and not too proud to try to divert some of that wealth towards themselves. A surprisingly large part of the surviving 18th Dynasty diplomatic correspondence is concerned with lists of valuable goods exchanged between kings, and there was a great deal of childish bickering over the relative values of presents expected, requested, received and sent. Tushratta of Mitanni, newly ascended to his throne, was certainly not too embarrassed to ask point-blank for a generous allocation of gold:

May my brother treat me ten times better than he did my father . . . May my brother send me in very great quantities gold that has not been worked, and may my brother send me much more gold than he sent to my father. For in my brother's country gold is as plentiful as dirt.[5]

Tushratta's letter was accompanied by a greeting gift which, although lacking the 'very great quantities of gold' which were so desirable, nevertheless included one inlaid golden goblet, twenty pieces of lapis lazuli, ten teams of horses, ten chariots and thirty men and women.

Egypt's New Kingdom population of approximately 4 million benefited from the strong economy. As the king grew ever richer he was able to pass his wealth downwards by creating employment for vast numbers of labourers and craftsmen. The civil service and the army had developed into efficient professional units; bureaucrats and soldiers were now rewarded for acts of outstanding loyalty or bravery by a gift of gold presented at a special ceremony by the grateful king. The priesthood of Amen-Re, already in receipt of a good income from its numerous assets supplemented by generous offerings from the royal palace, was now entitled to a large share of all foreign tribute, and the enormous temple storehouses were slowly filling. The new-found affluence of the Egyptian élite was reflected in the fashions of the day, which rejected the pure lines of the classic linen sheath dresses, kilts and tunics popular during the Old and Middle Kingdoms in favour of more frivolous garments; voluminous pleated, folded and fringed clothes were worn with full make-up, an array of semi-precious jewellery, earrings – a new fashion for men and women – and long, heavy wigs. The brightly painted tombs of the nobles on the west bank at Thebes suggest a relaxed hunting, fishing and banqueting lifestyle which makes the more muted Old and Middle Kingdom scenes appear positively austere.

Amenhotep, officially head of the army, the priesthood and the civil service, relied heavily upon the small core of bureaucrats who ran the country on his behalf. Included in his cabinet were men of high birth, born to inherit their fathers' positions, who had been raised alongside the king in the royal school, and men of more humble origin who had, by their exceptional intelligence and ability, earned promotion to the most influential positions in the land. Amenhotep gathered around him some of the finest administrators in his country's history, and Egypt's prosperity throughout his reign bears witness to their success. Most famous of all his bureaucrats was Amenhotep son of Hapu, a relatively humble man from the Delta town of Athribis who rose to become 'Scribe of Recruits' and 'Overseer of All Works of the King', and who was the mastermind behind the tasteful elegance of many of Amenhotep's

Theban monuments. Amenhotep son of Hapu was richly rewarded for his services; he was allowed to place his own statues in the temples of Amen and Mut at Karnak and was eventually given the unprecedented honour of a splendid mortuary temple close to that of his master on the west bank at Thebes. For many years after his death Amenhotep son of Hapu was revered as a wise man and worshipped as a demi-god at the Theban site of Deir el-Bahri. His cult continued until the Graeco-Roman period.

Freedom from expensive and time-consuming foreign campaigns allowed Amenhotep and his ministers to turn their attention inwards, towards the improvement of their own land. Making full use of the vast wealth and surplus labour at his disposal, and deploying some of the best architects and craftsmen which Egypt was ever to produce, Amenhotep instigated a building programme for the glorification of Egypt's gods and, of course, the commemoration of his own name. Construction started on an unprecedented scale up and down the Nile as insignificant mud-brick chapels were demolished to be replaced by impressive stone temples dedicated to an array of local gods. Heliopolis (temple of Horus), Sakkara (the Serapeum), Hermopolis (temple of Thoth) and Elephantine (temple of Khnum) were among those regional centres which benefited from the king's generosity. Nubia received more than her fair share of new monuments, while at the northern capital of Memphis the 'Castle of Nebmaatre', a temple dedicated jointly to the god Ptah and to Amenhotep himself, dazzled all who saw it.

At Thebes the Karnak complex, home of the state god Amen-Re and his family, saw building works at the temples of Mut and Montu. The beautiful White Chapel of Senwosret I, now demolished, was used as filling inside a magnificent decorated pylon or gateway which Amenhotep built to face the river, while a smaller undecorated pylon flanked by two colossal statues of the king was constructed on the south side of the temple of Amen. Gazing from an elegant plinth over the sacred lake, an outsized stone scarab-beetle observed the aquatic processions of the god and his entourage. All these monuments, erected with surprising speed given that Amenhotep's architects and builders were working without the modern benefits of steam power and the combustion engine, were well designed and well built, each lavishly decorated by master-craftsmen using the finest materials that the treasury could supply. Amenhotep himself tells us that his temple of Montu combined every type of noble and precious metal; the principal materials used included vast amounts of electrum (a mixture of silver and gold), gold, bronze and copper, augmented with lapis lazuli and turquoise.

Three kilometres to the south of Karnak stood the hitherto rather shabby Luxor Temple, a shrine dedicated jointly to Amen, to the ithyphallic god Min and to the celebration of the divine royal soul or *Ka*. Amenhotep rebuilt Luxor as a sandstone palace fit for the gods, so that it formed a suitable theatre for the annual Opet Festival, a lengthy celebration during which the king's own identity would effectively merge with that of Amen. This connection with the divine soul made Luxor an eminently suitable place for Amenhotep to tell the story of his divine conception as the son of Mutemwia and Amen-Re, a story-line which he had copied wholesale from the walls of King Hatchepsut's mortuary temple at nearby Deir el-Bahri.

The new Luxor Temple was linked to the Karnak Temple by an avenue of sphinxes, which allowed the gods to travel in public splendour between their various homes. Amenhotep was particularly fond of public processions, and he covered Thebes with a network of sacred routes connecting all the major east and west bank temple sites. On festival days the whole city celebrated as the gods emerged from the darkness of their shrines to sail along the processional avenues in their sacred boats carried high on the shoulders of their priests, accompanied by an entourage of soldiers, musicians, acrobats and dancers. The proper enjoyment of festivals was taken very seriously. At the west bank village of Deir el-Medina the workmen were given official leave from their labours in the Valley of the Kings in order to brew festival beer, while those afflicted with severe post-festival hangovers were allowed further time off work to recover.

On the west bank at Thebes Amenhotep built himself an immense mortuary temple of unprecedented luxury, recording its splendours on a stela housed within the temple itself:

A fortress made out of fine white sandstone, wrought entirely with gold, its floors decorated with silver and all of its doors decorated with electrum . . . Its lake was filled by the high Nile, possessor of fish and ducks, and brightened with baskets of flowers. Its workshops were filled with male and female servants . . .[6]

The temple functioned during the king's lifetime as a temple of Amen. After his death it would become more specialized, dedicated to servicing the cult of the dead king for all eternity.

Unfortunately, the mortuary temple intended to last for ever did not survive the vandalism of later pharaohs, most notably the 19th Dynasty King Merenptah, who demolished it in order to re-use its stone in their own buildings. However, the two seated quartzite statues of the king, each measuring 21.3m from pedestal to crown, which had originally flanked the temple entrance, remained untouched. There they still stand, isolated and battered but unbowed, beside the modern tourist road which leads to the west bank ferries. During the Graeco-Roman period these figures became known as the Colossi of Memnon, a corruption of Amenhotep's throne name, Nebmaatre, into the name of the legendary Ethiopian hero who had been killed by the Greek Achilles at Troy. Visitors to Thebes were taught that Memnon himself was buried at the feet of the northern monument, and when every morning an eerie moaning sound was heard to emanate from this figure, the noise was understood to be Memnon greeting his mother Eos (Aurora), goddess of the dawn. In fact the noise was the result of structural damage caused by an earthquake; its exact cause is not known and various theories have been suggested including the evaporation of night-time moisture from within the statue, wind whistling through the fissures in the figure, or the expansion of the stone warmed by the morning sun. When the Roman emperor Septimus Severus restored the monument, Memnon was heard to cry no more.

Every Egyptian king needed a queen to complete his role and supply the next heir to the throne. The divine triad of Osiris, Isis and Horus set the pattern for the ideal royal family and, just as Egypt could not function without a king, the king who took the role of Osiris could never be complete without his wife (Isis) and the son who would eventually replace him (Horus). Amenhotep III had inherited his father's harem and was not short of female companions, but he needed an official consort. He was therefore married within two years of his assumption to a young lady named Tiy, and Tiy, at twelve or thirteen years of age, became queen of the most powerful country in the world.[7]

. . . King of Upper and Lower Egypt, Nebmaatre, son of Re, Amenhotep ruler of Thebes, given life, and the king's principal wife Tiy, may she live. The name of her father is Yuya and the name of her mother is Thuyu; she is the wife of a mighty king . . .[8]

During the first eleven years of his reign Amenhotep 'published' a series of large scarabs inscribed with several lines of text commemorating important events. These scarabs, issued in the same way that a contemporary monarch might issue a commemorative medal or coin, were distributed throughout Egypt and sent abroad to impress his fellow kings. The undated scarab issued to publicize the royal marriage makes it clear that Tiy was the daughter of a non-royal couple named Yuya and Thuyu who hailed from the prosperous town of Akhmim on the east bank of the Nile, opposite the modern town of Sohag. That an 18th Dynasty king should select a queen who was not already a high-ranking member of the royal family was curious but certainly not unprecedented. Marriage with a close relative may have had many advantages but it was not compulsory and, although many kings chose to marry a full or half-sister, Tuthmosis III and Amenhotep II had both selected non-royal women as their principal wives. Amenhotep's own mother, Mutemwia, although she used the non-specific title of 'Heiress', never claimed to be the daughter of a king.

Amenhotep seems to have intended his marriage scarab to make an unusual situation clear to his people; to confirm that Tiy, although of relatively humble extraction, was not to be classed as a minor wife or a concubine. She was his consort, the queen of a great empire, and it was her son who would one day inherit the throne of Egypt. In fact Tiy was of humble birth only when compared to her exalted in-laws. Yuya and Thuyu were certainly not the 'Egyptians of mediocre, if not of low, extraction' identified by Gaston Maspero and others;[9] they were members of the wealthy and educated élite who effectively formed non-royal dynasties parallel to the royal dynasty, handing positions of trust and power from father to son. Such families were often linked by marriage both to each other and to the royal family, and it is possible that Yuya was already related to the young king, perhaps as the brother of Mutemwia. Yuya, a former army officer, held several important posts including 'Overseer of the King's Horses' and 'God's Father' and served as a high-ranking priest of Min. Thuyu, like many upper-class women, was included among the musicians of the state god Amen, and she was also active in the more local cults of Min and Hathor. Like her husband, she held a series of positions at court but, not surprisingly, the title which gave her most pleasure and which was repeated over and over again in her tomb was that of 'Royal Mother of the Chief Wife of the King'.

The queen's brother, Anen, was a man of some standing who served as an official of Re at Karnak and, more importantly, as the Second Prophet of Amen at Thebes at a time when the cult of Amen was one of the most powerful and wealthy presences in Egypt. Anen was eventually interred alongside the great and the good in the prestigious Sheik Abd el-Gurna burial site on the west bank at Thebes, where curiously his damaged tomb makes no mention of the fact that he was brother-in-law to the king. His sister's marriage may well have helped his career, but royal patronage via a sister was not something which Anen cared to acknowledge. Indeed, Anen's parentage is confirmed only because Thuyu includes his name on her sarcophagus, suggesting that he may have predeceased both his mother and his sister.

Circumstantial evidence suggests that Tiy had a second brother, a man called Ay. We know that a courtier of this name rose to prominence under Amenhotep IV, but unfortunately Ay does not include details of his parentage in his elaborately decorated tomb. We can tell that Ay was close to the royal family as he refers to himself as the 'One trusted by the good god' and 'Foremost of the companions of the king'. He includes among his many accolades some of Yuya's titles, including 'Overseer of the King's Horses' and 'God's Father'. As it was common practice for the first-born son to inherit his father's titles, and as Ay is known to have dedicated a chapel to Min at Akhmim, home town of Yuya and Thuyu, a link to the family of Tiy seems indicated. Even the names of Yuya and Ay hint that the two may have been related; we are not altogether certain how Yuya was pronounced but it is likely to have been something close to 'Aya', and both names may in fact have been nicknames or shortened forms of a more traditional Egyptian name. Cyril Aldred has even suggested that there was a close physical similarity between Yuya and Ay, with both displaying a large nose, receding forehead, protruding cheek-bones, prominent lips and a deep jaw. However, as we do not have Ay's body, this resemblance is based on Ay's portraits and statuary and is therefore not as clear-cut as we might wish.[10]

'Yuya' – perhaps because it was a nickname – was certainly an unusual name in ancient Egypt; the semi-literate artisans who were charged with labelling their patron's monuments and funerary goods had trouble with the spelling and each eventually produced his own Yuya variant. Mis-spellings were by no means uncommon in Egyptian tombs, but Yuya's name seems to have caused more problems than most, and this has led to suggestions that Yuya may have been an Asiatic with an unfamiliar foreign name.[11] The idea that Tiy may have been of foreign blood, possibly a Syrian princess, seemed an attractive one to those who first studied her. Flinders Petrie was quite firm in his belief that Tiy, who he felt bore a striking resemblance to depictions of Asiatic prisoners at Karnak, was of northern Syrian extraction and Wallis Budge concurred, agreeing that the queen, with her fair complexion and blue eyes, 'has all the characteristics of the women belonging to certain families who may be seen in North-eastern Syria to this day'. Others proclaimed Tiy to be of Lebanese extraction.[12] In stark contrast, Tiy has also been claimed as a woman of Nubia-Kush with 'full dark Africoid looks'.[13]

The suggestion that Tiy and Yuya were blue-eyed blondes can be dismissed at once; the blue eyes were the unfortunate result of a modern misinterpretation of an ancient portrait. The idea that Tiy may have been of Nubian or Central African origin is worthy of more serious consideration as Tiy does appear, on some of her sculptures, to have typical Nubian features, with a broad nose and full lips. The famous wooden head recovered from Gurob actually shows Tiy as black (Plate 3); this is, however, carved from a dark wood and is counterbalanced by other representations which depict Tiy as white. Added to this evidence is a sudden vogue for short curly Nubian-style wigs among the ladies of the court, and the rising importance of the queen, which some have linked to the more matriarchal nature of the Nubian royal family. Against this theory is the undisputed fact that Egyptian sculptures were never intended to be exact likenesses; they conveyed the essence of the person rather than his or her appearance, and a lady with a light-brown skin could be painted as white (living), or black or green (deceased).

In fact, the remarkably well-preserved mummified bodies of Yuya and Thuyu (Plates 6, 8) do not show the Central African appearance which has been assigned to Tiy and, while Yuya has been interpreted as having an unusual, almost European, physiognomy, Thuyu is generally regarded as a typical Egyptian woman. There is no reason to view Tiy as anything other than an Egyptian although it remains possible that her father may have been of (unspecified) foreign descent. Egypt, a corridor linking Africa to the Near East, had always been racially well-mixed and most families would have contained their quota of lighter- and darker-skinned members. The preoccupation with 'colour' and the idea of 'race' cutting across national boundaries is a very modern one. The Egyptians themselves drew a simple distinction between the people of *Kmt* who spoke Egyptian and followed Egyptian customs, and the foreigners who did not.[14]

Yuya and Thuyu lived to a good old age, eventually receiving the ultimate accolade of a double burial in the Valley of the Kings, the graveyard normally reserved for the tombs of the pharaohs. Although their tomb, now numbered as KV 46, was robbed soon after it was sealed and their mummy wrappings were disturbed by the thieves, the two white-haired bodies remained encased in their nests of wooden coffins until 1905, when their tomb was rediscovered by an American expedition led by Theodore M. Davis. Davis has described the opening of the tomb, apparently a highly dramatic and almost fatal occasion, in an account which perhaps owes more to dramatic licence than to historical accuracy. Davis was accompanied on this momentous occasion by Arthur Weigall, acting Chief Inspector for the region, and Gaston Maspero, Director General of Cairo Museum. When opened, the tomb proved confusing, very dark and very hot, lit only by the candles carried by the archaeologists. The eager explorers were forced to descend a steep passageway and then scramble through the small hole made by the robbers in the doorway which blocked the burial chamber. Maspero, the stoutest member of the party, could only enter the chamber after much pushing and shoving from his colleagues. Once inside, however, it was Maspero who, bending over the gilded coffin, first read the name of the deceased as 'Yuya'. This gave Davis a great thrill:

Naturally excited by the announcement, and blinded by the glare of the candles, I involuntarily advanced them very near the coffin, whereupon Monsieur Maspero cried out, 'Be careful!' and pulled my hand back. In a moment we realized that, had my candles touched the bitumen, which I came dangerously near doing, the coffin would have been in a blaze. As the entire contents of the tomb were inflammable, and directly opposite the coffin was a corridor leading to the open air and making a draught, we undoubtedly should have lost our lives . . .[15]

The expedition beat a hasty retreat and returned some time later, having rigged up an electric light. They found that Yuya and Thuyu had been buried with a magnificent collection of goods for use in the Field of Reeds, including two Osiris beds of growing corn[16] and a full-sized chariot suitable for a former 'Overseer of the King's Horses'. Although Maspero offered him a share of the treasure Davis rightly felt that such an important collection should not be split up and, although some items eventually made their way to the Metropolitan Museum, New York, most of the contents of the tomb are now housed in Cairo Museum.

Amenhotep III may have made an unconventional choice of bride, but his selection was a wise one. Tiy was to prove not only a fertile queen, but an astute woman of great political ability, well able to play an active part in her husband's reign. Almost immediately she became a force to be reckoned with; a powerful and influential figure with a high public profile and a string of impressive titles: 'King's Great Wife . . . The Heiress, greatly praised, Mistress of All Lands who cleaves unto the King . . . Mistress of Upper and Lower Egypt, Lady of the Two Lands'. Mutemwia was quickly relegated to the background as Tiy became Egypt's first lady.

Although strong queens had been a feature of the earlier 18th Dynasty, Tiy's immediate predecessors had been remote figures of little political importance. Tradition dictated that the queen, or rather the 'King's Great Wife', for there was no word for queen in Egyptian, should remain in the background, supporting her husband as and when required. The absence of the specific title 'Queen' both reflects the general shortage of kinship terms within Egypt and reinforces the overwhelming importance of the king. Only at times of dynastic crisis, usually following the premature death of a king, did the queen step forward. Tiy, however, soon abandoned the customary queenly reticence. She became the first consort to be regularly depicted beside her husband and the first queen whose name was consistently linked with that of the king on both official inscriptions and more private objects. A colossal statue designed for inclusion in Amenhotep's mortuary temple even shows Tiy at the same scale as her husband, an important development in a culture where size really did matter because size was directly equated with status.

Her religious profile rose equally high, and Tiy was allowed an increasingly prominent role in the rituals of her husband's reign. The queens of Egypt had traditionally been associated with the ancient goddess Hathor, who herself could appear as a royal wife and mother, and the features and actions of the two had often been blurred together so that the queen could appear as the living representative of Hathor on earth. Hathor, the cow-headed goddess of love, motherhood and drunkenness, was allied to the solar cults through her roles as the daughter of Re and the mother of the solar child, and was the alter ego of the fierce lion-headed goddess of war Sekhmet. Tiy became the first queen to adopt Hathor's cow horns and sun disc in her formal head-dress, and the first queen to be consistently associated with the use of the sistrum, a religious rattle whose handle usually featured Hathor's head. The sistrum was used to provide the music which would soothe the gods during worship. Its inclusion as part of the iconography of queenship emphasizes Tiy's new dual role of queen-priestess.[17]

At the same time Tiy became closely identified with Maat, daughter of Re and personification of truth, who, in an ideal world, would be the constant companion of the king. In the Theban tomb of the Queen's steward Kheruef (TT 192), Tiy and Hathor accompany the seated Amenhotep III. Tiy is here taking the role of Maat, and indeed is specifically described as 'The Principal Wife of the King, beloved of him, Tiy, may she live. It is like Maat following Re that she is in the following of Your Majesty [Amenhotep III].'[18] In the contemporary tomb of Ramose (TT 55), where we see Amenhotep IV sitting on a throne with Maat beside him, Maat has been given Tiy's features.

Towards the end of his reign Amenhotep established a cult to a deified form of himself, 'Amenhotep, Lord of Nubia'. Tiy, as consort of the semi-divine king, developed her own divinity until a temple was dedicated to her at Sedeinga in Nubia, the complement of her husband's fortified temple at nearby Soleb. Here Tiy appears in the guise of Hathor-Tefnut, 'Great of Fearsomeness', and she is seen in the form of a striding sphinx stalking across the tops of the temple pillars. This is not our only representation of Tiy as a sphinx. A carnelian bracelet plaque now held in the Metropolitan Museum, New York, shows Tiy as a winged sphinx holding her husband's cartouche in her human arms, while in the tomb of Kheruef she assumes the role of defender of Egypt as a sphinx trampling underfoot two bound female prisoners. Although the queen-sphinx was by no means an unusual symbol in 18th Dynasty art, such sphinxes had hitherto been essentially passive. Now we see Tiy, as she dominates the enemies of Egypt, appropriating a role formerly reserved for the king. The origins of the queen-sphinx motif are obscure, although it is generally agreed that she is connected with the solar deities as a daughter of the sun god. Some experts identify the queen-sphinx with Hathor in the form Sekhmet, while others have suggested that she may be linked to Tefnut, daughter of the creator god.

Convention dictated that husbands should love their wives, and Egyptian kings always took care to be seen to be behaving in a conventional manner. Nevertheless, the pride which Amenhotep obviously took in his bride, the unprecedented prominence which he allowed her and his habit of linking her name to his on all possible occasions, must be taken as a sign that Amenhotep felt a deep affection for Tiy. Seldom are we able to detect such a genuine emotion amid the conventions and calculated formulae of Egyptian monuments.

Tiy was not – to modern eyes at least – a great beauty. Her image, preserved in sculpture and painting, shows a determined-looking lady with a triangular-shaped face and the heavy-lidded almond-shaped eyes typical of the art of her time. Her face is often dominated by the long, heavy wig which dwarfs her features. Tiy rarely smiles, and her mouth frequently has a decided downward cast which gives her a dissatisfied expression. Beauty is, however, in the eye of the beholder, and at least one observer has seen in Tiy's portraits 'a face of pure Egyptian type, youthful and sweet, with a slightly projecting chin'.[19] Others have sensed the power behind the mask, noticing 'a realistic interpretation of imperious royal dignity',[20] and interpreting Tiy as a ruthless and determined woman, initially pretty but growing increasingly 'pinched and shrewish'.[21]

Although Tiy was the beloved of Amenhotep III, she was by no means his only beloved. The kings of the New Kingdom were polygamous, maintaining large harems which included their numerous wives, sisters and aunts plus a multitude of children and the servants and administrators who looked after them. The royal harem was housed in one or more permanent harem-palaces, which the king visited as he travelled between the royal residences which were dotted up and down the Nile. The harem of Amenhotep III, as befitted the ruler of a vast empire, was enormous, and throughout his reign the king took a keen interest in increasing its numbers so that by his death it housed well over 1,000 women. There was no disgrace in being a secondary or minor wife – indeed it was an honour to be selected for the king – but with one husband among so many it could never be a full-time occupation. In the secluded seraglios of the Ottoman Empire the women idled away their days in preparing themselves for a royal visit that might never come. In more down-to-earth Egypt the ladies of the harem were semi-independent, receiving an income from the palace and from their own estates, but also running a highly profitable textile business supervising the women who wove the linen cloth which Egypt consumed in such great quantities in her funerary rites.

The majority of the royal women were Egyptian ladies who provided the king with pleasure, status, and doubtless many children, but who had no political or ritual importance. Their names go unrecorded, and their children are ignored in the royal histories. Occasionally a harem lady would have the great good fortune to give birth to a future king. She would then be elevated to the status of 'King's Mother' and enjoy national prominence during her son's reign. This was, however, exceptional, as it depended upon the failure of the queen consort to produce a surviving male heir, and the ability of the mother to promote the cause of her own son.

Included among the women of the harem were a number of foreigners. Some were girls of lowly birth, sent as tribute or booty to the Egyptian court, while others were the daughters and sisters of minor rulers bound by oath of allegiance to Amenhotep. These vassals could not resist the demands of the 'father' who controlled them, and sent their daughters as brides – and perhaps hostages – as and when required. A few privileged royal brides were the daughters or sisters of rulers of importance who could confidently address the mighty king of Egypt as 'brother'. We know that Amenhotep contracted several of these diplomatic unions and was married to at least two princesses from Mitanni, two princesses from Syria, two princesses from Babylon and a princess from the Anatolian state of Arzawa. This trade in royal brides was strictly one-way traffic: Amenhotep demanded and received his foreign wives, but when Kadashman-Enlil of Babylon requested an Egyptian princess, Amenhotep turned him down with a flat refusal, even though Kadashman-Enlil's own sister was already a bride in the Egyptian harem. Amenhotep's original letter on this subject is unfortunately lost, but the Babylonian's indignant reply, quoting Amenhotep's words, was preserved in the royal archives:

. . . When I wrote to you about marrying your daughter you wrote to me saying 'From time immemorial no daughter of the king of Egypt has been given in marriage to anyone.' Why do you say this? You are the king and you may do as you please. If you were to give a daughter, who would say anything about it?[22]

Amenhotep stood firm. As ruler of the dominant world power he had no reason to change his mind. Kadashman-Enlil, constantly threatened by the volatile political situation outside the stability of the Egyptian empire, could not afford to be offended. He needed a powerful big brother. He therefore took steps to assure himself that his Egyptian sister was still alive and well. 'You are now asking for my daughter's hand in marriage, but my sister whom my father gave to you is already there with you, although no one has seen her or knows whether she is alive or dead',[23] and then sent his daughter to join her aunt.

The diplomatic marriages were celebrated as a means of linking two mighty rulers rather than two mighty states. The bond was always a highly personal one between the bridegroom and his father-in-law, and should either party die a new union would be necessary. Thus, although Amenhotep was already married to a Babylonian princess, the daughter of King Kurigalzu, the accession of Kurigalzu's son Kadashman-Enlil had to be marked by marriage with one of the new king's daughters.

Negotiations with Mitanni followed a similar pattern. Tuthmosis IV had married the daughter of Artatama I but this link was severed by the death of the two kings. Therefore, in the tenth year of his reign Amenhotep III married Gilukhepa, the daughter of Shuttarna, king of Mitanni, and a scarab was issued to commemorate the arrival of the bride and her retinue:

Year 10 ... The King of Upper and Lower Egypt, the Lord of Ritual,
Nebmaatre chosen of Re, Son of Re, Amenhotep ruler of Thebes, and the
king's principal wife Tiy, may she live ... The wonders that were brought to
his majesty were the daughter of Shuttarna, King of Mitanni, Gilukhepa, and
the chief women of her entourage, totalling three hundred and seventeen
women.[24]

We have to wonder how happy the 317 women of Gilukhepa's entourage would have been to accompany their mistress into effective exile in
a distant land.

Several years later Shuttarna died and, after a struggle during which
his elder son was assassinated, his younger son, Tushratta, brother of
Gilukhepa, took the throne. The now elderly Amenhotep III immediately opened negotiations for the hand of Tadukhepa, daughter of
Tushratta. The two kings exchanged magnificent gifts, Amenhotep
supplying a bride-price 'beyond measure, covering all the earth and
reaching to the heavens'[25] and Tushratta providing an extensive dowry
which included a chariot, four swift horses, and a variety of expensive
household and personal items including linen garments, shoes, a golden
bread shovel and even an inlaid lapis-lazuli fly-whisk.[26] Eventually, all
negotiations complete, Tadukhepa and her retinue followed her aunt to
Egypt.

Once the foreign princesses arrived in Egypt, they and their retinues
were absorbed into the harem and to all intents and purposes disappeared.
Although their families never forgot their Egyptian womenfolk – Tushratta was punctilious in remembering his sister and his daughter in his
correspondence, on one occasion sending Gilukhepa a greeting gift of
golden trinkets including toggle pins, earrings, a finger ring and a phial
of perfumed oil[27] – they played a peripheral role in the everyday life of
the royal family. The queen consort led a very different, and far more
public, life. Although Tiy had her own quarters in the harem, she also
had a place at court. She owned property in her own right, and derived
a good income from her estates which were administered by her stewards
and worked by her servants. Most importantly, Tiy, as queen, was at
the centre of royal family life. It was the queen, the king and their young
children, together with the king's mother, who formed the true royal
family.

Tiy bore her husband at least six children: two sons, Tuthmosis and Amenhotep, named after their grandfather and father respectively, and four daughters, Sitamen (Daughter of Amen), Henut-Taneb (Mistress of All Lands), Isis (the name of a goddess which literally means 'throne') and Nebetah (Lady of the Palace). Princess Sitamen, almost certainly the eldest daughter, was her father's favourite and as such was accorded an unusually prominent position within the royal family until, at around Year 31, Sitamen received the ultimate promotion becoming a royal wife alongside her mother. Sitamen's affairs were controlled by the great Amenhotep son of Hapu who held the post of 'High-Steward of the Princess Sitamen'. She had her own palace, her own estates, and her own furniture, some of which was included among the grave goods within her maternal grandparents' tomb. A scene on the back of an ornate chair recovered from this tomb shows Sitamen, 'the Eldest Daughter of the King, whom he loves', sitting to receive an offering of a golden necklace proffered by a servant.[28] Sitamen is dressed in a long skirt and an elaborate collar. On her head she wears a short wig and an intricate crown of lotus blossom but the double uraeus (or cobra) at her brow has been replaced by a pair of gazelle heads whose significance is not now apparent but which may be intended to designate a subordinate or minor queen. In her hands she holds the sistrum and *menit* beads which associate her with the cult of Hathor. Eventually Sitamen received the high accolade of 'Great King's Wife', although we can see from contemporary illustrations that she never took precedence over her mother.

Isis and Henut-Taneb may also have become royal wives. Their names were written in royal cartouches but they were never important enough to be named in their grandparents' tomb. Nebetah, however, does not appear to have become a queen, and it seems that she may have been the family afterthought, too young to follow in her sisters' footsteps.

Amenhotep III enjoyed a lengthy reign, celebrating three *sed* festivals, or jubilees, during his regnal years 30, 34 and 37. The *heb-sed*, a tradition which stretched back to the dawn of Egyptian history, was originally a public ceremony of rebirth intended to reaffirm the king's powers after each successive thirty years on the throne. However, kings who had achieved their first three decades felt free to bend the rules in subsequent years. As life expectancy at birth throughout the New Kingdom was less than twenty years, thirty years on the throne was by anyone's reckoning a remarkable achievement, and the celebration of an official jubilee gave the king and his people the excuse for a magnificent and lengthy party. Amenhotep, who was evidently something of an antiquarian, claimed to have discovered, hidden in the palace archives, an ancient order of service for the celebration of the *heb-sed*, and to have revised his own ceremony accordingly.

Although the *heb-sed* was traditionally celebrated at Memphis, Amenhotep chose to duplicate his festivities at a site now known as Malkata, literally in modern Arabic 'the place where things are picked up', on the west bank opposite Thebes, where he already had a royal residence. Here, in good time for his first extravaganza, he built a gaily painted mud-brick festival hall and a T-shaped ceremonial lake for use in the water procession. A vast array of tempting food was prepared, some of which was 'donated' by local officials, numerous jars of wine were made ready, and a host of dignitaries, both mortals and gods, was invited to witness the celebrations and enjoy the feast. Among the court officials present was Tiy's steward Kheruef, who recorded the highlights on his tomb wall:

The glorious appearance of the King at the great double doors in his palace, 'The House of Rejoicing'; ushering in the officials, the king's friends, the chamberlain, the men of the gateway, the king's acquaintances . . . Rewards were given out in the form of 'Gold of Praise' and golden ducks and fish, and they received ribbons of green linen, each person being made to stand in order of rank.[29]

After the jubilee the festival palace was demolished in order to expand the sacred lake in time for the second celebration. The excavation of this lake, still visible in modern times and now known as the Birket Habu, was one of the largest civil-engineering projects ever undertaken in dynastic Egypt. It measured two kilometres by one kilometre, and tens of thousands of labourers must have been involved in the excavation of many tons of earth. For a long time it was thought that the Birket Habu was the pleasure lake ordered by Amenhotep for his beloved queen and recorded on yet another scarab:

His majesty commanded the making of a lake for the great Queen Tiy in her home lands of Djarukha, its length being 3700 cubits and its breadth being 600 [or 700] cubits. His majesty made a festival of the opening of the lake in the third month of the inundation season, day six, when his majesty sailed in the royal barge 'The Sun Disc Dazzles'.[30]

Unfortunately the measurements do not tally. Queen Tiy's pleasure lake took only sixteen days to construct and, given that a dynastic cubit equalled 52.5 cm, must have been far narrower than the Birket Habu.

A new mud-brick festival palace was built beside the Malkata lake where it was serviced by the extensive royal village. Here, the contrast between the formal and well-planned architecture of Amenhotep's stone-built temple precincts and the rather rambling and disjointed layout of his own home is striking. The king's palace fronted on to a large open courtyard and included private quarters, a bedroom, bathroom and robing room, plus the necessary harem accommodation and an audience chamber, and was served by an untidy cluster of kitchens, offices and storerooms. Although the walls and ceilings of the palace are largely destroyed, painted plaster fragments show that the walls of the king's bedroom were decorated with an elaborate and entertaining frieze of naked Bes figures above a pattern of false door panels and alternating *ankh* (life) and *sa* (protection) signs, while the ceiling was painted with stylized vultures with outstretched wings. Next door was a smaller residence intended for the queen (now known as the South Palace). The crown prince had use of a large porticoed palace (the Middle Palace), while a fourth palace built without harem accommodation (the North Palace) was probably the home of Queen Sitamen. Also included within the complex were several great houses for high officials, smaller cottages for lesser courtiers, servants' accommodation, storehouses, workshops, a temple of Amen, sundry small chapels, a workmen's village and formal pleasure gardens. The complex was linked to the Nile by a canal, and to the king's mortuary temple by a causeway.[31]

We have a mere handful of scenes showing Amenhotep towards the end of his lengthy reign.[32] His earlier portraits had depicted a prime physical specimen displaying all the manly vigour expected of a New Kingdom monarch. His later images are less stereotyped. The king appears languid to the point of lethargy, his clothing is unconventional, and there has been a general consensus of opinion that we are looking at a fat and tired old man suffering from some unspecified but debilitating sickness. On one battered limestone stela, recovered from the Amarna house of Panehesy and now housed in the British Museum (Plate 4), we find the king propped limply in a chair 'with drooping head and with his corpulent body collapsed to a certain flabby lethargy, with his hand hanging listlessly to his knee'.[33] Beside him sits Queen Tiy who, although her image has been badly damaged, is always interpreted as bursting with rude health. In other representations we see the bloated king dressed in a long pleated linen garment which some have considered more suited to a woman than a man. Despite his idiosyncratic style, James Baikie speaks for many when he describes what he takes to be the king's obvious decline into obesity and mental decay:

The great king was still well short of his fiftieth year; but he had doubtless 'warmed both hands before the fire of life', with the consequences which usually follow on such indulgence of the relishing and enjoying faculties; and now he had to put conclusion to the verse – 'It sinks and I am ready to depart'.[34]

Obesity may be associated with various diseases including arteriosclerosis, inflammation of the gall bladder and gall-stone formation, all of which were to be found in ancient Egypt. However, the portraits of Amenhotep do not show a clinically obese old man. Indeed, they do not even show a particularly old man. Amenhotep appears singularly free of wrinkles and he does not display excessive folds of fat as shown on the Deir el-Bahri portrait of the Queen of Punt. It therefore seems likely that the king's extra pounds are nothing more sinister than the inevitable results of a lifetime of overindulgence which were not seen as a matter for shame. Indeed, rolls of fat and pendulous breasts were the well-respected signs of male old age in dynastic Egypt.

Amenhotep had certainly had every opportunity to overeat and drink to excess, and his only physical exercise seems to have occurred during his regular visits to the harem. Although he was still actively seeking new brides, the days of hunting wild lions and shooting fierce bulls were long gone, if indeed they had ever occurred; quite often the daring hunts commemorated in royal inscriptions involved the slaughter of 'wild' animals which had already been captured and penned. Similarly Amenhotep had avoided, through accident or design, all military action. He had not led the fight against the vile Ibhat in person, delegating the command of the army to the viceroy Merimose, and he had never felt the need to embark on a military campaign or to make a tour of his foreign possessions. While it may be going too far to suggest on such limited evidence that Amenhotep was basically a lazy man who enjoyed his creature comforts, there is certainly no evidence to suggest that he was ever tempted to exchange the luxury of the palace for the rigours of an army tent.

The king's new limpid pose and his unconventional garb probably owe little to his actual physical condition. Amenhotep's last portraits, which may have been produced some time after his death, were composed during a period when Egyptian artistic conventions were undergoing a profound change. It is therefore not surprising that we find Amenhotep being depicted in the exaggerated manner soon to be favoured by his son. His 'dress', which is again very similar to the garments worn by his son, may well have been a contemporary garment; long gowns were by no means confined to women.[35] Some observers, however, have chosen to read these portraits as indications of something far more sinister. They have seen a king in moral and physical decline, prematurely aged by his sexual decadence. The marriage with his own daughter is the ultimate indication of aberrant sexual taste, while the public donning of a woman's robe is an indication that Amenhotep had abandoned heterosexuality in favour of public cross-dressing and 'Greek love'.[36] As the king had now totally given himself to the pleasures of his decaying flesh, Queen Tiy, still very much *compos mentis*, must have taken effective control of Egypt. Again Baikie has summed up the thoughts of many:

There can be little doubt that during the later part of his reign, at all events, while it was Amenhotep who wore the Double Crown, it was Tiy who ruled; and probably the easy-going, good-natured king was quite content with the arrangement. Tiy's supremacy over her husband's mind leaves little question as to where we are to look for the chief influence in the upbringing of her young son. His vivid, capable mother must have been almost everything to the young prince, and increasingly so as the years went on, and his father gradually sank into the lethargy of premature decay.[37]

While we have absolutely no proof that the king had become senile, and indeed madness through sexual excess is more common in fiction than real life, there is some evidence to suggest that he was suffering very badly from toothache. Painful teeth were an unfortunate fact of Egyptian old age, as the desert sand and particles of grinding stone which invariably became incorporated in the food wore away the surface of the teeth until the sensitive pulp was exposed and became infected. Not only was this persistent toothache very painful, it undermined the general health of the sufferer. The skill of the Egyptian doctors was famed throughout the Near East, but even they could suggest no cure for the ailing king. Even a dedication of 600 statues to Sekhmet brought no relief. In despair, Amenhotep wrote to his brother-in-law Tushratta, asking if he could help. Tushratta responded by sending the cult statue of the goddess Ishtar of Nineveh, another female warrior with the power to heal:

May Ishtar, Mistress of Heaven, protect my brother and myself for a hundred thousand years, and may our mistress grant us both great joy. And let us act as friends.[38]

As Egypt's king suffered, the political situation in the Near East was shifting. Egypt remained the dominant world power but the Hittites, a non-Semitic people based on the Central Anatolian plateau, were pursuing expansionist policies which posed a threat to Mitanni's north Syrian possessions. At the same time in central Syria, Amurru or 'the West', a region populated by disparate bands of semi-nomadic peoples and bandits, was now united under the Canaanite-speaking Prince Abdi-Ashirta and making a determined effort to assert itself as an independent state. Both Tushratta and Amenhotep took steps to restrict the growth of Amurru but neither was entirely successful, and Abdi-Ashirta and his son Aziru – both nominally Egyptian vassals – were able to continue their expansionist policies unchecked. Amenhotep, perhaps because he had grown used to international inactivity, continued his friendship with Tushratta but took no effective action to intervene. He seems not to have realized, or not to have cared, that Mitanni was under increasing pressure, and he showed very little concern over the fate of his lesser vassals. Indeed the peoples of Tunip – a small independent state eventually overrun by Amurru – were later to complain that they had begged for help from Egypt for twenty years, in vain.[39]

The goddess Ishtar travelled to Egypt, but it was a wasted journey. Soon after her arrival Amenhotep died at Thebes during the seventh month of his regnal year 38. Tuthmosis, the crown prince, had predeceased his father, and so it was his younger son, now Amenhotep IV, who performed the funerary rites and buried Amenhotep III in a suitably regal tomb in the Western Valley, close to the Valley of the Kings (WV 22). Amenhotep was not, however, destined to lie in peace. His tomb – which almost certainly housed the richest royal burial Egypt had ever seen – was robbed during the 21st Dynasty, and his battered mummy, rescued by the necropolis officials, rewrapped and labelled, was eventually stored with other displaced royal mummies in the cache held in the tomb of Amenhotep II. Here, in 1898, a mummy bearing the label of Amenhotep III was discovered by Victor Loret and transferred to Cairo Museum. The unfortunate king was by this time in a sorry condition. He had suffered a severe mauling at the hands of the tomb robbers: his head, right leg and left foot had been snapped off and his back had been broken. G. Elliot Smith, who unwrapped the body in 1909, found that the mummy had been packed with resin, which had set hard under its covering of skin. 'It was a great disappointment to find only these broken and blackened bones to represent the body of

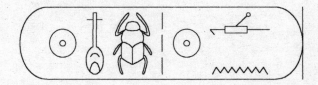

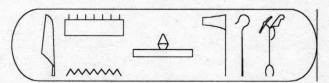

Fig. 1.2   The royal names of Amenhotep IV

Amenothes "the Magnificent" '.[40] More recent scientific analysis has cast grave doubts on our acceptance of this body as the remains of Amenhotep III. It seems that the necropolis officials who 'rescued' the king may well have muddled up their charges and lost the magnificent Amenhotep III.[41]

2

A Beautiful Woman Has Come

She pure of hands, Great King's Wife whom he loves, Lady of the Two Lands Nefertiti, may she live. Beloved of the great living Sun Disc who is in jubilee . . .[1]

Amenhotep IV emerged from an obscure corner of the royal court to become pharaoh of Egypt under the throne-name Neferkheperure Waenre (literally 'The transformations of Re are perfect, the Unique one of Re'). Little is known of him before his assumption and, while his sisters and his brother are known to us from their statues and inscribed possessions, the young Amenhotep is to all intents and purposes invisible. Although we do have a few formal scenes showing him alongside his father, it is probable that these images were not carved during the old king's lifetime. Our only certain mention of the young prince comes from the Malkata Palace which has yielded a wine-jar seal labelled 'the estate of the King's True Son Amenhotep'. We may deduce from this seal that, by the final decade of his father's reign, Amenhotep was old enough to have his own establishment, and therefore that he was probably born before Year 29 when the court moved from Memphis to Thebes.

It is highly unlikely that the young Amenhotep had been sent abroad to be raised and educated outside Egypt. This idea, put forward by those who would like to interpret Amenhotep's religious beliefs as Near Eastern rather than Egyptian in origin, shows a lack of understanding of the political situation throughout the later part of the 18th Dynasty. At this time Egypt was universally regarded as the centre of the civilized world, and the Egyptian royal court was acknowledged as the epitome of sophisticated luxury. All foreigners wished to emulate the Egyptians, and the Egyptians themselves were firmly convinced of their own cultural superiority. No Egyptian was likely to see a foreign education as in any way beneficial to an Egyptian prince, and the Egyptian royal sons did not enjoy the ancient equivalent of the Grand Tour. Instead, Egypt was in the habit of demanding that the sons of vassals and allies be sent to Egypt for their education. These young men, educated alongside the Egyptian princes in the school attached to the royal harem, served as hostages who would ensure the good behaviour of their fathers. They became so steeped in Egyptian customs and beliefs that, when they returned to rule their own countries, their loyalties in theory lay not with their own people but with the Egyptian king who had become their friend.

If Amenhotep was not raised away from Egypt, could there have been something about the young prince – perhaps something about his appearance or even his mental condition – which caused his family to shield him from public gaze?[2] With the benefit of hindsight this seems possible, although it begs the question why, if the young Amenhotep was so badly disfigured, should he ever have been allowed to become king? Amenhotep III was free to choose his successor and, although custom and divine precedent made his eldest surviving son the natural choice, the Egyptians had no objection to a reigning king adopting a less obvious heir before his death. The royal harem, with its hundreds of wives, could surely have yielded a replacement prince, and the fact that Tiy was not herself of royal blood would have made it relatively easy for Amenhotep III to reject her son in favour of one more suited to be king.

In fact we should not be too surprised by Amenhotep's hidden childhood as almost all New Kingdom royal children led sheltered lives away from the bustle of the court. Prominent royal offspring were very much the exception, and sons were particularly well hidden as, while daughters were almost always included in the traditional 'family groups' which adorned their fathers' monuments, sons rarely were. Indeed, a casual examination of 18th Dynasty royal scenes could give the impression that, at a time when the royal harem contained many hundreds of women, Egyptian kings were incapable of fathering male children. Such scenes can be very misleading. They were never intended to be accurate portraits detailing every family member, but were formal representations of the monarch supported by his close female dependants – those included in the nuclear royal family – who were present in the scene as symbolic appendages enhancing the status of the king.

Our lack of knowledge concerning Amenhotep's adolescence is more unusual, but probably reflects the fact that he was a second son born late in his parents' marriage. As first-born son, or crown prince, Amenhotep's older brother, Tuthmosis, would have inherited a well-defined role within the royal family. He was the Horus who would eventually inherit the throne of his dead father, Osiris. His future was assured, and there was an established training programme to ensure that he would grow into a conventional New Kingdom monarch. Since the reign of Tuthmosis I the crown prince had been educated in the school attached to the harem, where he learned his lessons alongside the sons of Egypt's élite who would one day become his ministers. His theoretical education complete, the prince was transferred to Memphis, the administrative centre of Egypt. Here he was able to experience the workings of the court bureaucracy at first hand, and his leisure time was spent perfecting his hunting skills so that he could become the brave and fearless warrior which Egypt expected.

Our only surviving image of Tuthmosis, an unusual statuette now housed in the collections of the Louvre Museum, Paris, shows the prince dressed in the kilt, side-lock and panther skin of a priest. He is lying prostrate to grind corn before the god Ptah, and the inscription identifies him as '. . . the King's Son, the *Sem*-Priest Tuthmosis'.[3] Other inscriptions tell us that Tuthmosis, who seems to have been something of an animal-lover, was accorded special responsibility for the burial of the Apis bulls of Memphis. The sarcophagus of his own pet cat, named Ta-Miu or 'The Cat', gives his full and final titulary as 'Crown Prince, Overseer of the Priests of Upper and Lower Egypt, High Priest of Ptah in Memphis and *Sem*-Priest of Ptah'. The tomb of Tuthmosis has never been found but, given his links with Memphis, it seems likely that he would have been buried at Sakkara.

There was no well-defined role for younger brothers who, unless some tragedy befell the crown prince, were unlikely ever to inherit the throne. In consequence younger sons played a relatively minor part in the official royal family while they waited to see whether they would be required to step into their older brother's sandals. Egypt's high infant and child mortality rates and low life expectancy meant that this happened more often than we might expect; within the Tuthmoside royal family both Tuthmosis II and Tuthmosis IV had inherited the throne after the death of their older brother(s). The gods themselves, immune to the scourge of child mortality, avoided the problem of surplus sons by restricting their own families to one child, and triads of local gods (father, mother and child, usually a son) were venerated as one family unit. At Memphis the god Ptah, his wife Sekhmet and their son Nefertum were worshipped together, while the Theban triad was made up of the great god Amen, his consort Mut and their son Khonsu. Where a divine family did include two sons there could be trouble. Seth, the younger brother of Osiris, eventually murdered his brother so that he could inherit the throne of Egypt.

Younger sons spent their earlier years as understudies to the crown prince, and those who did not eventually become king sank into obscurity once the succession was assured. This restricted the immediate royal family to the king, his principal wife, his sisters, aunts, mother, grandmother and children; brothers and uncles, and of course their children, were no longer regarded as fully royal although they enjoyed a well-respected place in Egyptian court life. Grown men were certainly wary of claiming a family relationship with the king at a time when others less well-connected were happy to boast of their monarch's patronage and, although we have examples of 18th Dynasty individuals classifying themselves as a 'King's Son', it seems remarkable that we have no one claiming to be a 'King's Brother' or 'King's Nephew'.

The new Amenhotep IV needed a consort to complete his role as king. Following the precedent set by his father he rejected his sisters and half-sisters and looked outside the immediate royal family to choose as his bride a previously obscure young woman named Nefertiti. Amenhotep is silent about his wife's origins and, although Nefertiti's name is constantly associated with that of her husband, her parents are not mentioned in any inscription or document. This in itself is not totally unexpected. Queens drew their status purely from their links with the king. The more links, the more status, so that the highest-ranking woman in the land was invariably a king's daughter who had become a king's wife and then a king's mother. It did not matter that such a lady would almost certainly be linked to three different kings (her father, her brother/husband and her son), as the role of king remained constant no matter how many individuals played it. A princess married to a king would always be given her correct titles which would include 'King's Daughter'. Non-royal women, however, were rarely given their filiation on their husband's monuments as their existence before their marriage was an irrelevance. Amenhotep III had been highly unusual in stressing his own non-royal bride's parentage.

With one exception, we know of no one claiming to be related to Nefertiti. This is somewhat unexpected as Egyptians routinely included within their tombs details of their more important and glamorous relatives, thereby impressing visitors and adding to their own status. There was a marked reluctance for men to make a direct acknowledgement of any link with the royal family forged via marriage, to the extent that neither Yuya nor Anen made any reference to their kinship with Tiy. This taboo, however, did not seem to apply to women, and Thuyu had certainly felt no need to suppress her pride in her daughter's achievements. As the discoverers of her tomb noted, her title of 'Royal Mother of the Chief Wife of the King' was everywhere:

... repeated jealously on the coffins, on the furniture, on the *ouashbaatiou* [shabti figures], in such a manner that the day an intruder should penetrate into the tomb, he would know from what to refrain on account of the quality of one of the persons resting there, and would not be able to plead the excuse of ignorance if he persisted in his intention of despoiling the mummy.[4]

It seems curious to modern eyes that Thuyu sought to impress visitors to her tomb by emphasizing her relationship with the queen, while the husband who lay by her side made no mention of his identical relationship. Indeed, if it were not for the commemorative scarabs which make Tiy's parentage clear, we would be justified in assuming that Tiy was not Yuya's daughter. The evidence provided by Yuya and Thuyu's tomb suggests that, while we might expect to find that Nefertiti's father and brother would stress their association with the king rather than their kinship with the queen, Nefertiti's mother would have felt free to boast of her daughter. As we have no woman claiming to be Nefertiti's mother, should we assume either that the tomb of Nefertiti's mother has yet to be discovered, or that Nefertiti's mother died before her daughter married the king? Could Nefertiti even have been born abroad?

As Nefertiti appears to have sprung from nowhere, speculation regarding her origins has been rife. Her name, an unusual one, translates as 'A Beautiful Woman Has Come'. This has naturally led to the suggestion that the new queen may have been a foreigner who, quite literally, arrived at the Egyptian court in order to marry the king. The idea of a foreign queen has a certain attraction, in the way that the theories of Amenhotep's Syrian education or Tiy's Near Eastern parentage had earlier appealed to egyptologists, because it allows Nefertiti to introduce strange, un-Egyptian religious ideas into the hitherto highly conservative royal family and thus provides a neat explanation for Amenhotep's defection from the traditional Egyptian gods. It also allows Nefertiti a certain romantic glamour to match her regal status. Although there is no evidence for the arrival of any foreign bride at the start of Amenhotep's reign, the harem which Amenhotep had inherited from his father already contained several suitable princesses. Could one of these have been transformed into Nefertiti?

We have no firm date for the royal marriage, although monumental evidence suggests that it occurred either just before or shortly after Amenhotep's accession to the throne. We can, however, deduce that Nefertiti was relatively young when she married Amenhotep, as she went on to bear at least six children. The most obvious candidate for the role of queen consort must therefore be the youngest of the foreign royal brides, Princess Tadukhepa, daughter of Tushratta of Mitanni. Tadukhepa had been sent to Egypt to marry the ailing Amenhotep III but the marriage was almost certainly unconsummated as her arrival coincided with the death of her elderly bridegroom. We know that Tadukhepa remained in Egypt, becoming the wife of Amenhotep IV, but from this point on she disappears from public view. Could she have become his consort, changing her outlandish foreign name to a more suitable Egyptian one? Tushratta had certainly hoped that his daughter would one day become queen of Egypt; during the original marriage negotiations he had stipulated that Tadukhepa should take the title of 'Mistress of Egypt' although, with Queen Tiy firmly in place, this must have seemed a remote possibility. A change of ruler, however, would have meant a change of circumstances, and a new name would certainly account for Tadukhepa's disappearance at precisely the time that Nefertiti emerges. Although there was no precedent for a foreign princess becoming queen of Egypt, this was in no way forbidden. Indeed, during the 19th Dynasty a Hittite princess, presented by her father as a peace offering to Ramesses II, was renamed Maathorneferure and made 'Great King's Wife'.

Flinders Petrie, a strong supporter of the Nefertiti as Tadukhepa theory, took matters one step further by suggesting that Tadukhepa was herself of mixed Egyptian-Mitannian parentage and an 'heiress' capable of transmitting the right to rule Egypt to her husband. He believed that she had never been intended as a bride for the old king, but had always been meant for his son.[5] Assuming, incorrectly, that Nefertiti/ Tadukhepa's daughters start to appear on their father's monuments only during his Year 6, and hazarding a guess that the first princess would probably have been conceived soon after her parents' marriage, Petrie decided that the royal wedding must have occurred during Year 4. However, Tushratta's correspondence with Amenhotep III makes it clear that the marriage was celebrated – but not necessarily consummated – before the death of the old king. For Petrie's theory to be correct, Amenhotep IV's Year 4 must have occurred during his father's lifetime, and the two would thus have spent at least four years as joint consorts.

Co-regencies had been an accepted feature of 12th Dynasty Egypt when many kings ended their reigns by ruling alongside their chosen successor. The Theban kings who founded the 18th Dynasty regarded the 12th Dynasty as the height of Egyptian civilization and, seeking to emulate their forebears in establishing an unquestionable line of descent, reintroduced the custom. These joint reigns must have posed many practical problems. How was such a reign to be dated, and who was to be the senior monarch? How could a co-regency be reconciled with the legend of the dying king Osiris passing his crown to his living son Horus, the myth which underpinned the whole dynastic system? However, the fact that the tradition persisted shows that, whatever the drawbacks of co-regencies, the benefits outweighed the obvious disadvantages. Co-regencies certainly had the advantage of making the succession crystal clear, an important message at a time when kings were fathering many tens of sons. Petrie's theory of a four-year co-regency, based as it was on flawed evidence, was quickly discarded but the suggestion of a joint rule between Amenhotep III and his son was revived in the 1930s with several experts proposing joint reigns of varying lengths ranging from three to twelve years.[6]

Co-regencies can prove almost impossible to detect. Does the presence of a king's name at an archaeological site confirm that he actually lived there? Is the image of a king standing alongside his successor intended to show two living monarchs or a dead father and his living son? Only when a monument is double-dated, that is it shows the dates of both the 'senior' and the 'junior' kings, can we be certain that there are two rulers on the throne. Unfortunately, New Kingdom co-regencies did not employ this double-dating system, and in all known joint reigns the 'junior' king started to count his own years only from the death of his co-monarch. All the 'evidence' put forward in favour of the proposed co-regency of Amenhotep III and Amenhotep IV is highly ambiguous and capable of a variety of interpretations; there are, for example, a handful of instances where the names or images of the two kings are linked on monuments, but filial piety may well have caused the new king to associate his name with that of his dead father. Similarly, wine dockets recovered from Amarna bearing the regnal years 28 and 30, and so assumed to belong to the reign of Amenhotep III, need not have been taken to Amarna during the old king's reign.

As yet there is absolutely no direct evidence to prove that Amenhotep III and Amenhotep IV ever ruled together. Indeed, King Tushratta's letter of condolence, written to Queen Tiy soon after news of her husband's demise had reached Mitanni, strongly suggests that the old king had been succeeded by the new without any period of joint rule. Tushratta manages to combine his expressions of sorrow at the passing of the old king with a lengthy grumble about the quality of gold statues sent to Mitanni by the new king. Apparently Amenhotep III (called Nimmuaria by Tushratta) had promised to send statues of solid gold ornamented with lapis lazuli, but Amenhotep IV (a.k.a. Napkhururiya) had substituted cheap wooden statues plated in gold:

Say to Tiy, the mistress of Egypt from Tushratta, King of Mitanni:
    With me all goes well. With you may all go well. With your household and your son, may all go well. With Tadukhepa my daughter and your daughter-in-law, may all go well ... You are the one who knows that I always showed love to Nimmuaria, your husband, and that Nimmuaria, your husband, always showed love to me ... You are the one that knows much better than all others the things that we said to one another. No other person knows them as well as you ... I will not forget my love for Nimmuaria, your husband. More than ever, I now show this love tenfold for your son, Napkhururiya ...

I had asked your husband for statues of solid gold . . . But now Napkhururiya, your son, has sent plated statues of wood. With gold being as dirt in your son's land, why has your son not given what I asked for? . . .[7]

This letter makes it clear that Tiy, now queen mother, was still widely regarded as one of the most important figures at the Egyptian court. Her influence over her son seems to have been as strong as her influence over her late husband had ever been, so that when Tushratta sought help in the matter of his missing golden statues it was to Tiy rather than to the new king that he turned. Amenhotep IV probably seemed something of an unknown quantity, and Tushratta may have calculated (wrongly) that his best chance of receiving the precious statues was to beg Tiy to plead his cause with her son. However, Tushratta may have already been aware that the new king was by no means as friendly towards Mitanni as his father had been. The two rulers went on to enjoy a less than brotherly relationship and none of Tushratta's letters to Amenhotep received the courtesy of a reply. After three abortive epistles Tushratta abandoned the correspondence. It is difficult to escape the conclusion that Amenhotep was indifferent to the fate of both Tushratta and his country.

The presentation of Nefertiti as an exotic foreign princess may have an appealing neatness and a certain romantic attraction. However, it is a theory completely unsupported by historical or archaeological facts. Nefertiti's name, although uncommon, was certainly not extraordinary. All but the shortest of Egyptian personal names had a meaning, usually reflecting either devotion to a certain deity or the particular attributes of the child; Tuthmosis, for example, is a Greek form of an Egyptian name which should more properly be written Djehuty-Mes and which translates as 'Born of Thoth', while Amenhotep means 'Amen is Satisfied'. A child's name was chosen by the mother at the birth, and it does not take too wide a leap of the imagination to envisage a proud mother choosing a name intended to reflect the beauty of her new-born baby girl. We know that other 18th Dynasty parents devised similar names for their daughters; the Theban tomb of Nakht, an official in the temple of Amen, which has been dated to the reign of Amenhotep III, includes the female names Nefert-Waty ('The Beautiful One is Unique') and

Neferteni ('The Beautiful One is for Me'), while one mother named her daughter Aneksi ('She Belongs to Me').

There is now enough evidence to confirm that Nefertiti, far from being a foreigner, must have been born a member of Egypt's wealthy élite.[8] In their unfinished Amarna tomb the lady Tey is shown alongside her husband Ay as they both receive a reward of golden necklaces from the arms of the king and queen. The receipt of gold was a great public honour which had originally been reserved for victorious soldiers, but which at the start of the 18th Dynasty had been expanded to encompass statesmen and high-ranking male court officials. For a wife to receive gold alongside her husband was, however, unprecedented and must be read as a clear message that the woman in question was of particular importance. The fact that Tey was permitted to share the most elaborate of the private Amarna tombs on an almost equal basis with Ay is further confirmation, if any were needed, that she was a lady of the highest rank. Tey was, indeed, no simple wife, and her titles include 'Favourite of the Good God, Nurse of the King's Great Wife Nefertiti, Nurse of the Goddess, Ornament of the King'. Nurse, in this context, is usually translated as wet-nurse.

A fragment of a relief recovered from Amarna and now housed in the Louvre Museum, Paris, has been hailed as confirmation of Tey's intimate relationship with the queen. The fragment appears to show a seated older woman wearing a distinctive golden necklace and holding a younger woman on her knee. Both women wear pleated linen dresses, and the older lady has one breast exposed. As Tey is the only woman known to have received gold as an official reward from the king, it has been assumed that the scene originally showed Tey holding her royal charge, or even offering her the breast. Such scenes were not considered in any way distasteful, and the wet-nurse, far from being a humble servant performing a rather basic task, was to be equated with the great mother goddesses. Earlier pharaohs had been depicted suckling from Hathor in her various guises, which included a woman, a cow and even a snake goddess, while references to nursing the king were made in several royal texts; we know, for example, that the Great Enchantress suckled the king in order to prepare him for his coronation. Unfortunately the Louvre relief is so badly damaged that the identification of the two figures as Tey and Nefertiti is by no means certain. It seems equally possible that the scene could represent Nefertiti's eldest daughter Meritaten sitting on her mother's knee, or even Nefertiti sitting on her husband's knee.[9]

The role of wet-nurse to the royal family was one of the most important and influential positions that a non-royal woman could achieve, conferring great honour on her husband and great privileges upon her own baby, who became a 'Child of the *Kep* [nursery]', raised alongside the royal children. Consequently, the royal wet-nurses were invariably the wives of the highest-ranking court officials. As we know that Tey was married to a man of high status, and as her tomb shows her to have been a woman worthy of great respect, could Nefertiti have been a royal baby? We know that she was not a daughter of Queen Tiy, but could she have been a half-sister of Amenhotep IV, born to a secondary wife? Perhaps even the daughter of Queen Sitamen, or of Gilukhepa? Theoretically, given the size of the royal harem, the list of potential mothers is extensive, although, as Sitamen only married Amenhotep III towards the end of his reign, it seems unlikely that she could have borne a daughter old enough to marry Amenhotep IV at the start of his rule. However, the fact that Nefertiti never refers to herself as a 'King's Daughter' makes such speculation fruitless. Nefertiti could not have been a royal princess.

We have already met Tey's husband Ay, the prominent court official who included among his many accolades the positions of 'Overseer of the King's Horses' and 'God's Father', the latter being his favourite title, used on all occasions until it eventually became a part of his name and he was universally known as 'God's Father Ay'. Circumstantial evidence makes it seem highly likely that Ay was the son of Yuya and Thuyu, and the brother of Anen and Tiy, while the shared title of 'God's Father' suggests an even stronger link between the royal family and the parallel dynasty from Akhmim. If 'God's Father' is not simply a priestly title but is to be taken literally, Ay, like his father before him, must have been the father-in-law of the king and the father of the queen consort Nefertiti.[10] Ay himself makes no mention of his relationship with Nefertiti but, as we have seen, that is only to be expected. Tey does claim a link with Nefertiti, although from her own words it would appear that she was merely Nefertiti's nurse and not her natural mother. Tey never lays claim to the respected title of 'Royal Mother of the King's Great Wife' which had earlier given Thuyu so much pleasure. We may deduce that

Tey was a second wife who had been called upon to raise the infant child of Ay's deceased first wife; such domestic tragedies were common enough in ancient Egypt. However, their joint tomb makes no mention of a first wife and the suggestion that Tey breast-fed the child poses certain problems. Did the widowed Ay marry his daughter's nurse? Could we be taking the title of wet-nurse too literally – does it really mean stepmother or adoptive mother? Whatever the answer, it is clear that the marriage of Nefertiti and Amenhotep IV raised the lady Tey and her husband to a position of great honour at court.

Although we know nothing of Nefertiti's parentage we do know that she had a younger sister who spent some time at the Amarna court.[11] As the term sister was used somewhat loosely throughout the dynastic period, it is equally likely that this lady could have been a half-sister, a stepsister or even a foster sister. Seven of the earlier tombs of the Amarna nobles include among their depictions of palace life a young lady referred to as Mutnodjmet, a Theban name meaning 'The goddess Mut (or mother) is the Sweet One'. The vast majority of the women of the queen's retinue remain anonymous background figures, and the very fact that Mutnodjmet is named is an indication of her importance,

Fig. 2.1   Mutnodjmet and her nieces

although strict Amarna etiquette ensures that she always stands behind the royal family. Mutnodjmet is consistently labelled 'Queen's Sister'. Like Nefertiti she never claims to be a king's daughter, and her parentage goes unrecorded. She is, however, often shown as a companion to the three older daughters of Nefertiti. Mutnodjmet is taller than her nieces and therefore older, although the fact that she still wears the side-lock of youth indicates that she was probably too young to act as their nurse or governess.[12] Mutnodjmet disappears from the scenes before Nefertiti's fourth daughter is born and we may assume that she left the immediate royal family at this time, possibly to be married.

In the tomb of Tey and Ay – most probably her parents – Mutnodjmet watches with the ladies of the court as Nefertiti and Akhenaten present the fortunate couple with a shower of golden gifts. She refrains, however, from participating directly in any of the Amarna celebrations, and does not seem to be a devotee of the sun disc. This aloofness, her apparent reluctance to join her sister and brother-in-law at worship, and the fact that Mutnodjmet is usually accompanied by two comical dwarfs who are encumbered with funny names, caused Norman de Garis Davies to speculate again on the fate of one of the lost members of Akhenaten's harem:

These servants, for whom ridiculous titles and names are invented, and their mistress, who stands apart without participating in the worship of the Aten, invite comment. Were it not for the evident youth of the princess and her Egyptian aspect, I would have ventured to suggest that it was Tadukheper [sic] herself under an Egyptian name, to whom the monogamous King would grant no higher title or relation than this . . . Her speedy disappearance would be easily explained by the king's repugnance to the alliance. The dwarfs' curious titles might then have some playful reference to their Syrian names.[13]

We have no contemporary written description of Nefertiti. However, as she was almost certainly of Egyptian descent, we can safely assume that she was relatively petite with brown eyes, a light-brown skin and wavy brown or black hair. Throughout the New Kingdom it was common practice for upper-class men and women to crop their hair and shave their bodies as a practical response to the heat, dust and bugs of the Egyptian climate; as Nefertiti frequently appears completely hairless, we

may assume that she too believed in total depilation. We do know that
Nefertiti used the make-up and unguents of her day, and excavations at
Amarna have yielded several intimate cosmetic items including a blue
glazed perfume bottle and kohl tubes inlaid with the names of the queen
and her daughters.[14] It is difficult to decide how much reliance to place
on contemporary depictions of the queen, as the Amarna artists did not
put a high premium on 'realistic' representations. However, her portraits
suggest that Nefertiti was slightly shorter than her husband and of slender
build at the time of her marriage, although she later became more
pear-shaped, with a trim waist but heavy thighs and a sagging stomach.
Whatever her shape, Nefertiti appears consistently graceful in her movements. Her epithets are to a large extent stereotyped expressions of
queenly virtues: 'Fair of Face, Mistress of Joy, Endowed with Charm,
Great of Love', but they do suggest that Amenhotep wished his wife to
be recognized first and foremost as a beautiful woman.

Our first glimpse of the new queen comes from the private tombs of
Thebes. In the badly damaged tomb of the royal butler Parennefer (TT
188), an unnamed lady, almost certainly Nefertiti, accompanies the king
as he worships the Aten and, in a scene reminiscent of earlier tombs, sits
beside Amenhotep as he receives the grovelling Parennefer.[15] In the
tomb of the Vizier Ramose (TT 55) we get a much better view of the
queen as she stands behind her husband at the Window of Appearance,
the palace balcony which allowed the royal couple to present themselves
to their subjects. Unfortunately the scene is only partially carved, and
Nefertiti is hidden from the waist downwards by the palace wall. She is
a slender young woman with a heavy jaw, dressed in a long, elaborately
pleated linen robe with sleeves. This is Nefertiti's standard attire, and
occasional depictions of an ankle-length sheath may simply represent
the same dress pulled tight in order to emphasize the body. On Nefertiti's
brow there is the uraeus which signifies royalty and in her hand she
carries an object which has been identified as a 'drooping queenly lily'
but which is more probably a fly-whisk.

Nefertiti's Nubian-style wig, a bushy layered bob cut at an angle so
as to leave the nape of the neck exposed while the longer side hair falls
to the clavicles, is something of an innovation.[16] This style, which is
believed to have been inspired by the naturally curly hair of the Nubian
soldiers who fought in the pharaoh's army, had hitherto been worn only

Fig. 2.2   The Window of Appearance: Theban tomb of Ramose

by men connected with the military or the police force. Its appearance
on a high-ranking woman must have had the same startling effect on
her contemporaries as the simple Eton crops of the 1920s had on a world
accustomed to seeing women with elaborate long hair. Judging by
modern standards of beauty the Nubian style was very becoming to
Nefertiti's gamine good looks; it is entirely possible that she adopted it
simply because it made her look good. However, the fact that this
hairstyle is henceforth reserved for women closely linked with the king,
suggests that it may have had a deeper significance for its wearer. In fact,
throughout her stay at Thebes Nefertiti varied her hairstyles, choosing

52   NEFERTITI

between the Nubian style, and the longer, more old-fashioned tripartite wig favoured by her mother-in-law, which Nefertiti wore either straight or curled. Generally the longer, heavy wig was worn with a tall feathered crown, possibly in order to counterbalance its weight.

Standing in front of his bride, Amenhotep appears in a long and voluminous pleated robe which very much resembles his wife's dress. Amenhotep is the active one; he leans forward with slightly outstretched arms to greet his people and in doing so reveals his trim waist, heavy hips and one breast. Nefertiti, entirely feminine in spite of her masculine wig, is passive, and seems quite happy with her traditional role as onlooker. High in the sky above, the sun disc of the Aten shines down on the queen and her husband.

Nefertiti bore six daughters within ten years of her marriage, the elder three being born at Thebes, the younger three at Amarna: Meritaten ('Beloved of the Aten'; born no later than Year 1), Meketaten ('Protected by the Aten'; probably born Year 4), Ankhesenpaaten ('Living through the Aten'; born before the end of Year 7, most probably before Year 6), Neferneferuaten-the-younger ('Exquisite Beauty of the Sun Disc'; probably born by Year 8), Neferneferure ('Exquisite Beauty of Re'; born before Year 10) and Setepenre ('Chosen of Re'; born before Year 10). All six daughters were depicted with their parents in a remarkable fresco painted on the mud-brick wall of the King's House at Amarna, dated on stylistic grounds to Year 9. Here the family was shown relaxing in a columned hall. Nefertiti reclined on a pile of cushions and cuddled the tiny baby Setepenre who may have only just been born. Amenhotep, dressed in a long robe and sandals, sat opposite his wife on a low stool, and the three eldest princesses, naked but adorned with jewellery, stood between their parents, secure in the shelter of their mother's extended left arm. Neferneferuaten-the-younger and Neferneferure, still babies themselves, sat on colourful cushions at their mother's feet and played together. Unfortunately by the time this mural was discovered by Flinders Petrie in 1891, it had suffered extensive damage caused by white ants and was in a highly fragile condition. The upper part of the scene was beyond reconstruction with Nefertiti and Amenhotep truncated at the waist, and baby Setepenre had vanished except for one tiny painted hand. The practical Petrie was forced to take drastic action to preserve what little he could:

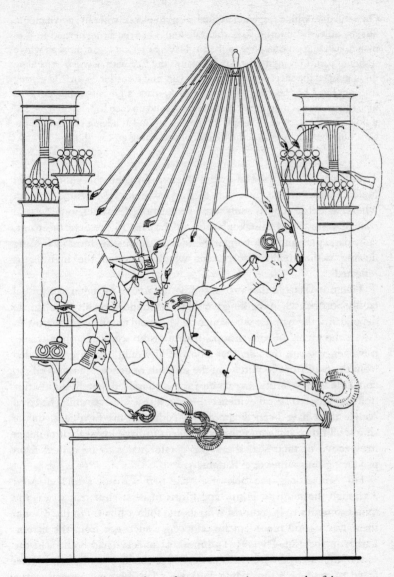

Fig. 2.3   The Window of Appearance: Amarna tomb of Ay

On a still day, with a carpenter's chisel, I cut to pieces, without any vibration, little by little, the mud-bricks of the wall, until I had the facing of mud 30 × 16 inches, standing on edge, free in the air. Having previously cut through where it should part, I brought up a box lid against the face with newspaper padding on it, grasped the sheet of mud against the lid, and turned it down. On getting it to my hut I brushed the dust off the back, made a grid of wooden bars an inch square, and as much apart, put a layer of mud on each bar and then pressed it down on the back of the mud, and put more mud as keying between all the bars. On reversal, there was the fresco unhurt resting on the grid.[17]

The fragment of mud showing Neferneferuaten-the-younger and Neferneferure at play was sent to the Ashmolean Museum, Oxford, where, as Petrie reports with some resignation, '. . . after some years a coat of varnish was mistakenly put on the face to preserve the paint, sadly darkening and yellowing it, besides destroying the most interesting dusting with powdered orpiment which indicated the high lights reflected'.

Tradition dictated that a royal son would not be included in a formal family portrait, when the king would be surrounded by his close female dependants, the women who supported him and emphasized his power. Given the highly unconventional nature of the scene described above, however, it seems unlikely that a boy child would have been excluded from the family group purely on the grounds of gender. It seems safe to conclude that Nefertiti never bore a son, and indeed there is no inscriptional or archaeological evidence to suggest that she ever did. The royal couple must have been disappointed. Although the Egyptians, unlike almost all other ancient civilizations, seem to have loved their children irrespective of their sex, there was greater status to be gained from producing sons rather than daughters.

For Amenhotep, the lack of a male heir was not a total disaster. Although the myth of Horus and Osiris made it clear that it was the king's son born to his consort who should follow him on to the throne, there was a good precedent for adopting a successor from the harem. Earlier in the 18th Dynasty Tuthmosis II and III had both been the sons of minor royal wives who succeeded to the throne when the queen failed to produce a son, while Tuthmosis I had been a general in the army until he was adopted by his predecessor. For Nefertiti the lack of a son was more serious, condemning her to a temporary role in Egypt's limelight. As Nefertiti was not of royal birth she was denied the title of 'King's Daughter', and her entire status was derived from her role as 'King's Wife' and mother of the royal children. Without a son this role would end with her husband's death and she could never become 'Mother of the King', the title which had ensured her mother-in-law's continuing importance at court.

The royal couple hid their disappointment well. From the moment they were born the little princesses were allowed an unprecedented prominence by both their parents, with the three eldest, and Meritaten in particular, being the favourites. All six are included in both formal and informal royal scenes, where they are portrayed as miniature adults rather than babies and toddlers, and all six are consistently associated with their mother who, as the Amarna boundary stelae make clear, took responsibility for their upbringing:

. . . My heart is pleased with the queen and her children. May old age be granted to the Great Queen Neferneferuaten-Nefertiti . . . for she is in the charge of the pharaoh, and may old age be granted to her children, the Princess Meritaten and the Princess Meketaten, for they are under the authority of the queen their mother, for ever and ever.[18]

So ubiquitous are the royal daughters that they have frequently been used as a means of dating their father's monuments, the assumption being that if a daughter is not depicted, she has not yet been born. While this is useful as a general rule of thumb, it can be dangerous to date a monument purely on the grounds of the number of daughters shown; we do not know, for example, whether a daughter would be included in a formal scene as soon as she was born, or whether the artist would wait until she was old enough to play a proper part in the ritual. Anachronisms did occur, the most obvious being an Amarna tomb scene showing the reception of foreign tribute during Year 12, where only three of the six princesses appear.

Throughout the first year of his reign Amenhotep IV acted as a conventional monarch, carrying on very much where his late father had left off. The royal court remained at Thebes, probably based at the Malkata

Palace, and building work continued in and around the Karnak Temple where Amenhotep undertook the decoration of his father's unfinished pylons with what at first sight appear to be irreproachably conventional images, although Re-Harakhty, the falcon-headed sun god who wears the sun disc on his head, was allowed unprecedented prominence. Pylon III was embellished with a scene showing the triumphant Amenhotep IV in the guise of a victorious pharaoh smiting the heads of a group of grovelling foreigners, while the southern pylon (now demolished) was garnished with a series of traditional offering scenes including the new king presenting to Re-Harakhty who is now designated '. . . he who rejoices in the horizon in his name "Sunlight that is in the Disc"'. At Soleb Amenhotep completed his father's unfinished temple, and here we see scenes of the son worshipping his deified father.

During Year 2 came the unexpected announcement that a *sed* festival was to be celebrated on the third anniversary of Amenhotep's accession. No official explanation for this celebration has been preserved, but we might hazard a guess that it marked some important event in the king's private life, perhaps his birthday or even his decision to dedicate himself and his people to a new god.[19] An unexpected festival would certainly have set the seal on the new king's popularity, as the *heb-sed* was a time of holidaying and feasting for all.

First, however, the festival buildings had to be prepared. There was a flurry of construction work and the opening of a new sandstone quarry at Gebel el-Silsila, where a tall stela cut high on the cliff shows the new king wearing the crown of Upper Egypt and offering to Amen beneath the winged sun disc, and an inscription records the cutting of stone for the 'Great *Benben* of Harakhty' at Thebes. Heliopolis, Memphis and Nubia received new sun temples, but Amenhotep's attention was focused on Thebes, the religious capital of Egypt, where Amen's supremacy was threatened by a disjointed series of temples and cult buildings, all dedicated in various ways to the worship of the sun disc or Aten who was to play a prominent role in the *sed* celebrations. These included a magnificent open temple named *Gempaaten* ('The Sun Disc is found') and its subsidiary, *Hwt-Benben* ('Mansion of the *Benben*-Stone'), which were situated to the east of the existing Karnak complex.

Unfortunately the archaeological evidence for this period is severely limited and none of these buildings still stands. This is due not to the ravages of time, which have not been particularly severe at Thebes, but to the deliberate actions of Amenhotep's successors who made a determined effort to wipe out all trace of their unconventional forebear. Amenhotep's name and image were ruthlessly erased and defaced wherever they were found. His monuments were torn down and his buildings were dismantled, the valuable stone being re-used in other constructions. A similar fate was to befall Amarna, Egypt's short-lived capital city. Here the stone blocks from Amenhotep's temples were salvaged and taken across the river to be incorporated in the building work of Ramesses II at Hermopolis (modern Ashmunein). In 1939 a German expedition to Hermopolis recovered over 1,000 limestone blocks which, originally from Amarna, had been re-used in the foundations of the temple pylon. Unfortunately the advent of war interrupted their work. The Germans hastily reburied their precious finds, only to have them re-excavated by enterprising locals who sawed the decorated blocks into slabs, 'improved' them with modern plaster and paint, and then sold them to eager collectors.

Not one of Amenhotep's Theban monuments has survived the harsh treatment meted out by his successors, and instead of a series of impressive temples we have been left with a vast number of inscribed and painted sandstone blocks of standard dimensions ($52 \times 26 \times 24$cm) which are today known as *talatat* blocks.[20] These relatively small blocks, Amenhotep's building bricks, were easy for his workmen to quarry and transport and very light for his builders to handle, allowing the king to embark on a rapid building programme which transformed the Karnak complex within three or four years. Ultimately, it was their size which saved the *talatat* blocks. They were preserved because they could be usefully employed as the filling inside later monuments; the cores of the second and ninth pylons at Karnak, for example, have been found to include thousands of blocks. Over 35,000 disjointed inscribed blocks have so far been collected from within the walls and gateways of the Karnak Temple, making a 3D jigsaw puzzle of such size, weight and complexity that many scholars believed the lost scenes would never be restored. Fortunately archaeologists cannot resist a challenge, and since the mid 1960s the Akhenaten Temple Project has been dedicated to the recovery of the lost images. By employing a combination of photography and 'space-age' computer graphics, it has so far been possible to reconstruct over 2,000 individual scenes of Amenhotep's early reign, although the buildings themselves remain a series of disjointed blocks.[21]

The indexing of the *talatat* blocks has made one thing very clear: Nefertiti enjoyed a far greater prominence in Theban state ritual than had ever been imagined. A brief analysis of the images of the recovered blocks makes fascinating reading.[22] By 1976 there had been 329 confirmed occurrences of the name or figure of Amenhotep IV and 564 occurrences of Nefertiti's name or image. When broken down these figures seem even more startling: for example, Nefertiti's name appeared sixty-seven times on offering tables, Nefertiti and Amenhotep appeared together thirteen times, and only three tables bore Amenhotep's name alone. This imbalance is likely to be at least in part a reflection of the fact that the recovered blocks – by no means a complete or randomly selected sample – include a disproportionate number of images from *Hwt-Benben*, a building which was particularly associated with Nefertiti. Nevertheless, Nefertiti's prominence in what until now had been a king-dominated sphere, is beyond dispute.

The *benben*-stone was an ancient pyramid or cone-shaped cult object which had been linked with the solar cult of Re at Heliopolis from the very beginning of the dynastic age. Amenhotep adopted and adapted this ancient symbolism, and his *Hwt-Benben* was a colonnaded temple associated with the vast Aten temple *Gempaaten* and focused not upon a true *benben*-stone, but upon the single Karnak obelisk set up by his grandfather Tuthmosis IV. Women had always been permitted to serve in temples as priestesses, musicians and dancers, and many queens had held honorary positions in the cult of Hathor. Some queens had enjoyed a more intimate relationship with the gods. It was recognized that the queen could stimulate or arouse susceptible male deities, and the king's grandmother Mutemwia had even conceived a child with Amen. Centuries of tradition, however, decreed that the king, and only the king, as chief priest of all cults, should offer to the gods. Within the precincts of *Hwt-Benben* it was Nefertiti and not Amenhotep who took the king's role of priest.

Each reconstructed square pillar of the *Hwt-Benben* colonnade has four sides, three of which show near identical full-length images of Nefertiti and Meritaten shaking their sistra beneath the sun disc while the fourth, the so-called 'special' side which is presumed to have faced the temple courtyard, is divided into four scenes showing Nefertiti offering to the Aten. On all the 'long' sides Nefertiti wears a long, heavy blue wig and a diaphanous pleated robe open to the waist and tied under the bust. She has a uraeus on her head and sandals on her feet, and holds out two large sistra. Behind her Meritaten – invariably described as the 'King's bodily Daughter whom he loves, Meritaten, born of the Great King's Wife whom he loves, Mistress of the Two Lands, Nefertiti, may she live' – appears as a perfect miniature adult, dressed in a similar flimsy robe and shaking a single small-scale sistrum. Directly above mother and daughter the sun's disc appears in the sky and the sun's rays reach down to extend their blessing. The scenes on the special sides vary slightly, but each register shows two Nefertitis in mirror-image, their open arms raised in worship, standing before an offering table under the Aten's loving rays. Her stance is that of a king offering to a god. Again Nefertiti

Fig. 2.4   Nefertiti and Meritaten in the *Hwt-Benben*

wears her flimsy robe, and again Meritaten accompanies her mother, shaking a miniature sistrum. Inside the temple the story is repeated. The queen, accompanied by one or occasionally two daughters, offers to the god, while the king is nowhere to be seen. Indeed, no males, neither human nor animal, are depicted on any of the *Hwt-Benben* blocks.

Hwt-Benben was dismantled during the reign of King Horemheb, when many of the blocks from the Nefertiti pillars were incorporated

in the Second Pylon at Karnak. The blocks were not, however, used in
a random or thoughtless manner. Henri Chevrier, the French archaeologist who worked on the Second Pylon during the late 1940s, discovered
that within it the Nefertiti blocks had been carefully reassembled so as
to make up partial scenes, but that curiously at least two of the scenes
had been deliberately reconstructed upside-down. Many of the images
of Nefertiti had been defaced within the pylon, and many of the hands
on the end of the Aten's rays had been slashed across the fingertips. We
do not know why Horemheb's workmen should have taken the trouble
to match up scenes which were to be hidden from view behind the
pylon facing, nor why some of the scenes should have been reassembled
in reverse order; the assumption that this may have been a symbolic act
of revenge against a heretic regime by the orthodox Horemheb is
probably correct. As Ray Winfield Smith has noted:

It is certain that the queen was held in contempt by those responsible for this
undignified treatment. To turn a beautiful female upside-down, to slash her
viciously, and to place her where she would be symbolically crushed by the
enormous weight of massive, soaring walls, can hardly be explained otherwise.[23]

The mutilation of the Aten's fingertips may have been intended to
suggest that the god would no longer be able to extend his love and
protection to the disgraced queen. It is not clear, however, whether
Nefertiti was singled out for this attack for political reasons, either
because she was usurping the role of a king or because she was worshipping a proscribed god, or whether Horemheb held a more personal
grudge against Nefertiti.

Nefertiti's prominence in the Mansion of the *Benben*-Stone could
perhaps be explained as an unprecedented aberration, the Mansion being
merely a minor temple dedicated to exclusively female worship of the
Aten as a subsidiary of the more powerful male temple *Gempaaten*.
However, other Karnak *talatat* confirm that at some point during the
first five years of her husband's reign, probably soon after the birth of
her first child, Nefertiti was able to abandon the traditional queen's role
of passive observer which we saw in the tomb of Ramose. In the
presence of her husband Nefertiti remains a supportive wife, appearing
at a smaller scale to shake a queenly sistrum, but she is now a woman of

action who may be shown riding in a chariot, travelling in a palanquin, or even enjoying a feast. In an echo of the scene in the tomb of Kheruef where Queen Tiy takes the form of a sphinx to trample two female enemies, alternating southern and northern female hostages now pay homage before Nefertiti's throne.

The most compelling evidence for Nefertiti's changed role comes from a disparate group of blocks which indicate her involvement in

Fig. 2.5   Nefertiti smiting a female enemy, scene on the royal boat

what are now known as 'smiting scenes'. *Talatat* blocks recovered from both Karnak and Hermopolis show Amenhotep's boat decorated with traditional images of the king slaying the foes of Egypt. Amenhotep stands beneath the rays of the sun disc, his right arm raised to deliver a fatal blow to an enemy who grovels at his feet, while Nefertiti, emulating the goddess Maat, stands impassively behind him and watches. These images are paralleled by unprecedented tableaux showing Nefertiti herself as a triumphal queen wielding either a mace or a sword in order to execute an enemy. The clearest of these scenes, recovered from Hermopolis, shows a fleet of at least three royal boats, although Nefertiti's is the only one which is substantially intact. Royal boats may be distinguished by the carved heads on the end of the steering poles, and here Nefertiti's poles show her wearing her trademark blue head-dress topped with a disc and two tall plumes, whose streamers flutter merrily in the breeze. On the deck, behind the central cabin, stands a small kiosk or canopy which possibly served as an audience chamber. The relief which decorates the back wall of this structure shows Nefertiti, again wearing her blue crown and dressed in a long skirt, raising her right arm to dispatch a female enemy who kneels in submission with her face turned towards the queen.[24]

These smiting scenes may well be representations of a disturbing ritual – we should not assume that they are merely symbolic. The image of the pharaoh as a victorious warrior subduing a representative of the enemies of Egypt was an ancient one, first seen on the ceremonial Narmer palette dating to the very dawn of the dynastic age. By the 18th Dynasty it had evolved into a visual metaphor used to depict the concept of the pharaoh triumphant rather than a specific event. Neither Amenhotep III nor Amenhotep IV was ever called upon to lead troops into battle, but both chose to be shown in this aggressive pose and both may well have been called upon to execute a token enemy. The message behind the scene is one of generalized victory – the enemy is always subdued and does not struggle to escape – and of sacrifice, and the action of the right arm raised to kill or sacrifice by a person of authority may be found in a scaled-down version in the tombs of the nobles, where the tomb owner, attended by his wife and children, holds decoy birds in his left hand and raises his right arm to throw a stick in the air.[25] However, the role of smiter had until now been exclusively a king's role, and by implication a man's role. The fact that Nefertiti was allowed to play the part of the king in this ritual must be read as an indication of her increased ritual and/or political importance.

It should not, however, be read as a sign that Nefertiti was now of equal importance to the king. The Egyptian love of symmetry dictated that Nefertiti's boat should as far as possible match Amenhotep's boat. In Amenhotep's scene, however, he is supported by the presence of the queen, his immediate inferior, while Nefertiti is supported by her eldest daughter, who we must assume to be her immediate inferior. The message seems clear. Just as Tiy had been separated by her marriage from the rest of humanity, so the gulf between Nefertiti and the common people has widened. The gap between Amenhotep and Nefertiti may have closed slightly, but it is still there. Nefertiti is indeed a powerful woman, and she has been allotted some of the privileges and duties of the crown. Amenhotep is happy for everyone to understand this. However, the basic chain of authority remains unaltered. Amenhotep is responsible to the Aten. Nefertiti falls under the authority of the king, and the little princesses remain under the control of their mother. Later, at Amarna, we occasionally see Nefertiti offering alongside her husband apparently as an equal. It is in these scenes that we may realize the true extent of her religious power.

The elaborate crowns worn by the queens of Egypt were, during the New Kingdom, intended to convey a symbolic message to the observer. The ancient Egyptians consistently made use of symbols as a means of communicating abstract concepts; it is this that makes their art so difficult for modern observers to understand at any but the most basic of levels. It should come as no surprise to find that Nefertiti's increased status is reflected in her choice of head-dress. For the first few years of her husband's reign she is invariably shown wearing the single or double uraeus which, as a symbol representing the eyes of Re, is often identified as the goddesses Hathor and Maat. The uraeus, which itself often wears a solar disc with cow horns thereby emphasizing the solar link, is frequently supplemented with a traditional queen's head-dress, and, like her mother-in-law before her, Nefertiti favours either the double feathers or the double feathers plus disc and horns which associate her with the solar cults of Re and his daughter Hathor. She consistently avoids donning the vulture head-dress which, as the vulture was primarily associated with Mut, the consort of Amen, may not have been acceptable in the new religious climate.

Now Nefertiti starts to wear her own unique head-dress, the tall, straight-edged, flat-topped blue crown familiar from the Berlin bust.[26] The origins of this crown are obscure, although it seems likely that it was developed as a female version of the tall blue leather war crown, covered with protective discs, which was worn by the kings of Egypt. Akhenaten himself favoured a rather high, narrow or bonnet-like version of the blue crown, which he often augmented with stylized ringlets or multiple uraei. Nefertiti's crown too was occasionally covered with decorative discs, which may themselves have had a symbolic meaning connecting their wearer with the cult of the Aten. The shape of Nefertiti's crown probably owes much to the head-dress worn by Tefnut, daughter of the sun god. Tiy, when depicted in the form of a sphinx associated with Hathor-Tefnut, had worn a tall crown of similar silhouette whose top was formed by sprouting plants, which some scholars have interpreted as a symbol of rejuvenation and fertility, perhaps even linked with the dishevelled hairstyles traditionally worn by women in labour.[27] Now we find Nefertiti herself associated with the form of the sphinx at Karnak.

It was during these early years, while the *Hwt-Benben* was under construction, that Nefertiti received a new name, Neferneferuaten or 'Beautiful are the Beauties of the Aten'.[28] From now on she was known to her contemporaries by the somewhat long-winded appellation Neferneferuaten-Nefertiti ('Beautiful are the Beauties of the Aten. A Beautiful Woman Has Come'), although the Karnak *talatat* blocks suggest that her shorter name was still used in scenes where space was limited. To avoid confusion she will remain Nefertiti, the name by which she is known today, throughout this book. Nefertiti's name, as queen, had always been written inside a cartouche, the hieroglyphic device representing a

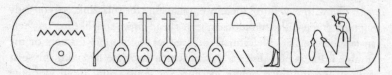

Fig. 2.6   The cartouche of Nefertiti

loop of rope which always encircled the throne-name and birth-name of the king. Her new name was similarly enclosed, although its length occasionally posed problems for imprudent masons who unwisely carved the cartouche first only to find themselves faced with the problem of trying to cram an unusual number of hieroglyphic signs into too small a space. Within the cartouche the writing of 'Aten' – an element of the name Neferneferuaten – was consistently reversed so that it faced the determinative sign which indicated Nefertiti's queenly status; the trans-position of the Aten was a great honour, likened to the inclusion of a capital letter within a modern name, which allowed the queen's image to face the name of her god. Occasionally Nefertiti was allotted two cartouches, so that her name resembled that of a king. At Thebes the juxtaposed cartouches contained her shorter name and her longer name, while at Amarna each of the cartouches contained the longer name.

Amenhotep's jubilee was celebrated during Year 3 with major festivities at *Gempaaten*. Recent excavation has shown that this was a vast temple built in the form of a rectangular open court surrounded by a roofed colonnade whose square pillars bore colossal painted statues of the king himself. Here, under the impassive gaze of his own image, Amenhotep reinterpreted the traditional *heb-sed* rituals celebrated by his father before him. Scenes recovered from the *Gempaaten talatat* blocks confirm that

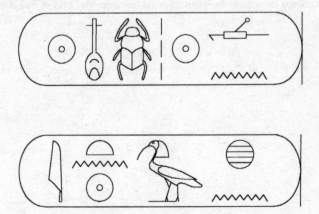

Fig. 2.7   The royal names of Akhenaten

the royal family and numerous anonymous dignitaries were present to observe the ceremonies and enjoy the feasting but, very significantly, many of the great state gods, including the hitherto all-powerful 'father of the gods' Amen, were excluded and the shrines which would normally have housed these deities all contained depictions of the king beneath the Aten's disc. Nefertiti played an obvious but not intrusive role in the celebrations – she supported her husband but never sought to usurp him. Dressed in a long-sleeved robe with two plumes on her head, she rode in a palanquin whose throne, the exact parallel of the king's, was carved with sphinxes in Nefertiti's own image. Even the rearing cobras fringing the palanquin had Nefertiti's face and feathered crown.

The deliberate exclusion of the major state gods from the *heb-sed* should have served as a warning to the priests of Amen. By the end of Year 5 the Aten had risen from obscurity to become the dominant state god. Offerings which had traditionally been presented to the temple of Amen were now diverted to the Aten temples so that the cult of the Aten grew rich as the cult of Amen grew poor. Eventually the old temples were closed, and all building work ceased as the decision was taken to relocate the court to a new purpose-built capital city, Akhetaten ('Horizon of the Aten'), now known as Amarna. Amen was now declared anathema and the king, rejecting the given name which linked him with the despised Amen, followed his wife in adopting a new name. Henceforth he was to be known as Akhenaten, or 'Living Spirit of the Aten'.

3

The Aten Dazzles

𓁹𓈖𓆓𓃀𓅱𓏏𓎟𓂋𓏤

Glorious, you rise on the horizon of heaven, O living Aten, creator of life. When you have arisen on the eastern horizon you fill every land with your beauty. You are gorgeous, great and radiant, high over every land. Your rays embrace all the lands that you have made.[1]

The kings of the 18th Dynasty openly acknowledged a great debt to the god Amen, for they well understood that it was Amen who had enabled the mighty Theban warrior Ahmose to unite Egypt after the civil unrest and foreign rule of the Second Intermediate Period. Amen's protection of Ahmose soon proved to be a shrewd political move, and the devotion of successive 18th Dynasty kings allowed him to evolve from a relatively insignificant local god worshipped in and around Thebes into the patron god of the Egyptian empire. Amen, appearing as a man dressed in a kilt and wearing a distinctive head-dress of two tall plumes, was recognized both as king of the gods and father of the king. He became associated with the most important Old Kingdom deity in the compound sun god Amen-Re and linked with the ithyphallic fertility god Min. Amen's mighty Karnak temple dominated the Theban skyline, and he was the presiding deity in each of the royal mortuary temples on the west bank of the River Nile. Within his temples, however, Amen was an aloof and secretive god; his name, which translates as 'the hidden', gives a clue to his character. Amen's home was a dark and lonely shrine hidden deep within the sacred precincts, inaccessible to the ordinary people and visited only by the priests who attended to the daily rituals of washing and dressing the god and making offerings of food, drink and incense. Even when on festival days Amen sailed out into the sunlight his sacred boat became a miniature temple and he remained concealed behind the doors of his shrine. This hidden aspect of the god allowed his priests – those privy to his divine wishes – great power.

Fig. 3.1   The god Amen

As the 18th Dynasty developed into an era of unprecedented prosperity successive pharaohs were faced with an embarrassment of riches. Much of their new-found wealth was used to enhance the Karnak temple complex, home of Amen, Mut and Khonsu, and the stonemasons were kept busy as succeeding kings vied with each other to express their devotion in stone. Amen's temple grew physically vast and, as royal endowments increased, developed into a significant semi-independent economic entity administered by an increasingly complex hierarchy of priests. Amen was now a major landowner in his own right with control over a variety of income-generating assets such as fields, herds, ships, vineyards and even beehives, some situated many miles away from Thebes. The revenue provided by these assets, plus taxes extracted in perpetuity from individual estates, were used to pay the priests and the temple servants; surpluses were hoarded, together with vast amounts of grain and the gold, precious stones and foreign loot donated by the king, in huge warehouses safe within the temple walls. Thus the king was able to convince all of his extreme piety and indifference to worldly goods, while the temple provided a convenient and secure bank for his treasures. If the annual inundation failed, or if the Nile rose too high and flooded the towns and villages, the temple stores could be requisitioned and their grain used to feed the people.

For many years the king and the priesthood of Amen existed side by

side in symbiotic harmony. The priesthood, which owned substantial
tracts of land in the south, assisted the vizier in the administration of
Upper Egypt, thus freeing the royal court to reside at Memphis. The
king in his turn supported the god financially, while making judicious
use of their relationship to reinforce his own position as divine ruler. By
the later 18th Dynasty, however, there are signs that the monarchy may
have started to feel itself challenged by the ever-increasing power of
Amen. Amenhotep II, Tuthmosis IV and Amenhotep III all attempted
to maintain control over the cult by appointing their own loyal followers,
natives of northern towns rather than southerners, as High Priest of
Amen. Amenhotep III, ruling over a peaceful empire, must have seen
little need for the protection of a mighty warrior god although he was
certainly not averse to exploiting other aspects of Amen's divinity. Amen
was chosen to be his heavenly father, and the extensive programme of
refurbishment at Karnak and Luxor which continued throughout his
reign is a testament to the king's loyalty.

Egypt's unprecedented wealth meant that the king's generosity need
not be confined to a single cult. Amenhotep had always been interested
in Egypt's past, as evidenced by his revision of the *heb-sed* ceremony.
Now he started to pay more attention to the other gods of the pantheon,
partially reverting back to Old Kingdom solar theology. He developed
a particular interest in one relatively obscure god, the Aten, whose name
simply means 'the disc', and who since the Middle Kingdom had been
recognized both as a physical manifestation of the sun god Re and as a
symbol of divinity closely affiliated with the king. The Aten was represented either by a winged sun disc or by a hawk-headed god, and at
this time had no cult centre or major temple. We now find the name of
the Aten appearing with increasing regularity, so that even the royal
barge which sailed on Queen Tiy's pleasure lake was named 'The Sun
Disc [Aten] Dazzles'.

Egypt is a land of hot sunlit days and dark cool nights. The contrast
between the two is both sudden and obvious, and it is therefore not
surprising that both the sun and its light played an important part in
Egyptian life and religion, the daily cycle of sunset followed by sunrise
being interpreted as a certain guarantee of life after death. The sun god
Re, represented either as a falcon-headed god or as a winged sun disc,
is known from the time of the earliest pyramids when to spend the

Fig. 3.2   The god Re-Harakhty

Afterlife with Re was one of the most important aspirations of the king. Indeed, the shape of the pyramid may well have been intended to represent the sun's rays in solid form, a straight-sided ramp which would allow the king to climb up to heaven. Re, the sun god, was occasionally combined with Horus, god of the horizon, to produce the hybrid deity Re-Harakhty, a man with Horus's falcon head.

The cult of the sun god was centred on the northern city of Heliopolis (ancient Iunu), one of the most magnificent cities of the dynastic age, which may well have provided vital archaeological clues to the development of the Aten cult. Here the original *benben*-stone, a pyramid or cone-shaped boulder, possibly a meteorite, took the place of a cult statue of Re as a focus for worship. Sadly, due to a fatal combination of ancient destruction and modern development, there is now almost nothing left of the ancient glories of Heliopolis. However, the 5th Dynasty sun temples of Abu Ghurab, only one of which now survives, may well have been built to the same plan. Here the temple consisted of an open courtyard with a central alabaster altar and, to the west, a large obelisk which acted as a sun totem or *benben*.

Amenhotep III used the cult of the Aten as a means of developing a cult of the king, stressing his own personal divinity through the newly established Aten priesthood. Although tradition dictated that the king should become fully divine only at his death, the mortal Amenhotep was already recognized as the living embodiment of Ptah and worshipped at the 'Temple of Nebmaatre-United-with-Ptah', Memphis. In Egypt's outlying regions Amenhotep was more obviously a god, and the Soleb temple included a relief showing the king making an offering to his own image, which bears the title 'Nebmaatre Lord of Nubia', a god who, judging from his head-dress, had lunar rather than solar connections. Later, after the king's death, Amenhotep IV is shown worshipping his father at Soleb, while in the Theban tomb of Kheruef, where we are shown Amenhotep III and Tiy associated with a variety of solar deities, a small scene shows the king and queen being pulled along in the evening boat of Re, an image which seems intended to symbolize the union of the dead king with the living sun god.[2] The Nubian cult of the deified Amenhotep survived the upheavals of the Amarna period and continued into the reign of Tutankhamen, while at Thebes it went on beyond the Ramesside period.

A major alteration in Amenhotep's status seems to follow the celebration of his first *heb-sed*;[3] it is after this date that we find an increasing emphasis on solar iconography and this goes hand in hand with the development of statues intended to commemorate the deified king. The Colossi of Memnon, placed immediately outside the king's mortuary temple, may well have served as an object of worship in their own right because, just as a cult statue was recognized as divine, a colossal statue of the king – particularly one which had been named – made an appropriate object of worship. By the time of Ramesses II, some sixty years later, colossal statues of the monarch were regularly named and worshipped and various cult temples included within their sanctuaries depictions of the divine Ramesses sitting alongside his fellow gods.

The king had always filled the role of an intermediary between the gods and mankind, a mortal born to a human mother who became semi-divine on the death of his predecessor. In his official persona the pharaoh was an *ex officio* god on earth, the only Egyptian who could speak directly to the gods and in consequence the chief priest of all religious cults, although he was forced to delegate his responsibilities to deputy priests, only stepping in to officiate at the major cult ceremonies. The king's most important duty, a function of his semi-divine status, was the maintenance of *maat* throughout his land. *Maat*, a word which cannot be translated literally but can mean 'justice' or 'truth' though it is better understood as status quo, was an abstract concept representing the ideal state of the universe and everyone in it. This ideal state had been established at the time of creation and had to be maintained to placate the gods. However, *maat* was always under threat from malevolent outside influences seeking to bring chaos to Egypt. Throughout the dynastic age the concept of *maat* combined with the divine nature of the kingship to reinforce the power of the royal family. By ensuring that the pharaoh's position could not be openly questioned without compromising Egypt's security by threatening *maat*, the ruling élite remained securely at the top of the social pyramid.

During the Old Kingdom his semi-divine status made the king very different from his subjects, and only he could look forward to an afterlife in the presence of his fellow gods. Mere mortals could continue to exist beyond death, but they were confined to the precincts of the tomb. By the Middle Kingdom, however, the afterlife beyond the grave had been opened to all. In consequence the king's perceived divinity on earth was weakened, although he still held sole responsibility for the preservation of *maat*. The New Kingdom saw an attempt to reverse this trend towards equality, with the introduction of the concept of the personal divinity of the king. This started during the reign of Hatchepsut who, in order to reinforce her right to the throne, claimed the god Amen as her bodily father. Theology had always recognized the reigning king as the theoretical son of the creator god, but Hatchepsut made it very clear that she was the fruit of a physical union between Amen and her mother, Queen Ahmose:

She smiled at his majesty. He went to her immediately, his penis erect before her. He gave his heart to her . . . She was filled with joy at the sight of his beauty. His love passed into her limbs. The palace was flooded with the god's fragrance, and all his perfumes were from Punt.[4]

Hatchepsut, as the child of a human mother and a divine father, was a demi-god, but she did not exploit this aspect of her persona, choosing instead to use her filial relationship to Amen as a justification of her reign. Amenhotep III chose to reintroduce the legend of divine birth by copying Hatchepsut's story, suitably amended, on to the wall of the Luxor Temple. Amenhotep III, the son of Tuthmosis IV, was a secure monarch with an incontestable right to inherit the throne; he used the story not as a means of justifying his rule, but as a means of confirming his own semi-divine status, promoting himself as personally divine rather than as a god through his office. It is no surprise that Amenhotep III chose to display this legend at the Luxor Temple, a temple dedicated to the celebration of the divine royal soul.

Within five years of his succession Akhenaten had radically simplified Egypt's polytheistic religion by abolishing most of the established pantheon, replacing a multitude of deities with one god, the Aten. The object of his worship was the light of the sun, rather than the sun itself. Two blocks containing the badly damaged and sadly disjointed text of a royal pronouncement – perhaps a justification of his unprecedented rejection of the old gods – hint at Akhenaten's perception of the traditional gods as worn-out and ineffective:

The king says . . . their temples fallen to ruin . . . they have ceased one after the other, whether of precious stones . . .[5]

At first the cult of the Aten was able to coexist with the old order. Then, perhaps because Akhenaten encountered opposition to his views, or became more entrenched in his beliefs, this peaceful coexistence became unacceptable. The Egyptian pantheon had always been willing to absorb fresh deities, and more traditional gods had simply faded in importance as they were gently displaced by the new. Akhenaten, however, demanded, and got, a rapid and somewhat ruthless rejection of the

Fig. 3.3   Worshipping in the temple

old order. Most of the traditional gods and goddesses could simply be ignored; it was as if they had never been. But from Year 5 onwards Amen, and to a lesser extent his divine family, was subjected to a persecution which was to increase in intensity as the new reign progressed. Amen's name and, more rarely, his image were erased or defaced wherever they were found. This persecution occurred throughout the length and breadth of Egypt although it is at Karnak that its true extent is felt. Here someone even took the trouble to remove Amen's name from the very tip of Hatchepsut's obelisk where, as obelisks are primarily associated with the solar cults, it had probably caused great offence. Throughout the rest of Egypt the desecration was somewhat haphazard and unsystematic, possibly because many of those charged with erasing the name of the god could not themselves read. Nevertheless, those prominent individuals unfortunate enough to bear personal names including the element 'Amen' found it wise to rename themselves at once.

As far as we can tell there had been no great quarrel with the old priesthood to precipitate this extreme reaction, although the Amarna boundary stelae drop dark and regrettably unspecific hints that the king had taken exception to something – possibly traditional cult practices – which had been repeated during both his reign and those of his forebears:

... it shall be worse than what I heard in Year 4; it shall be worse than what I heard in Year 3; it shall be worse than what I heard in Year 1; it shall be worse than what Nebmaatre [Amenhotep III] heard; it shall be worse than what Menkheperure [Tuthmosis IV] heard . . .[6]

Nor was there any apparent resistance to the imposition of the new state religion, although it is of course unlikely that any such resistance would have been recorded in official documents. By stopping all royal offerings Akhenaten ensured that the old temples were quickly and efficiently closed down and that their wealth was diverted to the Aten making this cult and its chief devotee, the king, extremely wealthy. The property confiscated from Amen was to be administered by centralized government officials rather than local priests.

Service of the state gods was at all times seen as a lucrative career rather than a religious vocation. It is therefore possible that many of Amen's priests, now redundant, may have changed allegiance and sought

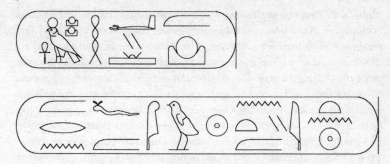

Fig. 3.4 The old names of the Aten

positions serving the Aten. Given the size of the Aten's endowments, their administrative experience would have proved invaluable. It is noticeable, though, that the Amarna court contained few members of the traditional ruling élite. The courtiers most prominent in the service of the king were men of more humble origins who owed their position to the king's patronage rather than to birth. The army now played a conspicuous role in daily life, lending their silent support to the king and his innovations. Although we know of no battles during Akhenaten's reign, the *talatat* blocks have revealed that the king, often viewed as a pacifist, chose to surround himself with soldiers and armed civilians. Even the 'Agents of the Harem Ladies' were armed and ready for action. This heavy military presence may, of course, explain why there was no open opposition to any of Akhenaten's reforms.

The old iconography of a falcon-headed god was abandoned and the Aten took the form of a faceless sun disc wearing the cobra or uraeus which signified kingship, whose long rays were tipped with miniature hands which could hold the *ankh*, symbol of life. Unlike Egypt's other gods the Aten was highly visible, yet at the same time very impersonal – an abstract symbol whose lack of a human body prevented him from appearing in the traditional religious scenes so that he was invariably depicted above the royal family, an observer rather than a participant in the tableaux below. This elevation of the god, and his relatively small size, allowed the king to become the most prominent figure in any religious scene: all eyes were now focused on Akhenaten himself. The Aten required little mystery, no hidden sanctuary and of course no physical host-statue as the sun was his own image, visible to king and commoner alike. We might have expected Akhenaten to extend this reasoning to its logical conclusion. The Aten, a democratic god, had no obvious need of a temple as he was accessible for anyone to worship at any time during the day. But Akhenaten needed his temples as a means of controlling access to his god, and so Aten worship followed the traditional pattern. Only the chief priest or his deputy could address the god, and it was only in the temple that the correct rituals of worship, including offerings, could be performed. The new temples were, however, a direct contrast to the gloomy precincts of Amen and the other traditional gods. Modelled on the solar temples of Re, they were in essence simple open courtyards which allowed the sun to shine down on the worship of the faithful.

Although Akhenaten set out to reform and simplify state religion he had no intention of weakening the position of the monarchy which, until his reign, had been closely linked with accepted theology. Indeed, he followed the example set by his semi-divine father and exploited his new god in order to emphasize the divine role of the king. Amenhotep III had already been linked with Re-Harakhty in the tomb of Kheruef. Now Akhenaten was the son of Re and, as the Aten was the visible, physical aspect of Re, Akhenaten became the earthly or human manifestation of the sun god. As the 'Beautiful Child of the Disc' he was effectively an interpreter standing between the god and his people. He alone could recognize and proclaim the will of his father. In many ways this was a continuation of the old theology, and the 'ordinary' middle- and lower-class Egyptians would have experienced little challenge to their personal beliefs. The biggest change was felt by Akhenaten's courtiers who, denied access to their official god yet needing to ingratiate themselves with the new regime, were compelled to worship via Akhenaten and Nefertiti.

Akhenaten's subjects, accustomed to a wide range of official deities, must have found it hard to understand the austerity of one simple abstract symbol. In the past there had been not one national creed but a series of overlapping religious spheres. These included what in modern terms may be classed as the 'major tradition' represented by the universally acknowledged state gods such as Amen, Isis and Osiris, the 'minor tradition' which included magic, superstition and witchcraft, and a whole series of local cults which fell somewhere between the two extremes.

1. Statue of Amenhotep III
with the god Sobek

2. The Colossi of Memnon at Thebes

3. Wooden head of Queen Tiy

4. Stela depicting Amenhotep III in old age, with Tiy

5. Gold mummy mask of Yuya, father of Tiy

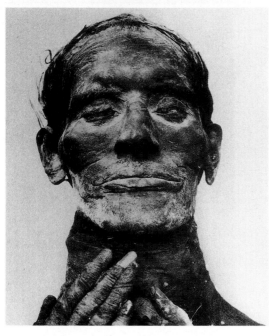

6. Head of the mummy of Yuya

7. Gold mummy mask of
Thuyu, mother of Tiy

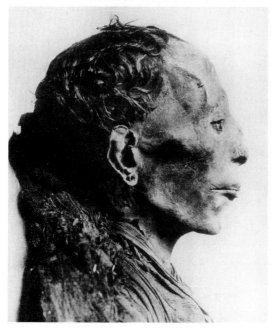

8. Head of the mummy
of Thuyu

9. A colossal statue of Akhenaten

10. An asexual colossus of Akhenaten/Nefertiti

11. Relief depicting Akhenaten

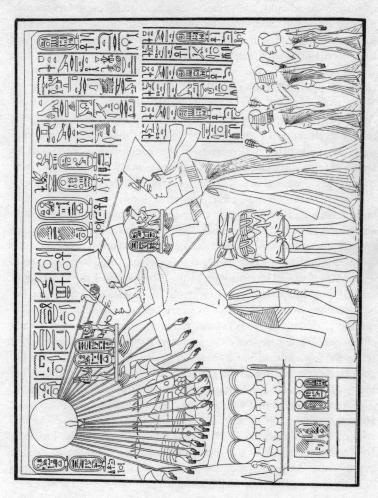

Fig. 3.5 The royal family worship the Aten

Most Egyptians worshipped a highly personal mixture of regional deities and family-based cults, with a heavy emphasis on the spirits responsible for pregnancy and childbirth, supplemented with strong doses of superstition and magic. The absence of the great state gods may therefore not have been a problem for the majority of the population, although they would certainly have missed the great festivals and processions which had so far provided regular breaks in their otherwise monotonous lives. There is no evidence that Akhenaten ever sought to develop national Aten festivals, and his intention seems to have been to replace public religious celebrations with semi-secular events such as the procession of the royal family through the streets, or the distribution of rewards to his loyal servants. This somewhat short-sighted policy must surely have contributed to the general lack of enthusiasm for the new, remote state god.

What obviously was a problem was the essential nature of the Aten itself. Like other creator gods the Aten combined male and female elements so that he could become the 'father and mother' of all things created. He was both asexual and androgynous, had no anthropomorphic association and, by his very nature as sole creator, could have no spouse. This in itself was neither unique to the Aten nor to Egypt.[7] In Egypt asexual gods had been known to create life single-handed; Atum, for example, had either masturbated or expectorated to produce his gender-specific children Shu and Tefnut. However, most gods were clearly either male or female; they coupled and produced their children by relatively conventional means. This cosy divine domesticity made the gods far more accessible to the Egyptian people who, valuing family life above all things, could understand gods who behaved in a human fashion. The Aten had no divine wife and no child to make up the usual triad. He was a remote, characterless entity and his role as a fertile god was very much a theoretical one. We have no equivalent of the Luxor or Deir el-Bahri legends of the divine conception of the king to explain exactly how Akhenaten became the son of the Aten, but it seems unlikely that any form of divine impregnation of Queen Tiy was ever envisaged. Furthermore, there was now no official equivalent of the essentially comforting mother-wife goddess who can be traced back to the female figurines of the predynastic age and who in recent times had been represented by state goddesses such as Isis and, more particularly, Hathor in her various guises. Female goddesses, especially those associated with safe pregnancy and childbirth, had always played an important role in both popular and state religion. Now, officially at least, they were anathema and even Hapy, the fecund male god of the Nile, had been suppressed, presumably because his existence was incompatible with the Aten's role of sole creator.

Akhenaten, who appears curiously androgynous in many of his portraits, spent much of his life conspicuous as the one male at the centre of a family of unusually prominent women. His grandmother, Mutemwia, his mother, Tiy, and at least three of his four sisters had been ladies of strong character. The highly publicized children in the nuclear royal family were all female, while Akhenaten's wife was not only a highly capable woman but was – if the evidence from Amarna is to be believed – the passion of his life and the centre of his universe. It is therefore not surprising that Akhenaten, conscious of the lack of a female aspect to the Aten and aware of just how useful an ally a strong queen could be, promoted Nefertiti to provide the absent element of the new cult. In a precept which extended to the royal family, a good Egyptian wife was always seen as her husband's most loyal supporter. As a consequence, some early New Kingdom queens had been allowed a prominent political role at times when the safety of the monarchy was at stake, and Tetisheri, Ahhotep and Ahmose Nefertari had all played their part in establishing the 18th Dynasty.[8] At the same time it was always recognized that the role of the queen, like that of the king, had semi-divine origins. Numerous queens had served the old gods as priestesses and, as we have seen with Tiy, queens were permitted to act as the mortal representative of the deity on earth. This aspect of Nefertiti's queenship was now to be emphasized as never before. Nefertiti was to become Akhenaten's religious twin, the female complement to his male role. The Aten, Akhenaten son of Re, and Nefertiti, his wife, now formed an inverted semi-divine triad which paralleled the ancient triad formed by the creator god, his son Shu, and Shu's twin sister-consort Tefnut.

Tiy, still very much alive and once believed to be the inspiration behind her son's beliefs, seems to have become a somewhat peripheral figure at this time. In the tomb of Kheruef, which spans the reigns of the two Amenhoteps, we see her alongside her son, offering wine to Re-Harakhty and Maat, and incense to Atum and Hathor. These scenes presumably date to the very beginning of Akhenaten's reign. With the advent of Nefertiti Tiy is forced to take a back seat, as Mutemwia had before her. Her part in the new religion is not clear and, although we know that Akhenaten built his mother a 'sunshade' temple where she could worship the Aten, there is no evidence to suggest that she ever abandoned the old beliefs to dedicate herself exclusively to the new. Where in earlier reigns we might have expected to find scenes of the king accompanied by his mother and his wife, we now see only the royal couple plus their daughter(s). Effectively there is a secondary triad of king, queen and royal offspring, with no place for the king's mother.

At first sight the Amarna letters suggest that in the field of politics the roles of the two queens may have been reversed with, for at least the first few years of her son's reign, Tiy remaining a powerful figure. We know that Tushratta chose to write directly to Tiy over the affair of the missing gold statues, in the hope that she could influence her son, who must have seemed very much an unknown quantity. In contrast Nefertiti is never specifically named in any of the letters and it would seem that to Akhenaten's correspondents she was of negligible significance. While it is possible to argue on the basis of this evidence that Tiy was, for a few years after her husband's death, required to act as regent for her young son, it seems more likely that Tushratta was appealing to Tiy as a friend, albeit a friend with motherly influence, rather than a powerful queen.

Nefertiti's curious exclusion from the Amarna letters does seem to suggest that her influence was confined to the religious sphere. It may also be, at least in part, a reflection of her husband's general lack of interest in all foreign affairs, although there is perhaps a danger that Akhenaten's pacifism and insularity may in turn be overstated. While no one could claim Akhenaten as one of the great Egyptian warrior pharaohs, the empire certainly did not collapse during his reign. Unfortunately, as the sequence of Amarna letters is obviously incomplete we are forced to draw our deductions from a markedly one-sided view of events.

The change in religion necessitated immediate changes in religious art, as scenes of the old gods and their rituals were displaced by scenes of the new. Just as the traditional temple scenes had to be replaced by images of Akhenaten and his wife offering to the Aten, so the non-royal tombs of Amarna, which under a more conventional monarch would have been decorated with happy images of the tomb owner and his wife plus detailed funeral tableaux, were now dominated by the royal family.

Depictions of the dead are few and far between in the Amarna tombs. Instead we are presented with scenes of Akhenaten, Nefertiti and their children – the living symbols of royal fertility – worshipping the Aten, visiting the temple and generally going about their daily routine, to the extent that the tomb becomes almost a shrine to the activities and achievements of the royal family. We see officials raising their arms to praise the royal couple, while the ordinary people bow low before the god's representatives on earth. Tomb owners, forbidden direct contact with their god, were forced to send their prayers via either Akhenaten or Nefertiti. The burial petitions in the Amarna tomb of the temple official Panehesy included prayers addressed to both king and queen, although the petitions directed to Nefertiti were to a large extent dependent upon her cultivating the good will of the king:

Akhenaten: May he grant a reception of loaves, presented at every festival of the living Aten in the hall of the *Benben*.

Nefertiti: May she grant the entrance of favour and the exit of love, and a happy recollection in the presence of the king, and that thy name be welcome in the mouth of the companions.[9]

The tomb of Huya, steward to Queen Tiy, even included a prayer addressed to the dowager queen:

Praise to your Ka, O Lady of the Two Lands, who makes the Two Lands bright with her beauty, the Queen Mother and Great Queen Tiy, Mistress of the Provisions, abundant in fat things . . .[10]

The formal scenes on the tomb walls were replicated in the highly conspicuous mud-brick kiosks found in the gardens of some, but perhaps surprisingly not all, of Amarna's élite. These buildings, originally misidentified as birth bowers or garden pavilions, seem to have functioned as miniature Aten temples where Akhenaten's most loyal subjects could worship the royal couple, and through them the Aten. Most of the chapels have survived in ground-plan only, although we can see that they were of varying complexity, ranging from a simple room built on a raised platform to an entire small-scale temple complete with forecourt, pylons, portico and subsidiary rooms. We might reasonably expect to find that the chapels were open to the sun, although in the absence of walls this cannot be confirmed. The fragments of evidence which have been preserved indicate that their walls were decorated with scenes of Akhenaten and Nefertiti offering before the Aten, and that they housed brick or limestone altars plus stelae and statues of the king and his family.[11]

More intimate scenes of royal family life were reserved for the stelae recovered from within the homes of prominent courtiers, where they almost certainly served as domestic shrines, a scaled-down version of the garden chapels. In the absence of the traditional myths and legends these stelae showed the royal couple and their offspring relaxing in the royal pavilion under the protection of the Aten's rays, and an accompanying inscription was usually provided to stress the subject's loyalty to the king. The affection between king and queen in these scenes seems both obvious and natural, and is a stark contrast to earlier royal couples whose affection was expressed by the queen placing one rather stiff arm around her husband's waist. Indeed, one badly damaged relief now housed in the Louvre appears to show Akhenaten sitting with Nefertiti and at least two of their children on his knee. If Akhenaten rarely appears alone with his daughters, it is presumably because he regards the children as being in the care of their mother. He would certainly not be the first father to be wary of looking after six small girls. In fact, 'off camera', the young princesses were cared for by their nursemaids; young women who hover in the background of the palace scenes and who generally remain anonymous, although we know that Ankhesenpaaten had a nurse named Tia.

Queen Tiy is remarkable by her absence from these scenes of Akhenaten, Nefertiti and their family, although the Amarna house of Panehesy has yielded the famous stela of Amenhotep III and Tiy where the old king is depicted in all his 'flabby lethargy'. It would appear that this stela, carved at the very end of Amenhotep's reign, was brought to Amarna by Panehesy as a mark of his devotion to the old regime.

Almost all Egyptian art is capable of an interpretation beyond the obvious, and these scenes of relaxed domesticity certainly held a symbolism for their original artists and owners which is now lost to us. The identification of the Aten, king and queen as a divine triad seems fairly obvious, as is the assumption that the royal children were included in the tableaux as physical manifestations of the couple's fertility. Akhenaten constantly stressed his role as the son of the god, and it is not surprising that he should use his own children as symbols of rejuvenation. Nefertiti, her lower body emphasized, is presented as the fertile Tefnut, consort to Akhenaten's Shu. A scene showing the queen serving the king by pouring him a drink, or by placing a necklace around his neck, is in many ways a distortion of the traditional scenes where a king would offer before a god. Such scenes continue beyond the Amarna age into the reign of Tutankhamen. Less obvious, but by no means improbable, is the suggestion that the reed matting and slender pillars of the royal pavilion may have been intended to represent a stylized birth bower, the temporary structure used by mothers during labour and the period of purification which followed delivery, and therefore may have served as a reinforcement of the theme of fertility and reproduction which was a constant underlying motif in Amarna art and religion.[12]

It seems that not everyone was enamoured of the new-style religion and its emphasis on the domestic life of the royal family, although resistance was very low-key and took the form of humour rather than obvious dissent. A series of crude limestone figurines unique to Amarna which show families of monkeys generally aping the behaviour of the royal family is probably best explained as an early attempt at political satire: the monkeys drive chariots, play musical instruments, eat, drink and even kiss their young.[13] Ordinary citizens seem to have encountered little difficulty in maintaining contact with their traditional spirits and deities, many of which were associated with age-old concerns over fertility, pregnancy and childbirth. Leonard Woolley, in his 1921–2 excavation of the Amarna workmen's village, discovered a range of Bes and Taweret amulets plus eye of Horus ring-bezels and even a few decorated Hathor heads.[14] Glazed Bes pendants, the remnants of broken necklaces, have been recovered from both private houses and the royal tomb, while an entire wall of the workmen's village Main Street House 3, one of the few Amarna houses whose walls have survived to yield traces of their original decoration, was painted with a frieze of dancing Bes and Taweret figures.[15] Beset, the uncommon female version of Bes, was also present at Amarna in the form of an amulet, while a cupboard in one private house yielded a small votive collection of two model beds, a fertility figure and a stela painted with a scene showing a woman, child and Taweret, the pregnant hippopotamus goddess of childbirth

and bringer of babies to the childless. As far as we can tell, no steps were
taken to hide these images and we must assume that Bes and his friends
were acceptable to Akhenaten, either because they had once been
included among the legendary followers and protectors of the sun god,
or because, as elements of the 'minor tradition', they fell outside the
scope of the prohibition extended to the mainstream deities.[16] Neither
Bes nor Taweret could have presented any real threat to the sovereignty
of the all-powerful Aten, and Akhenaten's tolerance of superstition may
well have been a tacit recognition of his inability to eradicate the beliefs
central to the family unit.

Bes, the male protector of women in childbirth, was a demi-god or a
spirit rather than a great state god. Nevertheless, or even perhaps because
of this, he was a universally accepted motif and as such was by no means
confined to the lower classes. We have already seen that the Malkata bedroom of Amenhotep III was decorated with comical Bes figures. Queen
Tiy seems to have been particularly fond of Bes, and her ornate chairs
and beds, recovered from the tomb of Yuya and Thuyu, were decorated
with both Bes and Taweret. An unusual cosmetic jar, now in Turin
Museum, even shows Tiy herself in the form of Taweret. Bes and
Taweret had always played an important role in popular – as opposed
to state – religion. Throughout the dynastic age the whole cycle of
human reproduction was seen as a dangerous yet desirable process, and
childbirth itself was a particularly worrying time when the entire family
would be brought into contact with inexplicable forces of creation far
beyond human control. All labour involved risk to both mother and baby
and conventional medicine could do little to help either. Mothers-to-be
therefore turned to the supernatural for protection and Bes and Taweret
seem to have remained acceptable as the protectors of the family – men,
women and children – throughout the Amarna age. The fact that images
of these gods were used to decorate the living rooms of the Amarna
workmen's houses, while at the Theban workmen's village of Deir
el-Medina Bes was joined by scenes celebrating women and childbirth,
is a strong indication that these female-centred cults were shared by the
whole family and were in no way restricted to women.

It is unlikely that a preoccupation with fertility and childbirth was
confined to the lower classes, although the walls of the houses of the
Amarna élite have not survived to tell their tale.

The upper classes, worshipping before their private shrines and in their garden chapels, were presented not with Bes or Taweret, but with images of Nefertiti and her children, who served as their living, and indeed highly fertile, symbol of the state god's creative powers. Akhenaten consistently stressed his wife's fertility, and the daughters who follow their mother in an ever increasing line play a symbolic as well as a literal role in all family portraits. It is almost certainly no coincidence that Nefertiti rose to public prominence following the birth of her first child.

Egyptian religion was never centred on a sacred text of divine revelation conveyed via a human prophet which could be equated with the Torah, the Bible or the Koran. However, Akhenaten's vision of the Aten as the creator of all life was celebrated in a series of hymns. The Great Hymn to the Aten, preserved on the wall of Ay's Amarna tomb and presumed to have been written by the king himself, was not in itself a great innovation, many of its sentiments having been expressed in earlier hymns to the sun god. However, the Great Hymn is unusual in the fact that it ignores the traditional gods of Egypt and makes reference only to the Aten. This monotheistic element, combined with the idea that there should be one supreme god for all races, has encouraged many observers to draw a direct comparison with Psalm 104, written some 500 years later in a different land and a different language. Weigall, for example, felt that

In the face of this remarkable similarity one can hardly doubt that there is a direct connection between the two compositions . . . in consideration of Akhenaton's [*sic*] peculiar ability and originality there seems considerable likelihood that he is the author in the first instance of this gem of the Psalter.[17]

It would, however, be wrong to see Atenism as the forerunner or inspiration of modern Christianity, or Judaism, on the basis of this text; the hymn is merely a reflection of the thinking which underlies many Near Eastern religions, and indeed a hymn dedicated to Amen and dated to the reign of Amenhotep II had already expressed many similar sentiments:

You are the sole one who made all there is. The unique one who made what exists . . . it is he who gives breath to him within the egg, and sustains the son of the worm . . .[18]

However, the Great Hymn to the Aten, originally written to be recited by the king and adapted by Ay for inclusion in his tomb, is worth quoting in full as, apart from its intrinsic beauty, it permits us a glimpse into the mind and beliefs of its composer. It is notable that Nefertiti, the composer's wife and most probably Ay's daughter, is barely mentioned. Here it is Akhenaten alone who is destined to enjoy an afterlife:

Glorious, you rise on the horizon of heaven, O living Aten, creator of life. When you have arisen on the eastern horizon you fill every land with your beauty. You are gorgeous, great and radiant, high over every land. Your rays embrace all the lands that you have made. You are Re and so you reach their boundaries, limiting them for your beloved son. Though you are far away, your rays are upon the earth. Though you are seen, your movement is not.

When you set on the western horizon the land is dark, like death. Night is spent asleep as in a bedroom with a covered head, one eye does not see the other. If the possessions under their heads were stolen, no one would notice it. Every lion comes out from its den, and every serpent bites. Darkness descends and the earth is hushed, because their maker rests on the horizon.

The earth is illuminated when you rise on the horizon and shine as the Aten in the daytime. You banish the darkness when you cast your rays. The Two Lands celebrate, lively and aroused now that you have awakened them; with bodies cleansed and clothed they raise their arms to adore your rising. Now the whole land begins to work. All the cattle graze on their fodder, trees and plants grow. Birds fly up from their nests, their wings stretched in praise of your spirit. All the flocks gambol on their feet and everything that flies and perches lives because you have arisen for them. Ships sail to the north and to the south, while roads open at your rising. The fish in the river leap before you, for your rays are in the middle of the sea.

You make the seed grow in women and create people from sperm. You feed the son who lies in his mother's womb and comfort him to stop his tears. You are the nurse within the womb, who gives breath to all that he has made. On the day he is born you open his mouth to supply his needs. When the chick in the egg chirps within his shell you give him breath to live, and when his time is ready to break out from the shell he comes out of the egg to proclaim his birth, walking on his legs. How many are the things you do, although hidden from view, O unique god, without compare. You created the world as you desired, alone – all people, all cattle, all flocks, everything which walks with its feet on the earth and everything which flies with its wings in the air. The northern lands of Asia, the southern lands of Africa and the land of Egypt

– you have set every person in their place and you have supplied their needs. Everyone has his food and his allotted lifetime. Tongues differ in their speech, and also characters and skins, for you have differentiated mankind.

You created the Nile in the Netherworld. You bring him forth at your will to feed the people, since you made them for yourself, lord of all, who toils for them. Lord of all lands, the Aten who shines for them in the daytime, great in dignity. You make all distant lands live, for you have made a heavenly Nile come down for them, to make waves on the mountains like the sea, to irrigate the fields of their towns. O Lord of eternity, how excellent are your designs – a Nile from heaven for people of foreign lands, and all the creatures which walk upon their feet and a Nile for Egypt coming from the Netherworld. Your rays suckle every field; when you shine they live and grow for you. You made the seasons to foster all that you made: winter to cool them and summer that they may feel you.

You made a distant sky in which you might shine and to see everything you have made. You are alone, shining as the Living Aten, risen, dazzling, far and yet near you have made millions of manifestations of yourself. Towns, villages, fields, roads and waterways – every eye sees you upon them, for you are the Aten of the daytime . . .

You are my beloved. There is none other that knows you except for your son Neferkheperure Waenre, whom you have made wise in your plans and your might. The creatures of the earth exist in your hand as you have made them; when you rise they live, when you set they die. You yourself are the duration of life, it is by you that men live. Eyes may behold your beauty until you set, but when you set in the west all work ceases. When you rise . . . You raise them up for the son who came forth from your body, the King of Upper and Lower Egypt, living in Truth, the Lord of the Two Lands Neferkheperure Waenre, son of Re, living in Truth, Lord of the glorious appearings, Akhenaten the long-lived. And as for the King's Great Wife whom he loves, the Mistress of the Two Lands, Neferneferuaten-Nefertiti, may she live and flourish for ever and ever.[19]

It is a characteristic of Atenism that it eliminates the old gods and the old traditions – many of them highly comforting to their believers – without ever finding a satisfactory replacement. The vivid scenes of the present which play a prominent role in Amarna art are a reflection of the fact that the Aten was purely a daytime god. His disciples have little reason to look forward, and indeed Akhenaten's hymn promises a grim future for the faithful. The myth of Osiris, god of the dead, and the promise of a golden afterlife in the Field of Reeds have vanished, a victim to the purges instigated in Year 5. The Aten takes responsibility for the deceased, and after death his devotees can look forward to a bleak existence haunting the altar of the sun temple by day, sleeping the sleep of the dead at night – an unwelcome reversion to Old Kingdom beliefs which allowed only the king to inherit eternal life.

Some traces of the old funerary ritual were permitted to remain, stripped of their original meaning. As we have seen at the Theban *Gempaaten*, Akhenaten was not averse to representing himself as an Osiriform figure. Mummification followed by interment in a rock-cut tomb remained the acceptable means of disposing of Egypt's élite, and canopic jars, scarabs and shabtis all remained a standard part of the funeral equipment, suitably adapted for Aten worship. A wooden shabti belonging to the Royal Ornament Py, for example, incorporated an acceptably edited text from the *Book of the Dead*:

Breathe the sweet breeze of the north wind which comes forth from the sky upon the hand of the living Aten. Your body is protected, your heart is glad. No harm shall happen to your body because you are sand. Your flesh will not decay. You will follow the Aten from the time when he appears in the morning until he sets in life . . .[20]

Is it correct to interpret the Amarna period as a true religious revolution, or was Akhenaten merely restructuring religious thought as a calculated means of serving his own ends and promoting his own divinity? Could it even have been an economic rather than a religious revolution, with Akhenaten deliberately diverting resources away from the priesthood of Amen in order to finance his new city? These unanswerable questions have vexed historians for many decades. At the turn of this century, when the extent of Akhenaten's reforms first became clear, many egyptologists were themselves Biblical scholars whose studies of egyptology were inspired by the need to explain the many mysteries of the holy book. To these scholars monotheism was obviously superior to polytheism. They tended to interpret Akhenaten's devotion to Atenism as an early and wholly admirable attempt to reach out to the one true God of Judaism or Christianity inspired by the religions of the Near East, which had in all probability been introduced into the Egyptian royal family via Tiy or Nefertiti, who were themselves believed to be of foreign extraction:

Akhenaten believed that his god was the Father of all mankind, and that the Syrian and the Nubian were as much under his protection as the Egyptian. This is a greater advance in ethics than may at once be apparent; for the Aten thus becomes the first deity who was not tribal or not national ever conceived by mortal mind. This is the Christian's understanding of God, though not the Hebrew conception of Jehovah. This is the spirit which sends the missionary to the utmost parts of the earth . . .[21]

Over the past hundred years we have gained a more complete understanding of both the nature of Akhenaten's new cult and the political climate of his reign, while at the same time losing the missionary zeal which affected so many early egyptologists. While the effects of Akhenaten's reforms should never be understated, the term 'revolution' now seems inappropriate; many of Akhenaten's 'innovations' were logical if extreme developments stemming from the religious climate of his father's reign, and there appears to have been little if any blood shed in defence of the old gods. Some modern historians have continued to view the introduction of Atenism as simple religious conversion, a great intellectual step forward fuelled by genuine religious conviction:

At no other time did anything approach the utter simplification of one creator as introduced by Akhenaten and Nefertiti, in place of the massive complexities that had gone before and followed after. Their thought was an intellectual breakthrough; a peak of clarity which rose above the lowlands of superstition that had existed until then.[22]

Others have taken a less charitable view, sensing the strong political and personal motivation behind Akhenaten's religious reforms. Donald B. Redford, biographer of Akhenaten, provides what is probably the most perceptive summary of his subject's character and beliefs:

For all that can be said in his favour, Akhenaten in spirit remains to the end totalitarian. The right of an individual freely to choose was wholly foreign to him. He was the champion of a universal, celestial power who demanded universal submission, claimed universal truth, and from whom no further revelation could be expected. I cannot conceive a more tiresome regime under which to be fated to live.[23]

As we have seen, Akhenaten's Atenism has frequently been interpreted as the world's first monotheistic religion with Akhenaten himself being the inspiration for Moses, and the Aten the forerunner of the Jewish-Christian-Islamic god. The Aten was never, however, intended to be a god in this mould. He remained remote and aloof, he created and observed but did not intervene in events and certainly did not require his devotees to adhere to any moral code. Egyptian morality was always separated from religion and, as an aspect of good social behaviour, was taught by scribes rather than priests. The religion of the ancient Egyptians was the equivalent of our modern science. It did not aim to teach men how to behave, but sought to provide explanations for the seemingly inexplicable. In fact it is highly debatable whether the new religion can be classed as true monotheism, the belief in a single supreme deity, rather than what Norman de Garis Davies, himself a Unitarian minister, has classed as 'little more than a beautifully expressed and humanized henotheism', henotheism being the belief in a single god without the assertion that s/he is the sole god.[24] Although the Aten was without question the most prominent deity, he was consistently linked with Re and the semi-divine Akhenaten. Several of the old gods remained in circulation for many years, and some were even included in the Aten's original name and titulary: 'May the good god live who takes pleasure in Truth, Lord of all that the Aten encompasses, Lord of heaven, Lord of earth, Aten, the living, the great, who illuminates the two lands, may the father live: Re-Harakhty appearing on the horizon in his name of Shu who is Aten, who is given life for ever and ever, Aten, the Living, the Great, who is in jubilee, who dwells in the temple of Aten in Akhetaten.'

Maat, the divine daughter of Re and personification of the concept of truth, *maat* or order already discussed, was originally acceptable to Akhenaten, although eventually she too was displaced as Nefertiti started to assume the role of companion to the god-king. Akhenaten constantly stressed his devotion to truth and even adopted the epithet 'who lives on *maat*'. As the reign progressed, however, the abstract nature of the god gained increasing emphasis until, during Year 9, the Aten was given

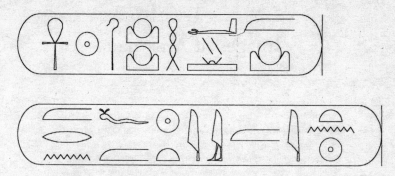

Fig. 3.6   The new names of the Aten

a revised titulary, his name purified by the exclusion of the names of Horus and of Shu. The reference to Re, shorn of its association with Horus, was allowed to remain: 'Long live Re, ruler of the two horizons, he who rejoices in the horizon is his name as Re the father who returns as Aten.'

This name was written in two cartouches suggesting that the Aten, who invariably wore the uraeus of kingship, was to be regarded as a king, and by implication that Akhenaten and the Aten could either be seen as co-regents, or even as one and the same person. Indeed, it would appear that Akhenaten's Theban jubilee was to be considered to belong as much to the Aten as to the king. Now all reference to 'gods' in the plural was banned, and the spelling of some words – including 'Mut', the name of Amen's wife which also translates as 'mother' – was changed to avoid the inclusion of a proscribed god's name.

4

Images of Amarna

*Giving adoration to the Lord of the Two Lands, and kissing the earth
for the sole one of Re, by the Overseer of Works in the red mountain,
the assistant pupil whom His Majesty himself taught, the Chief of
Sculptors in the many great monuments of the king in the house of the
Aten, in the Horizon of Aten, Bak, son of the Chief of Sculptors Men,
born of the lady of the house, Ruy of Heliopolis.*[1]

For over a thousand years the 'rules' of artistic representation had decreed
that all upper-class Egyptians should be physically perfect with no obvious flaws or deformities. Men should either be eternally young with
firm, slender bodies and tanned skins or, towards the end of their
successful lives, mature statesmen with drooping breasts and pronounced
rolls of fat around the waist. Women should be beautiful, slender and
pale with no concession paid to the ravages of time, although very
occasionally during the New Kingdom an older woman such as Queen
Tiy might be presented as a wise elder, the wrinkled female equivalent
of the plump successful man. It was particularly important that the
pharaoh should be depicted as a flawless male with a handsome face and
a firm, athletic body as this was the image which his people expected to
see. There had been variations on this theme – monarchs of the Old
Kingdom had been shown to be remote, god-like creatures, while
the pharaohs of the Middle Kingdom had appeared more caring and
compassionate – but these were subtle differences in expression, and the
underlying principle had remained constant for centuries.

So strong was this belief in the correct presentation of the king that
the female pharaoh Hatchepsut had, for all her official portraits, assumed
the body and clothing of a man. The royal artists never allowed less than
perfect physical specimens to deflect them from their goal, and simply
overlooked such undesirable features as buck teeth, a deformed foot, or,

in the most extreme case, a female body. By producing essentially the same portrait of successive monarchs they sought to inspire confidence in the eye of the beholder by confirming the continuing presence of a traditional king on the throne. This in turn served as confirmation of the presence of *maat* in its widest context. A true likeness to any individual king may have been regarded as an added benefit but it was certainly not a necessity as the pharaoh was not to be seen as an individual, but as merely the latest in a long line of identical rulers. A name, carved or painted on to the portrait, would confirm the identity of the individual.

At the start of his reign Akhenaten adhered to tradition, and his early portraits show a conventional New Kingdom monarch performing typical kingly deeds. By the end of Year 5, however, the king had developed a startling range of features. His narrow head, perched atop a long, thin neck, was now elongated, its length deliberately emphasized by his preference for tall head-dresses plus the traditional pharaoh's false beard. His face, in spite of its narrow almond-shaped eyes, fleshy earlobes, pendulous jaw, long nose, hollow cheeks, pronounced cheekbones and thick lips, had a curious sensuality in its knowing and secretive smile. His body had become the exact opposite of the king's traditional manly physique. His shoulders, chest, arms and lower legs were weedy and underdeveloped and his collar bone excessively prominent, and yet he had wide hips, heavy thighs, pronounced breasts, a narrow waist and a bloated stomach which bulged over his tight-fitting kilt. The colossal statues which once lined the colonnade at the Theban *Gempaaten*, when viewed as intended, from below and in profile lit by the uncompromising Egyptian sunlight, must be classed among the most effective and disturbing pieces of dynastic art. Even today, housed in the less appropriate setting of Cairo Museum, they retain a haunting power to disturb. Weigall, a great admirer of Akhenaten, chose to see in these portraits of the young king:

. . . a pale sickly youth. His head seemed too large for his body; his eyelids were heavy; his eyes were eloquent of dreams. His features were delicately moulded, and his mouth, in spite of a somewhat protruding lower jaw, is reminiscent of the best of the art of Rossetti.[2]

Others have been less kind, employing emotive words such as hideous,

travesty, grotesque and weird in their descriptions of Akhenaten's face
and physique:

A son of more unlikely appearance than Amenophis IV [Akhenaten] could
hardly have been born to altogether normal parents. Though his earliest monuments do not present his features and figure as markedly different from those
of any earlier Egyptian prince, the representations of only a few years later
provide us with frankly hideous portraits the general fidelity of which cannot
be doubted . . . the standing colossi from the peristyle court at Karnak have a
look of fanatical determination such as his subsequent history confirmed all too
fatally.[3]

The feminization of the king's body has been obvious to everyone,
while to Grimal, the swollen body of the king is representative of death
itself:

The accentuation of his facial features and the deliberate sagging of his torso
produce such a disease-ridden appearance in the colossal Osirid statues
(executed by the sculptor Bak) that their bloated stomachs might even be
interpreted in terms of bodily fluids inflating the decomposed corpse of Osiris.[4]

   The royal artists must have found it difficult to break away from the
old tradition of standardized realism and adapt to a new, more surreal
way of expressing themselves. It has generally been assumed that their
eagerness to change combined with their lack of expertise in the new
style causing them to overcompensate, producing bizarre portraits of the
king and queen with the new elements inadvertently exaggerated
beyond the point of realism. In fact we have no reason to suppose that
these new representations are in any way accidental or a mistake, and it
seems equally, if not more, valid to assume that we are witnessing a
deliberate experimental phase inspired by Akhenaten and implemented
by his chief sculptor, Bak. Bak, trained in the classical Theban style, was
responsible for the earliest and most unusual monuments of his patron's
reign, and it was only following his replacement by the chief sculptor
Tuthmosis that Akhenaten's art mellowed into a softer, more relaxed
realism. With the move to Amarna and the subsequent employment of
locally and northern-trained sculptors, the king became more human in
form. His face seemed less haggard and his body appeared altogether

more masculine, although still flabby and out of condition. Even with these modifications Akhenaten remained the most striking and instantly recognizable pharaoh in Egypt's history. The art of his reign, with its increased sense of movement and expression plus its emphasis on informal scenes from daily life and nature, is now widely recognized as one of the high points of Egyptian culture, yielding what Egyptian art expert Cyril Aldred has considered to be 'more than its proper quota of masterpieces'.[5]

Akhenaten must have been the inspiration behind his own revised image. No artist would have taken it upon himself to challenge tradition in such a dramatic fashion, and indeed Bak explicitly tells us that he was merely 'the pupil whom His Majesty taught'. Bak would have learned his technical expertise from his father, Men, chief sculptor to Amenhotep III and probable author of the Colossi of Memnon. Father and son are shown together on a rock relief at Aswan, where a miniature Men worships before a seated statue of Amenhotep III, possibly one of his own colossi, offering 'every good and pure thing; bread and beer, oxen and fowl and every good vegetable', while Bak presents an offering table heaped with delicacies to a statue of Akhenaten which is now erased from the scene.

The move from the old art style to the new seems to come as a sudden and shocking change, a swift response to the king's abandoning of the old religious beliefs. Indeed, the Theban tomb of Ramose, where the two contrasting styles sit uncomfortably side by side, gives the impression that the change occurred overnight. In fact Akhenaten was not so much inventing a new style as speeding up and exaggerating a natural evolution and, just as his religious 'revolution' was rooted in the theology of the past, so several of Akhenaten's innovative artistic features may be traced back to the art of his forebears.

Egypt's increased internationalism during the 18th Dynasty had already allowed foreign influences to infiltrate the hitherto insular arts and crafts. Gradually the strict artistic conventions of the Old and Middle Kingdoms had started to relax and informal poses, flowing draperies, modern clothing and hairstyles, and pierced ears had already made their way into the repertoire. This trend towards modernism was reflected in the literature of the period which now showed a greater freedom of composition and an increased awareness of modern language; the New

Kingdom was the period of divine hymns, lyrical love poetry and action-packed fiction. At the same time had come an increasing tendency towards realism in royal portraiture. The wooden head of Tiy recovered from Gurob (Plate 3) shows the queen not only with her habitual down-turned lips but with heavy eyelids and deep furrows running from her nose to her mouth; it is the portrait of an individual rather than a stereotyped queen, and it shows a woman who is well beyond the first flush of youth. While his father and grandfather had already appeared more stolid than their predecessors, Amenhotep III, towards the end of his reign, became the first pharaoh to be depicted as a fat and frail human rather than an immortal demi-god. Some of Amenhotep's statues show the almond-shaped eyes, full curved lips, sharp features and obvious breasts of the early Amarna pieces, and he also adopts the more relaxed poses and informal garments which have contributed to his diagnosis as a sad and worn-out failure.[6]

Many early egyptologists sought to interpret Akhenaten's new image as a true representation of the king himself. Akhenaten consistently stressed his devotion to *maat*, which in its simplest form may be translated as truth. Thus they reasoned that the king, in the grip of religious mania, had decided to 'come clean' about his unfortunate appearance. This led, not unnaturally, to the assumption that Akhenaten suffered from some serious medical complaint. His body as seen in both two- and three-dimensional art, with its breasts, narrow waist and wide hips, is certainly not the body of a healthy male. Indeed the Egyptian historian Manetho had recorded the succession as passing from Amenhotep III to an unknown Orus and then to 'his daughter Acencheres' who is presumably the effeminate Akhenaten, although some have taken Orus to be Nefertiti, and who is reported to have ruled over Egypt for a little over twelve years. Flinders Petrie, writing in 1894, was able to dismiss what was perhaps the most bizarre suggestion then current:

It has been proposed that Amenhotep IV died after a very few years; and that Akhenaten, a man, or a woman was raised by intrigue into his vacant place, adopted his throne name, and his diadem name, and introduced the new style. It has been proposed that the new ruler was a woman, masquerading with a wife and suppositious children; such a notion resting on the effeminate plumpness of Akhenaten, and the alleged prevalence of feminine courtiers. It has also been proposed that he was a eunuch.[7]

As Petrie reasoned, with logic which holds good today:

Is it credible that the most uxorious king of Egypt, who appears with his wife on every monument, who rides side by side with her in a chariot, and kisses her in public, who dances her on his knee, who has a steadily increasing family – that this king was either a woman in masquerade or a eunuch?[8]

Needless to say, speculation over the nature of the king's supposed medical condition was rife. Unfortunately, as Akhenaten's mummy has never been identified, all diagnoses had through necessity to be based on the artistic evidence and were therefore, to say the least, highly speculative.

Weigall's suggestion that Akhenaten was an epileptic whose condition caused him to hallucinate and therefore inspired his devotion to the sun's disc can be dismissed as mere guesswork perhaps inspired by the epilepsy attributed to Alexander the Great and Julius Caesar. Most plausible is the suggestion that Akhenaten may have suffered from the feminizing Fröhlich's syndrome, a group of symptoms caused by damage to the pituitary gland and thalamus.[9] Sufferers from Fröhlich's syndrome may experience a female-type distribution of fat over the breasts, hips and thighs, while the genitalia may be so underdeveloped as to seem invisible amid the surrounding folds of fat. As this disease generally becomes apparent only at puberty, it would conveniently explain the change from the conventional images of the young king at his accession to the new style some four years later.

The major stumbling block in attributing any such feminizing disease to Akhenaten is the fact that he appears to have fathered at least six children, and most sufferers of Fröhlich's syndrome are impotent. Of course, the father of a baby is not always the husband of its mother, but if Akhenaten was not the father of the princesses, who was? His fertility was obviously a matter of huge importance to the king, who displayed his ever-increasing brood of daughters as a means of reinforcing his link to the Aten, the most powerful creator god. Is it possible that Akhenaten, aware but ashamed of his illness, sanctioned or turned a blind eye to the use of an anonymous, surrogate father? Perhaps, but lacking the bodies of both Akhenaten and his daughters for DNA testing, this is something which would be very difficult to prove.

No specific clue to their paternity is provided by the titles of the
princesses, who are most frequently described as:

King's bodily daughter whom he loves, [Meritaten], born of the Great King's
Wife whom he loves, Mistress of the Two Lands, Nefertiti, may she live

As we have already noted, all the women in the royal family bore
titles which reflected their relationship with the king. The closer this
relationship, the more important was the lady. Therefore just as there
was no Egyptian title of 'queen', merely 'King's Wife' or 'King's Great
Wife', so there was no equivalent of princess and all the king's female
offspring were 'King's Daughters', a title which they would carry all
their lives without necessarily needing to mention the name of the king.
It is not therefore unusual that the princesses' father goes unnamed.
What is unusual is that they are specifically identified as the daughters
of Nefertiti; we would not expect to find a queen's name included in
her children's title in this way, as the queen was very much the minor
parent. Just as Tiy's high status seems confirmed by her inclusion on the
commemorative scarabs of Amenhotep III, so the inclusion of Nefertiti's name in her daughters' titles can be read as a sign of her own
prominent position. Their affiliation thus seems entirely in keeping
with the hierarchy within the royal family where the line of authority
descended downwards from the Aten to the king, then to the queen
and finally to the royal children. In fact, towards the end of their father's
reign, two of the princesses are directly affiliated to Akhenaten on blocks
recovered from Hermopolis Magna.

More recently it has been suggested that Akhenaten may have suffered
from Marfan's Syndrome, a genetically determined abnormality caused
by defective collagen formation; sufferers from Marfan's Syndrome tend
to be tall, with long faces and chest deformities. There may also be a
high palate and eye defects, but a female-type distribution of fat as shown
in Akhenaten's statuary would be unusual.

One curious colossal statue recovered from the Theban *Gempaaten*
must be considered before concluding any discussion of Akhenaten's
health and sexuality. *Gempaaten* took the form of an open courtyard
surrounded by at least twenty-four colossal figures of the king. These
statues, which were carved at the start of his reign and were highly

exaggerated in style, were based on traditional Osirid mummiform statues but show Akhenaten dressed in his favourite pleated linen kilt, carrying the crook and flail in his crossed arms and wearing head-cloth plus either the double crown of Upper and Lower Egypt or the plumed head-dress of Shu. His upper body and arms are carved with the double cartouche of the Aten and his kilt, which bears his name on its belt, is actually carved into the stone of the statue and would originally have been painted. One unfinished and slightly damaged statue, however, displays a naked torso without any sign of a kilt and without any genitalia (Plate 10). The long thin head seems to be that of Akhenaten and the figure wears the king's beard and double crown, although unusually the head-cloth is missing. The upper torso again has the crossed arms carrying the crook

Fig. 4.1 Nefertiti's trademark blue crown and flimsy linen robe

and flail, and is decorated with the cartouches of the Aten. The lower torso has a well-defined waist and an indented navel. The upper legs appear in proportion to the body, while the lower legs and most of the crown are missing.

It would be wrong, in view of the evidence discussed above, to leap to the conclusion that the figure must be true to life. Had Akhenaten been born without any genitalia he would undoubtedly have been classed as a woman and would never have become king. Nor is it likely that the genitalia would be omitted simply for reasons of modesty; the god Min was always depicted with a larger than life-sized erect penis and this does not appear to have caused any offence. While it was very unusual for the king to be portrayed without any clothing, on those occasions when a monarch was depicted naked he was shown as nature made him. Egyptian art was very literal and, as the king was in one of his aspects a fertility god, it would have been inappropriate to have presented him as in any way disabled.

Given that all the other *Gempaaten* statues are clothed, it is possible to argue that this unfinished figure was not in fact intended to be naked and would have eventually been carved or painted to show a kilt. However, given the shaping of the torso, the definition of the upper legs and the apparent completeness of the navel, this seems unlikely; the kilt would have needed to be a micro-skirt which would have hugged the king's figure in an unprecedented and impractical fashion. It may be that the sculpture would eventually have been dressed in clothing made from some separate material, perhaps a skirt of precious metal. The genitalia may therefore have been omitted either because they would not be seen or in order to allow the garment to hang flat. However, this again is not a particularly convincing explanation. The torso bears no sign of any attachment for a permanent garment of metal or stone, while the sheer size of the piece makes it unlikely that the body would have been clothed in a less permanent linen kilt. There are so far no known examples of colossal statues clothed in this way and, while composite statues do occur during Akhenaten's reign, these were made by manufacturing separate body parts to be attached to much smaller-scale bodies.

Worthy of more serious consideration is the suggestion that the figure is that of a woman, Nefertiti rather than Akhenaten. The lower body certainly has feminine curves and the breasts, although partially obscured by the arms and perhaps slightly small for a woman, could have been equally at home on either Akhenaten or Nefertiti. Male breasts were, however, a feature of the royal family and Akhenaten's father and grandfather before him had both been depicted with well developed chests. The fact that the figure lacks a pronounced female pubic triangle is perhaps slightly inconsistent with this interpretation, since Nefertiti is usually shown as decidedly feminine with a prominent pubic mound. To Julia Samson, the interpretation of the figure seems obvious:

The breasts are carved more like those of a woman, although Akhenaten was plump-chested. It must have been one of several colossal statues of Nefertiti

. . . Presumably this nude feminine figure was to have been finished as Nefertiti, wearing her open robe and the tall crown of the kings of a united Egypt, a part of which remains on the statue.[10]

However, it is possible that Samson is influenced in her interpretation by her belief that Nefertiti ruled alongside Akhenaten at Thebes, as previously she has indicated her belief that the incomplete figure is male.[11]

The suggestion that the statue would eventually have been carved or clothed with Nefertiti's open robe again presents certain difficulties, as the definition of the legs combined with the carved cartouches and the positioning of the arms across the upper body would have made it very difficult to apply to the figure a voluminous full-length robe with sleeves or shawl. Representations of Nefertiti did not necessarily conform to modern ideas of feminine modesty, and her garments are occasionally so clinging that they can only be detected by the presence of the thin line denoting the neckline. If the statue does represent the queen it is entirely possible that a skin-tight sheath dress would eventually have been carved or painted over her form, or that she would have been left naked. If this is the case, the statue might have been intended to portray Nefertiti in the guise of Tefnut, a parallel figure to the colossi depicting Akhenaten as Tefnut's twin Shu. Alternatively, the figure may have been intended to show Nefertiti in her most regal aspect, as the female counterpart of the king. This interpretation of Nefertiti's role would be entirely in keeping with her appearance in the smiting scenes where she acts as a substitute for the king, and is perhaps paralleled by her appearance at Akhenaten's *heb-sed* celebrations where she is shown riding in a palanquin carrying royal regalia.

Despite the scholarly reasoning outlined above, the identification of the figure as Nefertiti is not entirely convincing to those who have seen the statue. 'Gut feeling' is certainly not a scientific means of analysing and interpreting ancient art, but in some cases it is all we have to go on. The long, thin neck and the gaunt face with its knowing smile seem so clearly to be those of Akhenaten, and the entire silhouette of the statue so closely resembles the other, kilted, colossal figures recovered from *Gempaaten*, that it seems almost perverse to argue that it could be anyone other than the king. So far, only one larger-than-life head recovered from Karnak has been identified as Nefertiti, an identification which has been made purely on the basis of the double uraeus worn on the brow and which, in consequence, is not itself as certain as we might hope. This head, now housed in Cairo Museum, has been severely damaged and most of the mouth and all of the chin are missing. It too is carved from sandstone and what remains of the face is strikingly similar to the *Gempaaten* representations of Akhenaten. The hairstyle is, however, decidedly different, and this head wears a curled wig with a deep fringe.

In spite of the number of paragraphs already devoted to the *Gempaaten* figure, it would probably be a mistake to worry overmuch about the precise meaning behind a single piece which is merely one of a series of colossal statues created at a time when artistic experimentation was the rule and departure from realism the norm. Given the disjointed state of the archaeological evidence recovered from Karnak, the figure is probably best interpreted as a non-literal portrayal of Akhenaten, a visual metaphor depicting the king in his most divine aspect as a genderless entity, denuded of all primary sexual organs in order to represent the sexless nature of the Aten himself. There is a tendency for archaeologists to assume that what they have unearthed is exactly the image that the sculptor intended to produce, with no allowance made for mistakes or a 'one off'. It would seem that in this case, while the artist (Bak?) set out to create a sculpture that depicted Akhenaten as both male and female, what was actually produced was an image which showed him as female rather than male and therefore lacking all the procreative powers of the Aten. This is the only representation of the king that we have in this form; presumably it is an image that proved unsuccessful and was abandoned soon after its conception.

Wherever the king led the court soon followed. While the ordinary people continued to be depicted very much as they always had been, we now find all high-ranking Egyptians from Nefertiti downwards developing flabby stomachs, breasts and languid poses. Even Bak felt it appropriate, or politically expedient, to be portrayed with a bulging pot-belly which gives him an unfortunate, almost pregnant, appearance. Nefertiti keeps her well-defined waist but develops a rounded abdomen, large hips, jodhpur-like thighs and pronounced buttocks which remind us of the fact that she has borne at least six children. Her stomach is often highlighted by a single curved line at the base of the abdomen just above the pubic mound, while Queen Tiy, perhaps because of her greater age, is endowed with two such lines to emphasize her sagging stomach plus a double line under each breast. Nefertiti's breasts receive little attention; they were not considered her most important attribute and, as we have seen, obvious breasts were not an exclusively female trait. Nefertiti's usual garment, a transparent, pleated linen robe tied with a sash worn either under the bust or around the waist, allows us a clear view of her body. Indeed, the dress is frequently shown with the front completely open so that the queen's body is displayed without any obvious form of undergarment. Alternatively Nefertiti dons a dress so fine and so close-fitting that her entire form can be seen through the folds.

It is highly unlikely that Nefertiti habitually wore such revealing and uncomfortable garments. Artistic convention had always required that the female form should be well defined although men, who frequently appeared topless and occasionally wore semi-transparent kilts, almost invariably had their genitalia concealed behind a belt or a thickness of cloth. We find élite Old and Middle Kingdom ladies dressed in sheath dresses so tight that they would have been unable to walk or sit down, the curves of their breasts, stomach, hips and pubic mound clearly visible to all. Linen, the material used for upper-class garments throughout the dynastic period, cannot be persuaded to hug the figure in this way without the addition of Lycra, and the garments are in fact an artistic ideal. During the New Kingdom goddesses continued to favour the tight sheath dress but there was change in human fashion towards more voluminous pleated and fringed garments, and Akhenaten's artists emphasized the female body beneath by making the robes appear so fine as to be transparent. Again this must be an exaggeration. Although Egyptian linen was the best in the world, it could never have been so fine. Actual garments recovered from tombs indicate that women wore a rather baggy linen dress with sleeves, often covered by a shawl, a practical response to Egypt's hot days and much colder evenings and nights.

Throughout the dynastic period it was widely agreed that a woman's fertility contributed to her sexual attractions. Nefertiti's role as a devoted wife and mother did not prevent her from being portrayed as a beautiful, even desirable, woman and the fact that she was known to have borne many children may even have added to her considerable charms. Nor did Nefertiti's religious duties conflict with her presentation as a sexually attractive or even sexually active woman. Sex, or more specifically reproduction, was acknowledged to be a fundamental aspect of human and divine life and no attempt was made to separate sex from religion. The gods and goddesses of ancient Egypt were in no way celibate beings and their varied and active couplings were well known to all. The gods' sexual needs were treated with a down-to-earth practicality which can occasionally appear shocking to those of us accustomed to more cerebral deities; under the traditional religion, for example, the queen assumed the role of 'God's Wife of Amen' in order to sexually arouse the god and ensure the continued re-creation of the world. The rituals associated with this are not now known. The more explicit title of 'God's Hand of Amen', also linked with the role of the queen, is an obvious reference to the masturbation which allowed the creator god Atum to produce Shu and Tefnut. The hand, which in the Egyptian language is feminine, is often associated with Hathor, a goddess who in turn is associated with the queens of Egypt.[12] The hands which terminate the Aten's rays may thus be interpreted as symbols of both femininity and queenship.

Although Nefertiti's new body-shape essentially mirrors that of her husband, raising the question of who is copying whom, there seems little doubt that she is being deliberately presented as a desirable super-woman, a living symbol of fertility.[13] On the strength of these images she has frequently been identified as a 'venus figure', a reference to the European ice-age figurines which, with their emphasized breasts and buttocks and rudimentary faces, are generally understood to be female fertility icons. A better parallel may perhaps be drawn with the 'mother goddess' figures recovered from the predynastic period, which place a heavy emphasis on the lower body, and with the naked female fertility figurines which, wearing long wigs and jewellery and often accompanied by a miniature child, started to appear in 18th Dynasty Egypt. These were originally interpreted as concubine figures placed in the grave for the enjoyment of deceased males. However, they are now known to come from both funerary and domestic contexts, and are often associated with model beds, snakes and convolvulus, suggesting a link with child-birth and all aspects of human reproduction. Approximately sixty of these figures have been recovered from Amarna. As the new images of Akhenaten, Nefertiti and their children at leisure are being held out to the people as an ideal semi-divine family worthy of adoration, it is perhaps not surprising to find Nefertiti assuming the role of mother-goddess or fertility symbol within the perfect family. What we cannot know is whether this role of goddess was attached to Nefertiti personally, or whether it was associated with her role as queen.

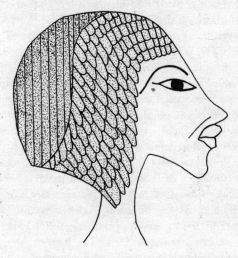

Fig. 4.2   Nefertiti, early Amarna style, in Nubian wig

Nefertiti's features quickly start to resemble those of her husband as his body becomes more like hers until she becomes as ugly and idiosyncratic as he. Following the move to Amarna, although she remains strikingly similar to Akhenaten, Nefertiti loses some of her angularity, with her face becoming slightly rounder and her body more feminine. As Nefertiti and Akhenaten were most probably cousins a certain facial likeness is perhaps to be expected, but at its most extreme, at Thebes, their resemblance goes far beyond realism. If Akhenaten and Nefertiti are to be interpreted as the earthly representatives of the divine twins Shu and Tefnut this resemblance might perhaps be understandable. However, it would seem more likely that Nefertiti and her daughters were being deliberately depicted in the image of the king as a means of associating themselves with his divinity while differentiating the royal family from the rest of humanity. This would explain why the placing of Nefertiti's feet so often copies that of the king's, and indeed why women of the Amarna royal family are often shown as red-brown in colour, a deliberate reversal of the tradition which decreed that all women should be a pale contrast to their tanned menfolk. The mirroring of features and postures was a well-established tradition used as a means of stressing the link between the king and the gods and Akhenaten's version of Re-Harakhty shown on the wall of the Karnak temple had already displayed a sagging stomach highly reminiscent of the king himself. Queen Tiy, who might also have been expected to resemble her son but who played a less prominent role in the worship of the Aten, was allowed to retain her own characteristic features, although the wooden head recovered from Gurob, which was almost certainly carved during her son's reign, is clearly influenced by the Amarna art-style, displaying a more triangular face and a more obvious bone structure than is usual in depictions of this lady.

As we have already seen in our consideration of the *Gempaaten* colossi, this deliberate similarity of facial features can make it very difficult to distinguish between damaged or unlabelled representations of the king and queen. To add to the confusion, Akhenaten and Nefertiti now frequently appear in the same type of clothing, although there are subtle differences if we know where to look. The hem of Akhenaten's long pleated dress, for example, always clears the ground, while Nefertiti's dress drops straight down. Similarly, while the folds of Nefertiti's dress hang vertically over her hips, the folds of Akhenaten's linen kilt mostly lie horizontally or diagonally. The back of Nefertiti's neck tends to be concave, while Akhenaten has a slightly convex neck – unfortunately, the back of the neck is all too often hidden from view. The so-called Amarna navel, a flattened oval rather than a circle, is usually but unfortunately not always placed higher on Nefertiti than on Akhenaten, while the Nubian-style wig worn by Nefertiti is tapered into the back of the neck in contrast to male wigs which tend to be cut straight across the neck. More subjective are the differences to the face, although it is generally agreed that Nefertiti's nose is smaller than Akhenaten's, her chin more pointed and her cheek-bones more pronounced.

As Akhenaten's reign progresses Nefertiti's angular face evolves until, before Year 12, she loses her drooping jaw and chin, developing instead a square jaw, obvious cheek-bones, naturally rounded cheeks and straighter lips.[14] At the same time the proportions of her head and neck are adjusted to allow her a more natural appearance. The famous Berlin bust, which will be considered in more detail in the Epilogue, is one of the earliest examples of the new-style, natural-looking queen. The reasons for this change are not immediately apparent. It could be connected with a change in sculptor or workshop but, although Akhenaten's face becomes slightly softer, there is no obvious corresponding adjustment to his features. It is certainly tempting to see Nefertiti's changed image, and her move away from Akhenaten's features, as in some way connected with her evolving role within the royal hierarchy.

The appearance of the disembodied Aten high in the sky above the royal family necessitated changes in artistic composition. The Egyptians loved symmetry, and so in more traditional scenes involving a king and a god the two figures had almost invariably been placed at the centre of the picture so that they balanced each other. With the elevation of the Aten the king became the most important standing figure and the queen was promoted from her usual position behind or beside her husband to stand facing him, thus providing a pleasing triangular balance and emphasizing the increased importance of the queen. The Aten now drew the eye upwards, and in order to emphasize this the proportions of the humans were adjusted. In particular, the torso above the navel was lengthened so that the legs appeared somewhat stocky in comparison with the body. The emphasized head and the hips, which at first appeared out of proportion, were soon readjusted to give a more natural effect and the fingers were lengthened, allowing the royal couple to make graceful fluttering movements with their hands, now clearly differentiated between left and right.[15]

Egyptian artists had never been particularly interested in portraying children who played a relatively minor role in public life. High infant- and child-mortality rates meant that children all too often led the briefest of lives. Where they were shown, they appeared either as miniature adults or as symbolic infants: naked, sporting the side-lock of youth hairstyle and with one finger permanently in the mouth. Now the royal children were to be included in family groups as symbols of their parents' fertility, and the Amarna artists were forced to rethink their approach. This resulted in a more natural representation of childhood, with the young princesses becoming individuals, free to move and perform child-

Fig. 4.3   Nefertiti pours liquid for Akhenaten

ish actions, although their bodies remained scaled-down versions of their mother, complete with her wide hips and skinny legs. The little girls are constantly associated with Nefertiti, and Meritaten, as the eldest, is always accorded the prominent role, playing most often with her father. All six daughters look like their mother (who, of course, looks like their father) and, although they are usually shown naked, they occasionally imitate her by wearing long, diaphanous robes. They are curiously free of symbolic head-dresses, and only their changing hairstyles give an indication of their increasing age as they advance from bald babies with strange egg-shaped heads to gawky girls with the side-lock of youth and finally elegant young ladies sporting a modified version of the Nubian-style wig favoured by their mother.

Their bald heads ensure that the curious elongated skulls of the Amarna princesses, emphasized by their long, stalk-like necks, mimic the profile of the king's head which is almost invariably elongated by his sloping crown. Again, the 'truth' behind these egg-shaped heads is open to doubt. If the princesses did indeed have grossly misshapen heads, was this the result of deliberate manipulation during childhood, a practice which is so far unknown in dynastic Egypt, or could they all have been born with some severe physical abnormality, perhaps inherited from their father whose head is invariably concealed beneath his crown? The fact that the adult Ankhesenpaaten displays a perfectly normal head several years after her father's death suggests that once again the royal artists were not attempting realistic portraiture, but were deliberately choosing to exaggerate the slightly elongated heads of the princesses in order to prove a theological point. The egg was accepted by Akhenaten as a symbol of creation, and was indeed included as such in the hymn to the Aten: '. . . when the chick in the egg chirps within his shell you give him breath to live, and when his time is ready to break out from the shell he comes out of the egg to proclaim his birth . . .'. Dorothea Arnold has suggested that the children's egg-heads may well have been intended to reinforce their role as embodiments of divine creation, comparing them to a unique but badly damaged alabaster sculpture recovered from Amarna which has been reconstructed to show Akhenaten in the form of a squatting child with one finger raised to his mouth.[16] In this figure Akhenaten is bald, although he wears the side-lock of youth, and he too has an elongated egg-shaped head.

5

Horizon of the Aten

𓇌𓊪𓏏𓊖𓇋𓏏𓈖𓏤𓇿𓈖𓇌

Behold Akhetaten which the Aten desires me to make unto him as a monument in his name for ever. It was the Aten my father that brought me to Akhetaten. Not a noble directed me to it saying 'it is fitting for his majesty to make Akhetaten in this place'. It was the Aten my father that directed me to it, to make it for him as Akhetaten . . .[1]

As Akhenaten tells us, the site chosen for his new capital Akhetaten or 'Horizon of the Aten' (now widely known as Amarna) was selected by the great god himself. Unfortunately, we are not told how the Aten made his choice known, although it is probably not too fanciful to suggest that Akhenaten was first attracted to Amarna by its topography; many modern travellers have noted how, particularly when viewed from the river, the natural shaping of the cliffs in silhouette resembles the hieroglyph for 'horizon'.[2]

The new capital was to lie on the east bank of the Nile in the Hare Nome of Middle Egypt, almost equidistant between the southern capital, Thebes, and the northern capital, Memphis, and several miles to the south-east of the ancient west bank town of Hermopolis (modern Ashmunein). The chosen site was a wide, hot and somewhat windswept arc of desert some eleven kilometres long and five kilometres wide, sandwiched between the river Nile to the west and a semi-circle of steep cliffs to the east. There was relatively easy access to water, but although Middle Egypt is in general a fertile area, a shortage of agricultural land on the east bank meant that all farming would have to take place on the west, with supplies being ferried over to feed the city. It was, however, a virgin site which, because it had never been built on, had never been dedicated to a particular deity. This may well have heightened its attraction for the king and his god who wanted to build the Aten's 'Seat of the First Occasion', a city which would belong exclusively to the

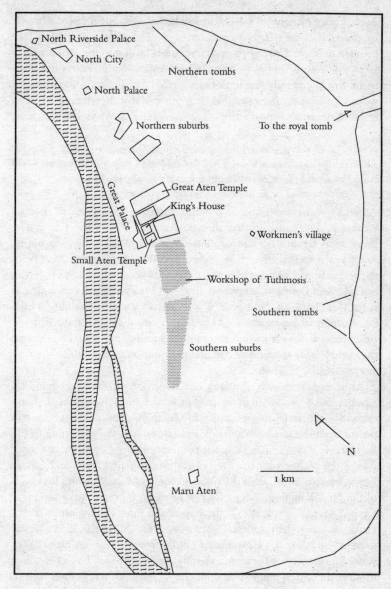

Fig. 5.1   Map of Amarna

Aten. In fact Akhenaten's decision was almost certainly inspired as much by practical as by religious considerations. The Nile Valley could not provide unlimited city-sites, and a late 18th Dynasty king looking for a large, completely untouched plot of land suitable for extensive development would certainly not have been spoiled for choice, as the best sites would have been long occupied. It is possible that Nefertiti recognized some of Amarna's shortcomings, as Akhenaten rather tersely informs us:

Neither shall the queen say unto me 'behold there is a goodly place for Akhetaten in another place' . . . I will not say 'I will abandon Akhetaten, I will hasten away and make Akhetaten in this other goodly place'.[3]

Amarna's main strength as a site also seems to have been its greatest weakness. The isolation that allowed Akhenaten to make a new start away from Egypt's traditional deities ensured that his city, despite its status as the capital of a great empire, remained very much apart from the rest of Egypt. As Amarna went about its unique business of serving the king and the Aten, elsewhere in Egypt life continued very much as it had for centuries. However, it is Amarna's very unsuitability which has ensured its preservation. Akhenaten's city may well have suffered from decay and both ancient and modern looting, but it has been spared the complete destruction of Amarna period monuments which we find at Heliopolis and Thebes.

Akhenaten's chosen site did not have the obvious geographical advantages of the other three capitals of the New Kingdom. It is no coincidence that the ancient capital of Memphis lay only a few kilometres distant from the modern capital, Cairo. As early as the beginning of the 1st Dynasty it was realized that the natural centre of Egypt was the point where the Valley met the Delta, the junction of Upper and Lower Egypt, and so, throughout the Old and Middle Kingdoms and for much of the New Kingdom, Memphis remained the administrative capital of Egypt.[4] Memphis was always the largest and most cosmopolitan of the Egyptian cities. In contrast Pi-Ramesses, the New Kingdom capital founded by Ramesses II, was sited not far from the eastern Delta backwater home town of Ramesses's family. Sentiment was, however, allied to shrewd political judgement since the location of Pi-Ramesses near to the old Hyksos capital of Avaris moved the centre of political life closer to the eastern border at a time when Egypt was feeling concern over her military, diplomatic and trading relationships with the kingdoms and empires of western Asia, particularly the Hittites who had superseded Mitanni as Egypt's main rival and competing international superpower. Thebes, although far to the south, was conveniently situated for overseeing the administration of Nubia, vast tracts of which had come under direct Egyptian rule early in the New Kingdom. Thebes was also a useful starting point for expeditions into the eastern desert, while access to the Red Sea via the nearby Wadi Hammamat provided another useful southern trade route.

The limits of the god's new territory were defined in a series of massive inscriptions carved at strategic points into the limestone cliffs of both the east (eleven stelae) and west (three stelae) banks. In fact, the area enclosed within these so-called 'boundary stelae', measuring some sixteen by thirteen kilometres, was far larger than the area eventually occupied by the city itself and included 'mountains, deserts, meadows, water, villages, embankments, men, beasts, groves and all things which the Aten shall bring into existence'. Akhenaten was providing his god with a small self-contained kingdom which allowed plenty of room for internal growth but which, the king swore, would never be expanded beyond its stated boundaries. It is difficult to calculate how much of this area was fertile land, but it has been suggested that the Amarna cultivation would have been capable of supporting a population of up to 45,000.[5]

The first three boundary stelae, most probably carved during Year 5, detailed the founding of Amarna. By Year 6 a further eleven stelae had been carved to mark the final boundaries of a city which was already substantially complete. Several of these stelae are now, due to a combination of ancient and modern vandalism plus natural damage, completely unreadable. One stela (known as stela P) was even blown up by local Copts searching for the treasure behind the 'door' in the cliff. Fortunately the stelae were fully documented at the turn of the century by Norman de Garis Davies, working on behalf of the Egypt Exploration Society, and this record, combined with the surviving sections, has allowed scholars to make a fairly complete composite reconstruction of Akhenaten's full message. From this we learn that the king first decided to abandon Thebes for Amarna during Year 4, formally establishing the limits of his new city in Year 6 when he swore an oath of dedication.

This oath was renewed in Year 8 when the king inspected his boundaries and a postscript to this effect was added to eight of the stelae. All the boundary stelae were carved to the same pattern; they were rectangular with straight sides and a rounded top which allowed the Aten to shine in an arched sky. Beneath the Aten there was inevitably a scene showing Akhenaten, Nefertiti and their daughters at worship, while beneath this came the text. To either side of all but three of the stelae, and standing free although carved from the same rock, were statue groups of the royal family, the king and queen holding large plaques inscribed with the names of the Aten, Akhenaten and Nefertiti.

The stela known as boundary stela S, which was by happy accident carved into a vein of exceptionally hard limestone, is the best preserved of all Akhenaten's proclamations. Measuring approximately one and a half metres wide by two and a half metres tall, it displays four columns and twenty-six lines of inscription. The scene at the top of the stela depicts Akhenaten, Nefertiti, Meritaten and Meketaten worshipping the Aten (Fig. 5.2). All are shown in the early, deliberately exaggerated Amarna style, so that 'the work in the scene above the inscription is beautifully fine, though the profiles are hideous and the forms of the body outrageous'.[6] Nefertiti wears her usual flimsy robe with sleeves, which partially conceals her breasts but highlights her stomach, hips and pubic region; on her head she wears the long wig and the uraeus, disc, horns and double plumes seen in the *Hwt-Benben* reliefs. Akhenaten wears a pleated linen kilt which emphasizes his paunch but conceals his genitals, and his favourite tall blue crown. The family, as always, line up in order of importance. Nefertiti stands behind her husband, yet she is virtually the same height as Akhenaten, and has abandoned the queen's sistrum to follow her husband in holding out her arms to the god. The rays of the Aten in turn hold the *ankh*, sign of life, before the faces of king and queen. The two little princesses, dressed like their mother in long transparent robes designed to emphasize their lower regions, but with elongated bald heads displaying the side-lock of youth, shake their sistra before the god. In the damaged statue groups to each side of the stela the king has his genitals covered by a belt, while Nefertiti and the princesses appear naked.

Akhenaten intended his new city to be Egypt's permanent capital, home of the one state god Aten and the bureaucracy which hitherto

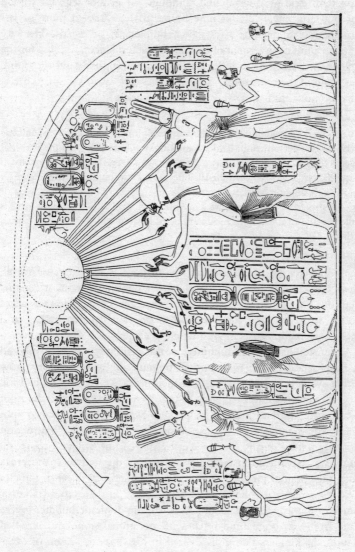

Fig. 5.2 Boundary stela S

had been centred on Memphis. He seems to have rejected the old peripatetic style of kingship and, although we cannot state for certain that the king never left his new home, to have settled more or less permanently in the one base which fulfilled all his needs. The city included a full complement of temples, royal residences, housing for the civil servants, army chiefs and priests, artisan housing and a burial ground. The siting of the royal tomb in the Amarna cliffs was a sign of Akhenaten's certain faith that his new city would outlast its founder:

A tomb shall be made for me in the eastern mountain of Akhetaten, and my burial shall be performed in it with a multitude of festivals which the Aten has ordered for me. If the Great Queen Nefertiti who lives, should die in any town of north, south, west or east, she shall be brought and buried at Akhetaten. If the King's Daughter Meritaten should die in any city of north, south, west or east, she shall be brought and buried in Akhetaten. And the sepulchre of Mnevis shall be made in the eastern mountain of Akhetaten and they shall be buried in them.

The Mnevis were sacred animals, living gods in the form of a bull, consecrated to the solar cult at Heliopolis. Their high status at Amarna is curious but perhaps indicates both Akhenaten's respect for aspects of the old solar cult, and his intention to develop Amarna, rather than Thebes or Heliopolis, as Egypt's religious capital.

Akhenaten had almost unlimited wealth at his disposal. Not only did he have access to the richest royal treasury in Egypt's history, now further swelled by the offerings withheld from Amen, he also had full control over the funds belonging to the Aten priesthood, plus the right to commandeer the labour of his people. Nevertheless, the speed with which Amarna rose from the barren desert is impressive. Construction had only started during Year 5, yet by the end of that year the royal family was ensconced in temporary quarters, 'the tent of apartments', while they waited for their palace to be finished.[7] By Year 9, the city was fully functional. The builders were helped in their task by a crafty choice of construction materials. As usual, the domestic buildings were made from sun-dried mud-brick with occasional stone and wooden features. As Flinders Petrie discovered in his 1891–92 season of excavation at Amarna, a simple mud-brick hut can easily be built in a day:

We settled to live at the village of Haj Qandil . . . building a row of mud-brick huts as we needed them. Such rooms can be built very quickly; a hut twelve feet by eight taking only a few hours. The bricks can be bought at tenpence a thousand; the boys make a huge mud pie, a line of bricks is laid on the ground, a line of mud poured over them, another line of bricks is slapped down in the mud so as to drive it up the joints; and thus a wall of headers, with an occasional course of stretchers to bind it, is soon run up. The roof is made of boards, covered with durra stalks to protect them from the sun; and the hut is ready for use, with a piece of canvas hung over the doorway.[8]

The inner walls of the ancient houses were plastered and painted with some of the most lively scenes of the natural world ever to be seen in dynastic Egypt, which allowed any defects in the structure to be hidden beneath a thick layer of plaster. The standard of painting was not, however, always of the highest, and Petrie was able to detect rooms in the palace where the work of a good artist was placed next to that of an obviously inferior craftsman.

Sandstone *talatat* blocks, even smaller than those used at Thebes, played a part in the construction of the Amarna temples, but now extensive use was made of both limestone and mud-brick, while mud-brick rather than stone was employed as a core. These buildings, although outwardly impressive, were again not of the highest standard. All too often the plaster which covered the walls, and into which were carved the sunken reliefs, served to conceal the inferior workmanship beneath. It seems likely that within its enclosure wall the Great Temple complex remained substantially incomplete; had Amarna continued as the capital of Egypt we would probably have seen successive monarchs vying to expand and embellish the temple just as Akhenaten's predecessors had competed over the development of the Karnak complex. Archaeological evidence suggests that this rebuilding had already begun towards the end of Akhenaten's reign, when mud-brick temple elements started to be replaced with stone.[9]

Naturally the intensive building created a huge demand for craftsmen, not only labourers but artists, architects, sculptors, painters and the bureaucrats who would supervise them, while the cult of the Aten demanded its full complement of priests. Within the city, although proper care was taken to ensure that the principal religious and administrative buildings were in the correct relationship to each other, there was no overall plan. Akhenaten seems to have resisted the temptation to regulate the private lives of his citizens, or maybe he lacked the resources to devise and build an entire city.[10] In consequence the city simply grew organically around its palaces and temples, while the magnificent walled villas of the nobles served as the focus for clusters of smaller houses which may well have been economically dependent upon the larger estates. The city may have been founded to serve the Aten, but it needed a sound economic basis to survive. It was provided with a full complement of transport, storage and manufacturing facilities many of which, but by no means all, fell under the control of the king. The southern suburb, home to some of the most influential of Akhenaten's courtiers, was also the site of the sculptors' studios and a large glass factory, while the northern suburb, where many merchants lived within easy reach of the quay, even developed what can only be classed as a slum area.

Like any other city, Amarna required a vast amount of water, not only for human and animal consumption but to maintain the elaborate pools and private gardens which were very much a feature of Akhenaten's palaces and temples. The city could thus not expand too far away from the river, and developed into a long ribbon-like entity running parallel to the line of the Nile and set slightly back from the thin strip of cultivation. Even so, an entire city could not rely on water transported from the Nile, and it proved necessary to develop a system of wells sunk deep into the subsoil. Sanitation throughout the city was primitive, and few homes had any form of toilet facility. Although the larger houses were furnished with stone-lined bathrooms and lavatories, there was no proper drainage system and the water which was poured over the bather simply collected in a vessel sunk into the floor or, in the more elaborate bathrooms, ran off through a conduit in the bathroom wall to sink into the ground outside. The lavatories, basic earth closets housed in a small chamber next to the bathroom, consisted of a wooden seat balanced on two brick pillars and set over a deep bowl of sand. It was customary to sweep the inside of the houses, but the sweepings were simply tipped out into the street. Large dumps developed, not necessarily confined to the outskirts of the city, which from time to time would be levelled or burned to allow building on the site. Such dumps are a conspicuous feature of Egyptian villages today where the heat brings about rapid decay, and there is a constant problem with vermin.

If Amarna was not a particularly well-planned city, nor even a clean one, it was certainly well defended. The task of protecting Amarna and its royal tombs was made easy by the geography of the site. To the west the Nile provided an effective barrier which could be patrolled by boat, while the cliffs to the east rendered a city wall unnecessary. The military and armed police who had been so prominent at Thebes maintained their high profile at Amarna, and both Egyptian and foreign troops were stationed within the city. The tracks worn by the soldiers who guarded the eastern cliffs and desert are clearly visible today. What we cannot tell is whether the guards were engaged in keeping foreigners out, or the citizens in. It would not be too surprising if some resented their enforced seclusion in the king's model city, and perhaps even more so their enforced burial away from their ancestral tombs. Elizabeth Riefstahl has gone as far as to compare Amarna with 'an embattled city, a luxurious concentration camp'.[11]

Mahu, Chief of the *Medjay* (police) and 'General of the Army of the Lord of the Two Lands', was an important figure at Amarna. He was assisted in his work by a 'General of the Army', a battalion commander and several commanders of the cavalry, including Ay. It was Mahu's duty to keep the peace within the city, a job which he obviously did well, as a badly damaged vignette in his tomb shows him receiving the gold which rewarded Akhenaten's favourites. In a more unusual tomb scene we see Mahu heading the king's bodyguard as Akhenaten, Nefertiti and Meritaten leave the temple and drive in state along the Royal Road in their chariot (Fig. 5.3). The people assume an uncomfortable posture, bowing low from the waist, as the royal family pass. As Mahu and his soldiers are compelled to run alongside the royal chariot, we must assume that their presence as bodyguards is a formality rather than a necessity. In fact the ride itself seems fraught with danger. Although Akhenaten holds the reins of the two prancing horses, his attention is on Nefertiti whom at first sight he appears to be kissing, although it is possible that the two were simply sharing the *ankh* of life held between them by one of the Aten's rays. Whatever the reason for their distraction, tiny Meritaten is taking full advantage of the situation as, ignored by her parents, she goads the horses with a stick.[12]

The long and fairly straight road which formed the backbone of

Fig. 5.3   A royal chariot ride

Amarna functioned as the all-important processional way, which allowed the royal family to display themselves to their subjects in a semi-secular version of the old religious processions, as shown in the tomb of Mahu. This road, now known as the Royal Road or the Sikket es-Sultan, ran from north to south, linking the North Riverside Palace, the fortified private home of the royal family which now lies largely under the modern cultivation, to the city centre which housed the main religious and administrative buildings. Beyond the city centre the road ran on to reach the outlying *Maru-Aten* cult centre, although by now it was no longer part of the processional way.

The North Palace lay between the northern suburbs and the North Riverside Palace. This unfortified 'palace' was an isolated complex of rooms first identified by its excavators as a kind of zoological garden,[13] but now believed to have been a palace for the use of the oldest royal daughter, Meritaten, whose name is found superimposed over that of another, as yet unidentified, female. The complex, centred around a large pool, incorporated a garden courtyard, an open-air court with altars for the worship of the Aten, a room with a dais usually interpreted as a throne room, private quarters including a bathroom and, most surprisingly, beautifully decorated accommodation for animals, including aviaries and pens complete with elaborate stone mangers. The 'Green Room', whose walls were painted with a papyrus thicket full of spectacular wild birds undisturbed by the hunters who so often intrude on Egyptian scenes of nature, has often been described as a masterpiece. A series of rooms within the complex has been tentatively identified as harem quarters although, as the excavators noted, 'it is astounding that these rooms are not larger than prison cells or bathing cabins and bear no reflex of any charm of life, no indications of great ceremonies or splendid equipage'.[14] Meritaten, of course, would have had little need for harem quarters in her palace, although her attendants would have needed their own accommodation.

To the south of the North Palace the Royal Road passed through the northern suburbs to reach the city centre. Here, to the west of the road, lay a vast group of buildings constructed partly of stone and partly of mud-brick. Although this complex is generally referred to as the Great Palace, argument over its exact purpose has been rife. To some the buildings are unquestionably the remains of a great royal residence whose apartments were home to the royal family, their dependants and servants and, of course, the royal harem. Others believe that the stone-built courts and halls, which originally included colossal statues of the royal couple plus decoration showing the royal family at worship, must have been in some way connected with the Aten cult. Unfortunately a great deal of this structure has been lost to modern cultivation while the stonework has been salvaged and re-used in both ancient and modern buildings; it seems unlikely that archaeology will ever be able to solve the question of its original purpose(s), although it would perhaps be surprising if such a large complex did not serve multiple functions.

The Great Palace, whatever its other duties, would seem to have been a suitable site for the royal harem which must have numbered many hundreds of women. Nefertiti is so consistently presented as Akhenaten's consort, and is so obviously at the centre of the nuclear royal family,

that there is a tendency to forget that Akhenaten followed New Kingdom tradition in having many secondary wives. His harem, which may
well have been home to his shadowy sisters and aunts, included not only
Akhenaten's own brides, but all the women inherited from his father,
including Gilukhepa and her niece Tadukhepa. All these ladies would
have needed appropriately regal accommodation for themselves, their
children and their retinues which, in the case of the foreign princesses,
could number several hundred women. Given Akhenaten's stated intention to have one capital city, and his apparent disinclination to travel
outside Amarna, it seems likely that he would have rehoused some, if
not all, of his women close to his home.

The tombs of Tutu, Ay and Parennefer allow us a tantalizing glimpse
into some of the more public rooms which normally remain hidden
behind the palace façade. However, these small-scale cartoon-like scenes,
which merely form the background to the all-important spectacle of the

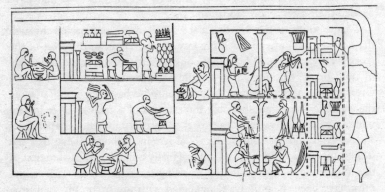

Fig. 5.4   The royal harem

tomb owner being rewarded by the royal couple, were never intended to be faithful reproductions of the palace interior, and in consequence are liable to pose more questions than they answer. In the tomb of Ay (Fig. 5.4) we are shown a group of women within two separate buildings whose doors are guarded, or perhaps protected, by men whom Davies, for no apparent reason other than cultural expectation, identifies as eunuchs.[15] Almost all the women are either making music or dancing, while the walls of their rooms are hung with an assortment of lyres, lutes and harps. The women in the upper rooms of both houses have strange, un-Egyptian-looking hairstyles, with their long tresses divided into locks and either curled or weighted at the end. One woman, again in an upper chamber, is squatting so that her friend may part and dress her hair in this atypical style. This, combined with the unusual skirt worn by at least one of the women, has led to the suggestion that they may be Syrian musicians, perhaps part of the retinue who accompanied Tadukhepa of Mitanni to Egypt.

Most high-ranking households maintained a troupe of female musicians and acrobatic dancers who, dressed in the most scanty of garments and with their long hair weighted to produce a seductive swing, would entertain guests at dinner parties. The full extent of the duties expected of these women is not clear. The connection between music and sexuality in ancient Egypt was well understood, with prostitutes often using music as a means of seducing their clients; this link is made clear by a scene in the Turin erotic papyrus where a prostitute throws down her lyre to copulate with a client, while a fragment of wood recovered from a New Kingdom Theban tomb shows a woman who, although engaged in intercourse, refuses to put down her lute.[16]

Less apparent is the link between music and religion, although we know that the gods were stimulated by sound and that their rituals had, since the start of the dynastic age, been accompanied by singing, chanting, clapping and dancing. The Aten, like all his divine predecessors, was worshipped through the music which encouraged him to accept the offerings placed before him,[17] and the temple precincts echoed with sound as 'musicians and chantresses shout for joy in the court of the *Benben* temple and every temple in Akhetaten'.[18] Music provided by the queen, whose traditional duties included the arousal of the gods, was particularly important. Nefertiti's sistrum was used to calm and soothe

the god, while references to her vocal charms, 'one is happy to hear her voice', or 'the one who pacifies the Aten with a sweet voice and whose hands carry the sistrum', should not be read as generalized compliments, but as specific references to her ability to complete her religious duties.

The King's House was situated opposite the Great Palace and was linked to it by a mud-brick bridge passing over the Royal Road. This was the king's official residence within the city and it was from here that he conducted his affairs of state. Here too, in a room on the north-east corner of the building, was the Window of Appearance where the royal couple appeared before their people to announce promotions, distribute gold to a faithful few and rations to the masses.[19] Consequently the house, although relatively small, included accommodation for the guards and servants who would have attended the royal family, plus storage facilities including a large granary which, under other more orthodox regimes, we might have expected to find within the temple precincts. Surrounding the house were the offices and archives of the civil service and it was here, in the remains of the 'Bureau for the Correspondence of the Pharaoh' that the Amarna letters were recovered.

Within the King's House there were private apartments, including bathrooms and lavatories, and a garden courtyard. Here John Pendlebury discovered an independent suite of six separate rooms, each with a niche to hold a bed; he tentatively identified this as the royal night-nursery, although it is perhaps more realistic to view the small rooms as accommodation for the large entourage of anonymous women who invariably accompanied the royal family on their travels. It was in the King's House that Flinders Petrie found and rescued the painting of the two little princesses, now housed in the Ashmolean Museum, which originally formed part of a much larger mural of the royal family.

The beautiful painted pavement within the Great Palace suffered a less happy fate. Petrie tells us how he went to great lengths to preserve the gypsum floor, painting it with a weak solution of tapioca applied gently using the side of one finger and building a gangway to make a walkway for visitors. As word of the magnificent floor spread Amarna became a tourist attraction, and eventually the Society for the Preservation of the Monuments of Egypt paid for the erection of a small protective hut. However, no path through the fields was provided for the visitors, and the fields were trampled by the eager tourists. Petrie describes with some bitterness how, on 1 February 1912, at a time when the German expedition led by Ludwig Borchardt held the Amarna concession:

... One night a man went and hacked it all to pieces to prevent visitors coming. Such was the mismanaged end of a unique find. I was never even informed and allowed to pick up the pieces.[20]

An alternative interpretation of events, that the pavement was destroyed by local guards who resented the *baksheesh* earned by their colleagues in charge of the floor, is perhaps more convincing but does not alter the pointless nature of the destruction.[21] The fragments were collected, transferred to Cairo Museum, and reassembled in a somewhat haphazard manner. Here we may still see the calm blue pool filled with contented fish and surrounded by a wonderful assortment of animals, birds and plants.

The two temples of the Aten lay on the east side of the Royal Road, on opposite sides of the King's House. Immediately to the south was *Hwt-Aten*, or the 'Mansion of the Aten', more commonly called the Small Temple of the Aten, a temple which although 'small' was of roughly the same size as the Theban *Gempaaten*. The Small Temple, however, lacked the colonnades and colossi found at Thebes; instead its outer wall was provided with towers and battlements with niches for flagpoles, and it is possible that it was at least in part roofed. This may well have been a centre for the celebration of the royal cult, perhaps even the king's version of a mortuary temple, and it may be no coincidence that it is aligned towards the distant royal tomb.

Per-Aten, the 'House of the Aten' or Great Temple of the Aten was a confusing complex of independent stone buildings bounded by a massive oblong enclosure wall some 229 metres wide and 730 metres long and entered via either a western gateway or a northern entrance pavilion. Unfortunately, all that now survive are the foundations, and much of the site has been lost beneath the modern cemetery of el-Till. We know that within the enclosure wall were a number of small shrines and so-called sunshade temples associated with the royal women, a vast open space, and at least three stone buildings. *Per-Hai*, 'The House of Rejoicing', led to *Gempaaten*, 'The Sun Disc is Found', a progression of open-air courtyards diminishing in size and housing many limestone offering tables arranged in neat rows. Two hundred and forty metres away, at the eastern end of the complex, was the sanctuary, occasionally called *Hwt-Benben*, or the 'Mansion of the *Benben* stone', which was sited close to a sacrificial butcher's yard and was associated with a collection of subsidiary buildings and a rubbish dump.

Conspicuous offerings had been a prominent feature of Aten worship at Thebes, but at Amarna this became more exaggerated, with a plot of land to the south of *Gempaaten* housing 920 mud-brick offering tables arranged in orderly ranks (forty-six tables by twenty tables). It has been suggested that a further array of tables may have existed on the opposite side of *Gempaaten*, but aerial photographs indicate that this is unlikely. The tables were used to hold the offerings of food, drink and flowers which were to be presented to the great god. Their presence in the temple highlights the illogical and contradictory mixture of tradition and innovation which was the cult of the Aten. Akhenaten, who had gone to considerable lengths to establish his god as a remote, non-anthropomorphic deity, never discarded the custom of making offerings. He may well have felt it necessary to retain the ceremony in order to stress his unique relationship with the god. The light of the disembodied sun – to modern eyes at least – appears to have no immediate need of offerings and, indeed, no means of consuming them. However, the rays of the sun with their tiny hands were able to reach down and touch or take whatever they wanted. The idea of the solid physicality of the sun's rays was certainly not a new one; the Old Kingdom pyramid texts describe the ramp of the sun's rays connecting Egypt with the sky.

The Amarna *benben* stone was no longer an obelisk, but a free-standing stela, most probably carved from quartzite. The change in form of the *benben*, which may well have been a practical necessity rather than a theological choice, seems to have gone hand in hand with a change in the pattern of Aten worship, for at Amarna there is no sign that the cult of the *benben* is exclusively connected with Nefertiti, as it appears to have been at Thebes. Instead the highest-ranking royal women, including Queen Tiy, were provided with individual sunshade temples for their exclusive worship of the Aten. Several of the Amarna tombs show the new-style *benben*-stone: in the tomb of Panehesy it takes the form of a large, round-topped stela which stands on a raised platform with a ramp or stairway, in front of several offering tables and next to a larger-than-life-sized sculpture of the seated king wearing the blue crown.[22] Although this stela has not survived, Petrie tells us how Howard Carter discovered its probable site:

The site of the temple, or shrine, which was entirely excavated by Mr Carter, is marked by heaps of broken pieces of mortar and stone; and the cores of the walls consisting of mortar and chips still remain to show the position. Mr Carter turned over nearly all of this without finding anything more than two or three blocks of the great stela. This was built up of small blocks, and bore a life-size figure of Akhenaten (of whom the head was found), and doubtless similar figures of the queen and princesses, whose titles were also found.[23]

During Pendlebury's 1933 excavation many broken pieces of purple quartzite were discovered in the area between the sanctuary and the butcher's yard.

Worship before the *benben*-stone, no longer an exclusively female ritual, was still a vital aspect of Akhenaten's religion. A large, rectangular, red quartzite stela recovered from Heliopolis, the original cult centre for solar worship, and now housed in Cairo Museum, provides a clue to its importance.[24] One face of this stela was recarved during the reign of Horemheb and now depicts an entirely conventional scene. The other, badly damaged face shows two aspects of the Amarna royal family at worship. The upper tableau is of Akhenaten, Nefertiti and Meritaten kneeling to pray to the Aten. Beneath this is a portrayal of the king, a princess and an unknown male prostrate before the Aten, whose rays can be seen holding the *ankh* of life to Akhenaten's lips. This is an unprecedentedly humble posture for Akhenaten to adopt.

The southern suburb housed some of Amarna's most luxurious private homes including the house of the Vizier Nakht, who owned one of the largest and most elegant villas. Situated on the fringe of the suburb, a somewhat inconvenient two kilometres from the King's House, Nakht's home was set in a spacious compound defined by a mud-brick wall enclosing the kitchens, storage areas, outbuildings, servants' quarters, animal pens, stables, a private chapel and a walled garden whose plants would be embedded in fertile Nile mud and watered from the private well. The villa itself was enormous. Its ground floor, which survives in plan form only, consisted of almost thirty rooms. The upper floor, which may have provided accommodation for the children and the household servants, has vanished, but it has been estimated that this would probably have represented an additional ten rooms, with further use being made of the flat roof. The villa, in spite of its exceptional size, followed the standard Egyptian tripartite house-plan, with the main door leading into public reception rooms. The reception hall, or 'north loggia', was a rectangular room with eight wooden pillars whose elaborately frescoed walls, blue ceiling and red and yellow floor were clearly designed to impress visitors. Beyond this lay a series of semi-private family rooms and finally the private area, including two en-suite bedrooms, which was probably restricted to women, children and immediate male family members.

The Royal Road, no longer a processional way, continued southwards, running beyond the southern suburb out into the desert until it reached *Maru-Aten*, an isolated complex of walled gardens, water and open-air shrines including sunshade platforms.[25] *Maru-Aten* was initially interpreted as a leisure centre where the royal family could spend a relaxed day eating and drinking away from the pressures of city life. The discovery of numerous fragments of wine vessels seemed to confirm this view. However, it is now recognized that, like so many of Akhenaten's buildings, *Maru-Aten* had an as yet unidentified religious purpose, and that it was firmly associated with one of the royal women. The inscriptions recovered from *Maru-Aten* now bear the name and titles of Meritaten, but her name is not original, it has been written over that of another royal woman. The erased name and titles are those of a hitherto unknown lady of the harem, Kiya, 'wife and greatly beloved of the King of Upper and Lower Egypt living on Truth, Lord of the Two Lands Neferkheperure Waenre, the perfect child of the living Aten who shall live for ever'.[26]

Kiya's name, unrecognized until the mid twentieth century, has since been found on a handful of objects recovered from Amarna, including a fragment of a badly damaged offering slab, various broken cosmetic pots and tubes and the broken lid of a small wooden box. On blocks recovered from Hermopolis it has even been found beneath the names of Meritaten and Ankhesenpaaten. Kiya's origins, however, remain even more obscure than those of Nefertiti, and our only clue is provided by her unusual name. It is likely that 'Kiya' was a contraction of a longer Egyptian name, although the theory that Kiya was simply a pet name

for Nefertiti must be ruled out as
we have enough evidence to confirm that Kiya was a separate individual. It is just possible that Kiya
bore a foreign name and that, even
though her titulary does not give
any indication of high birth, she
may have been one of the foreign
princesses who were, as far as we
know, still housed in the royal
harem. Kiya could have been Gilukhepa, the contraction being spelt
with a 'K' in transcription, but
Gilukhepa, who was married to
Amenhotep III during his Year 10,
may well have been too old to have

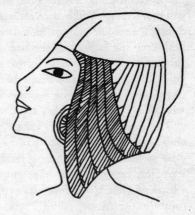

Fig. 5.5   Kiya

borne Akhenaten's children.[27] Tadukhepa, who was probably of a similar
age to Nefertiti, seems the more likely candidate. It has even been
suggested that the romantic story of Kiya, a princess of Mitanni, may
have been incorporated into the New Kingdom Tale of Two Brothers,
a fable which tells how the pharaoh fell in love with a beautiful foreign
woman after smelling a lock of her hair: 'His majesty loved her very
much, and he gave her the rank of Great Lady.'[28]

Kiya never bore the consort's title of 'King's Wife' and never wore
the royal uraeus, but she was clearly an important and highly favoured
member of the harem, accorded great respect in her lifetime and allowed
to play a part in the rituals of Aten worship which had previously been
confined to Akhenaten and Nefertiti.[29] Not only did Kiya have her own
sunshade, which would have come with its own endowment of land
and therefore its own income, she was allowed to officiate both alongside
Akhenaten and, surprisingly, alone. We have no confirmed portrait of
Kiya in the round, but her two-dimensional image has survived, enabling
us to recognize her calm and slightly smiling face which appears
altogether softer and less angular than that of Nefertiti. Both women
favoured the true Nubian wig which may well have served as a symbol
of their status. We know that Kiya bore the king at least one daughter
as we have a relief showing the proud parents together with their

unnamed offspring. There is also strong circumstantial evidence to suggest that Kiya gave Akhenaten at least two sons. Kiya remained in favour during the middle years of Akhenaten's reign and her name is associated with both the earlier and the later forms of the Aten's name. By Year 12, however, Kiya had vanished, possibly disgraced but more likely dead, and her name and image had been erased from *Maru-Aten*. She disappeared without making use of the elaborate grave goods which were being prepared for her and her mummy has never been found.

The Amarna workmen's village was tucked into a little valley in the cliffs a discreet 1.2 kilometres to the east of the main city and conveniently close to the southern group of tombs. Here were housed the labourers – possibly experienced workers imported from the Theban workmen's village of Deir el-Medina – occupied in cutting the royal and other tombs in the Amarna cliff.[30] Here also lived their wives, children and dependants and the officer in charge of the workforce, who was provided with a larger and more elaborate home. In contrast with the more haphazard city proper, the village was laid out with a strict regularity and was enclosed by a wall with a single guarded gate. Within the complex each workman was allocated a small unit measuring a mere five by ten metres, and seventy-three such houses were built in six straight terraced rows facing on to five narrow streets. The workmen were provided with only the basic shell of their home, and each house was finished off by the family using local mud-bricks. This allowed a degree of diversity in the internal planning of the houses, although the standard home was divided by cross-walls into four small rooms: a reception area, a family room, a bedroom or storage room and a kitchen which did not necessarily have an oven. None of the village houses contained a bathroom.

Conditions within the houses must have been, to modern eyes at least, unacceptably crowded, and we may assume that good use was made of the flat roof which could have served as an additional living and sleeping area. It is even possible that some of the houses were extended upwards to provide a second storey, perhaps a large private room reserved for the women of the family and their rituals. Some of the painted plaster fragments recovered in the earliest excavations at the village show what appear to be convolvulus flowers twisting around a papyrus stem; these plants were important elements employed in scenes of childbirth and suckling.[31] Outside the village wall individual families built small private chapels where they could not only worship but sit in peace, eat meals and perhaps even keep animals. Some enterprising villagers, undaunted by the lack of soil and water, every drop of which had to be transported from the main city, maintained small allotments where they raised pigs and even attempted to grow vegetables.[32]

The geography of the Amarna cliffs meant that the tombs of the nobles fell into two distinct groups on either side of the royal wadi. Generally speaking, Akhenaten's officials chose to be buried, as they had lived, close to their place of work, so we find the tombs of the priests and the officials of the royal residence included in the northern group, while the southern group houses the tombs of the great state officials such as Mahu, Parennefer and Ay. Forty-five tombs were started for Amarna's élite although, due to the short-lived nature of the site combined with a shortage of skilled workmen, only twenty-four were inscribed and few were completed. These élite tombs must represent Akhenaten's innermost circle of trusted friends who would have had little choice but to be seen to support every aspect of the new religion including the establishment of the new burial ground, and whose tombs may well have been the gift of the king himself; the decorative scheme within the tombs certainly suggests that Akhenaten, if not actually their designer, would have been fully aware of their content. No cemetery for the wider population has yet been found at Amarna, although there was a small graveyard associated with the workmen's village, and it seems likely that those who could afford it may well have chosen to be interred in their ancestral home towns. The less important members of society were presumably buried, as they were at other cities, in relatively simple tombs and graves dug into the desert sand.

Under normal circumstances the king's advisers would be the sons of his father's ministers who would have been raised alongside him in the royal school attached to the harem. Throughout the dynastic age we can trace many families of statesmen who pass down their royal duties from father to son. Akhenaten, however, displays a clear and unusual preference for new, but not necessarily young, blood, and many of his courtiers, whom Alan Gardiner has classed as *novi homines*,[33] claim to have been discovered, taught or raised to their present position through the generosity of the king. Clearly, Akhenaten relished his role as a creator and teacher. Tutu, a statesman so distinguished that he was

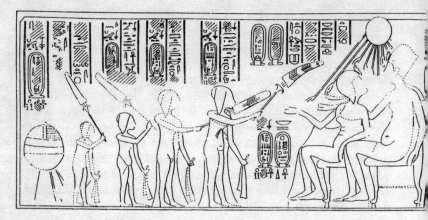

Fig. 5.6   The families of Amenhotep III and Akhenaten

mentioned in the Amarna letters, admits to being 'a servant favoured by
his Lord; his teaching and his instruction are in my innermost heart',
while the mayor of Amarna bore a name which translates as 'Akhenaten
created me' – a name which can hardly have been given to him at birth.
Even Ay, who almost certainly came from a distinguished line of civil
servants, tells us that 'my Lord taught me and I do his teaching'. The
Royal Scribe and Chancellor, May, was perhaps the most fulsome in his
public appreciation of his patron:

Listen to what I say . . . for I tell to you the benefits which the ruler did for
me. Then truly you shall say 'How great are those things that were done for
this man of no account!' . . . I was a man of low origin on both my father's
and my mother's side, but the prince established me. He allowed me to grow
. . . He gave me provisions and rations every day, I who had once been one
who begged bread . . .[34]

Parennefer, the royal butler, is the only official known to have followed
the royal court from Thebes. This preference for new blood may simply
have been a reflection of the king's wish to avoid the advice of those
closely associated with the old traditions and the old cults, but it may
perhaps add some support to the suggestion that Akhenaten did not enjoy
an entirely normal royal childhood networking in the royal nursery. The

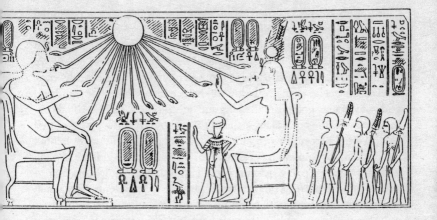

old families, whose sons would have expected to serve the king, seem to have been excluded from the delights of Amarna life. Perhaps generations of political experience encouraged them to keep a low profile during such an innovative regime.

The rock-cut tombs are, due to their nature, in a much better state of preservation than the mud-brick city, although here too there has been a great deal of deliberate destruction both ancient and modern, plus damage due to a variety of natural causes and problems resulting from post-dynastic usage as homes, burial sites and even Coptic churches. Bats have proved a particular nuisance in many of the tombs, not only corroding the walls, but causing an extremely unpleasant odour. Norman de Garis Davies, whose inspirational work of recording the tombs at the turn of the century has ensured that they are today accessible to scholars, gives some idea of the extent of the problem while working in the tomb of the Chamberlain and Treasurer, Tutu:

The surface of the stone . . . is most unsightly and sadly corroded; indeed in the upper parts the sculpture is almost effaced. This is due to the countless bats that infect the tomb and make their presence known to the nose as unpleasantly as to the eye . . . [in a footnote] When working here I cleared the tomb of them in an hour or two by a massacre of about a thousand victims – a good proof of how easily the pests could be kept down or exterminated.[35]

It is in the scenes that decorate the tomb walls that we are permitted a glimpse of the royal family as they go about their daily duties in a city whose architecture is represented in a somewhat idiosyncratic form. The most elaborate tomb is that belonging to Ay and Tey and here, as we might expect, Nefertiti features prominently. We have already considered the scene at the Window of Appearance where both husband and wife receive gold from the king and queen (Fig. 2.3). Here Nefertiti, in contrast to the equivalent scene in the tomb of Ramose, is permitted to play a full part in the ceremony and, although she still stands behind Akhenaten, she joins in the presentation. The three little girls are making a valiant attempt to be helpful; Meritaten is actually holding a tray of collars and also presents directly to her putative grandparents. Meketaten holds a tray but stands with one arm around her mother's neck – it looks as if she too has the right to present gold, but is too young to cooperate – while baby Ankhesenpaaten, perhaps bored with the ritual, turns to caress her mother. All the royal family appear to be completely naked, although it seems likely that the garments of the king, if not those of the queen, are merely hidden behind the balcony wall. Both Ay and Tey are clearly having a wonderful time. Ay already has five necklaces around his neck as he reaches out to catch another, and included in a pile of loot at his feet is a remarkable pair of red leather gloves. The next scene shows Ay departing the palace, wearing his gloves and holding them out to the admiring crowds.

The Amarna tomb of Parennefer, 'he who washes the hands of His Majesty', includes a Window scene which was largely completed and painted in antiquity, but which has suffered extensive modern damage. Fortunately, with the help of earlier copies, Norman de Garis Davies was able to restore the scene to a remarkable extent.[36] His reconstruction shows the royal family again on the balcony, with the Aten caressing Nefertiti in an almost sexual way; one ray encircles her waist, a small hand is placed on her left breast which is exposed by the folds of her dress, and a third hand appears round the side of her crown. Akhenaten too is gripped firmly around the chest by the Aten 'as if to prevent them [i.e. the king and queen] losing their balance as they lean over the window-sill'. Nefertiti, shown at a slightly smaller scale than Akhenaten, stands behind her husband and observes while the king leans forward and waves his arms. Her face is largely destroyed, but we can see that both king and queen are blessed with remarkably long necks and exaggerated Amarna profiles. It is very obvious that the queen has two left hands; the Amarna workmen only mastered the distinction between left and right hands and feet at some time between Years 6 and 9, and even then this distinction was reserved for the royals, with the less important citizens condemned to hop through life on two left feet. The three royal daughters are in the room behind the window, in the company of two bowing attendants and their aunt, Mutnodjmet.

Elsewhere in the tomb of Parennefer we see the royal family enjoying a stroll, possibly on a visit to the tombs. The king is grasped firmly by the Aten, while he in turn has his right arm passing around Nefertiti's neck so that the fingers of their right hands are somewhat clumsily entwined. The artist, evidently wishing to stress this unusual handhold, has both extended the length of Akhenaten's right arm and exaggerated the size of the two right hands. Nefertiti's dress is again transparent and open to reveal her abdomen, hips and thighs, and she has abandoned her trademark crown in favour of a simple wig and uraeus. She is of even smaller stature than in the Window scene; here the top of Nefertiti's head barely reaches Akhenaten's armpit.

The tomb of Huya is of particular interest to those following the movements of the extended royal family. Huya, 'Superintendent of the royal harem, Superintendent of the Treasury, Steward in the house of the King's Mother, the King's Wife, Tiy', was, as his titles imply, the major-domo of Queen Tiy and a favourite of Akhenaten. His tomb, which includes the standard scene of its owner receiving gold from the king and queen, is in many ways a celebration of Tiy's visits to Amarna. Although we know that Tiy had her own Amarna sunshade, and is likely to have had her own Amarna home, there is no evidence to suggest that she took up permanent residence at the new city. For a long time egyptologists were convinced that, following the death of her husband, Tiy had gone into semi-retirement at the palace of Medinet el-Gurob on the edge of the Faiyum. Here stood a mud-brick complex which has yielded many inscriptions of Amenhotep III and Tiy, including the famous yew head which shows Tiy as an elderly woman (Plate 3). However, the assumption that the building functioned as an 18th Dynasty harem palace is by no means proven; many of the recovered artefacts are religious or even funerary rather than domestic, implying that Gurob

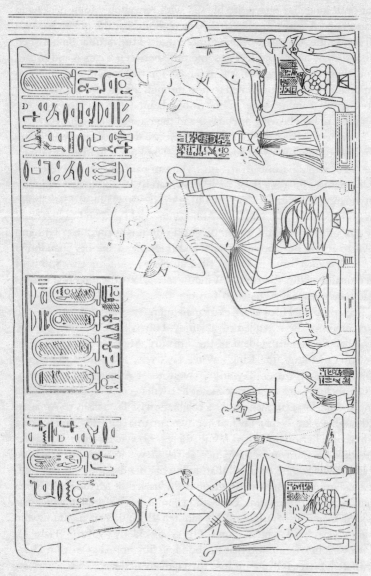

Fig. 5.7   Nefertiti and Akhenaten entertain Tiy

may well have been a cult centre for the worship of the dead Amenhotep III.[37] Tiy, a commoner queen who owed her exalted position to her marriage with the king rather than to her birth, may well have been determined to keep her deceased husband's memory alive. Her inscriptions, which come complete with references to Osiris, make it clear that she at least had not entirely abandoned the old ways of thinking:

The King's Chief Wife, his beloved, the Lady of the Two Lands Tiy made it as her monument for her beloved brother [husband] for the Ka of the Osiris the King [Amenhotep III] justified.

Tiy's devotion to her dead husband, and Akhenaten's respect for his father, may explain why Amenhotep III appears on the lintel to the north doorway of the first hall in the tomb of Huya (Fig. 5.6). The decoration of this lintel is curiously asymmetrical and unbalanced by Egyptian standards. The lintel is divided in two by a vertical line. The right-hand side shows Amenhotep III seated to face Tiy and one of the royal princesses, while the left-hand side shows Akhenaten and Nefertiti who both face left, although Nefertiti's head is turned towards Akhenaten, and four of their daughters who are approaching from the left.

In the same tomb we see Queen Tiy enjoying a meal with Akhenaten and Nefertiti. The royal couple sit side by side opposite the dowager queen, their feet raised on hassocks, with the two eldest princesses seated on small chairs beside their mother. Huya appears as a small, bowing figure at his mistress's feet. Scenes of the royal family eating and drinking are very rare, yet here Akhenaten is tucking into something which looks very much like a giant kebab or even a rack of ribs, while Nefertiti gnaws on a duck. Beside the royal diners, individual food stands are piled high with every delicacy Egypt could offer. Drink flows freely, and in a parallel scene we are shown Tiy, Akhenaten and Nefertiti with goblets raised to their lips (Fig. 5.7). This conspicuous consumption and obvious enjoyment of the bounties of the Aten, which brings to mind the generous offerings which Akhenaten felt it appropriate to supply for the enjoyment of his god, may perhaps go some way to explaining Akhenaten's less than streamlined shape.

Amenhotep III is absent from the scene, but seated beside Tiy is a young girl wearing a side-lock who is identified merely as the 'King's

Daughter' Beketaten. Neither her father the king nor her mother is named. Beketaten, whose name means 'Handmaiden of the Aten', is clearly associated with Queen Tiy and we would expect her to be Tiy's daughter by the late Amenhotep III. Confirmation of this parentage is suggested by her inclusion in Huya's 'lintel scene' where she appears with Tiy before Amenhotep III. However, this is the first time that we have heard of Beketaten, who seems to have sprung from nowhere. Her obvious youth, the observation that her name includes the 'Aten' element and the fact that she is never specifically identified as the daughter of Amenhotep III have combined with a mistaken assumption that Queen Tiy's visit to Amarna must have occurred during Akhenaten's Year 12, and have led to speculation that Beketaten must have been born after the start of Akhenaten's rule. That would imply either that she was not the daughter of Amenhotep III, who was presumably dead when she was conceived, or that Amenhotep III was alive during his son's reign.[38] Unfortunately, Huya neglects to date this intriguing scene, and we have no idea which year or years Tiy visited her son.

Neither her size nor her side-lock should necessarily be taken as an indication that Beketaten was a very young child at the time of her visit to Amarna. The artists who decorated the tombs were not always consistent in their depictions of the royal children and Beketaten may well be much older than her portrait suggests, maybe as old as thirteen or fourteen. If we are correct in the assumption that Tiy married at the age of twelve and remained fertile into her mid-forties, it is perfectly possible for her to have had a five-year-old daughter at the time of Amenhotep III's death. All these assumptions, although nothing more than educated guesswork, allow little difficulty in inserting Beketaten into the royal family as Akhenaten's sister, and it is tempting to speculate whether Beketaten could in fact be the renamed Princess Nebetah, Akhenaten's youngest sister, about whom so little is known. An alternative theory, that Beketaten may have been Tiy's granddaughter adopted by her grandmother, is plausible but suffers somewhat from a lack of evidence,[39] while the suggestion that Beketaten was Tiy's daughter by her son Akhenaten, which was first put forward by Velikovsky and then taken up by some of the more sensational writers of historical 'biography', is entirely groundless.[40]

6

Queen, King or Goddess?

I breathe the sweet breath that comes forth from your mouth and shall behold your beauty daily. My prayer is that I may hear your sweet voices of the north wind, that my flesh may grow young with life through your love, that you may give me your hands bearing your spirit and I receive it and live by it, and that you may call upon my name eternally, and it shall not fail . . .[1]

A private devotional stela of unknown provenance (Plate 16) allows us to catch a glimpse of the royal family at the time of their arrival at Amarna. The family relax in a stylized tent whose walls are denoted by slender papyrus pillars. The tent has a floor of reed matting but no roof – it is open to the sky, allowing the rays of the sun to offer the *ankh*, symbol of life, to the royal couple and their children.

Akhenaten sits on a simple padded stool with his feet raised on a hassock. He is dressed in his favourite pleated kilt and sandals, and wears a blue crown ornamented with multiple uraei, a decorated band and two streamers. He is holding his eldest daughter somewhat awkwardly in his arms and is slightly bending forward, apparently about to kiss her. Meritaten twists to stroke her father's chin with her right hand while pointing towards her mother and sisters with her left. Akhenaten's long but not unduly grotesque face is emphasized by his tall crown. His neck, too, is long and sinuous, while his upper arms, shoulders and lower legs are strikingly underdeveloped. His kilt does nothing to hide his paunch. Behind the king is a stand holding four pairs of wine jars.

Facing her husband Nefertiti sits on a more regal looking but slightly lower stool decorated with the *sma-tawy*, the bound papyrus and lily symbol of the Unity of the Two Lands. Her sandalled feet rest on a footstool. Nefertiti's face has the plain features of the early Amarna period and her slightly slumped body mirrors that of the king. She wears a long, delicately pleated gown casually tied with a sash under the bust. The pleated sash hangs downwards, partially obscuring the *sma-tawy*. While her upper arms are covered, her rounded stomach, oval navel and inner right calf are exposed. She wears no jewellery, but her trademark blue crown is embellished with a decorated fillet and banded streamers that, with artistic licence, flutter in the breeze in the opposite direction to the streamers on the king's crown.

Nefertiti has Meketaten on her knee, and the child is looking over her shoulder at her mother while gesturing towards her father and sister with her right hand; this overlapping of bodies gives the scene a feeling of depth not usually found in Egyptian art. Meanwhile baby Ankhesenpaaten, a miniature adult, is clambering over her mother's left shoulder and reaching for a tempting ornament suspended from Nefertiti's crown. All three daughters are naked and have elongated bald heads, although the eldest two wear ear-ornaments and we may assume that all three sport a side-lock which, in the cases of Meritaten and Ankhesenpaaten who have their heads turned towards the left, cannot be seen.

At first sight this stela offers the simple image of a perfect family in an ideal world far beyond the experiences of most Egyptians. A second glance, however, reveals a curious mixed message. Akhenaten, as we might expect, appears the taller and more dominant figure. He is associated with the eldest and most important princess while Nefertiti, a typical wife, cares for the babies. Yet he is allocated the plain stool while his wife occupies the seat decorated with an unmistakable regal motif. Under normal circumstances we would expect the more important person to sit on this stool. What are we to read into this? Is it a simple, irrelevant mistake in a private stela that was never intended to be an accurate portrait, and certainly never intended for public display? Or is it a deliberate message from the artist? Who exactly is the dominant partner here?

This stela has fuelled heated debate over the precise nature of Nefertiti's role at Amarna. Everyone accepts that Nefertiti was Akhenaten's consort – the evidence for this is overwhelming. But some historians have gone much further, suggesting that she acted as Akhenaten's co-regent and, maybe, ultimately as sole ruler of Egypt. This theory, first proposed by Gaston Maspero, is perhaps best expressed in the work of Julia Samson who, in writing about the earlier Theban images of Nefertiti, comments:

12. Sandstone portrait of Nefertiti

13. Relief depicting the family of Akhenaten offering to the Aten

14. Quartzite head of Nefertiti

15. Relief showing Ay and Tey receiving royal gold

16. Stela showing Akhenaten and Nefertiti with their family

17. Statuette of Nefertiti in old age

18. Painted relief depicting Smenkhkare and Meritaten

19. The most widely recognized image of Nefertiti

Here was not a goddess but a Regnant Queen. The determined and powerful purpose is obvious behind the numerous carvings, and they spell aloud that Akhenaten wanted no mistake made! He was writing and displaying in the various carved scenes the new social and religious development as well as showing to his people his wife's equality at his side. In Thebes this policy was pictured many years before their co-rule was actually recorded at Amarna . . .²

One could, of course, argue that the best way for Akhenaten to ensure that 'no mistakes were made' with regard to his wife's unusual status would be to publicly proclaim his wife's co-regency and carve it in stone throughout his land. But perhaps he did, and it has been lost or deliberately destroyed along with much else of Akhenaten's world?

Here, straightaway, we come to the heart of the Nefertiti-as-co-regent problem. A complete and utter lack of any positive evidence. Nowhere is the precise nature of Nefertiti's role spelt out to us. Those who would argue that she did rule Egypt alongside her husband are compelled to rely on inferences and deductions and, at the end of the day, can offer no real proof to support their theory. Those who would argue that she did not rule must rely on an absence of evidence; the fact that there is no record of Nefertiti ever using a full king's titulary, no record of her coronation, no writing which unequivocally refers to her acting in a kingly capacity. It can be hard to disprove a popular theory without appearing negative and stick-in-the-mud. And certainly for many readers (and publishers), the image of Nefertiti as king of Egypt makes a far more satisfying end to her story.

Could Nefertiti have acted as king? In theory, yes. The ideal king of Egypt was the son of the previous king, the Horus to his dead father's Osiris, but the father-son chain occasionally snapped. Tuthmosis I, great-great-great-great grandfather to Akhenaten and head of his dynastic bloodline, had himself been adopted into the royal family when the elderly Amenhotep I found himself in need of an heir. Nor did the king have to be a man, although again that was considered the ideal. Sobeknofru, the one queen known to have inherited the throne in the absence of a male king, had been accepted by her people.

If it was rare for a woman to rule alone, it was relatively common for a widowed queen to rule on behalf of her infant son. Egyptian history is littered with competent queens whose successful rule was destined to be absorbed into their sons' reigns. Ahhotep and Ahmose Nefertari, the mother and daughter who were the last queen of the 17th Dynasty and the first queen of the 18th respectively, fall into this category as they ruled Egypt temporarily on behalf of their sons Ahmose and Amenhotep I. Hatchepsut, the best known of Egypt's female kings, can also be included in the group of queens who ruled through their link with a young king, although Hatchepsut's case is complicated by her refusal to give up the throne when Tuthmosis III came of age.

So, there are precedents for female kings inheriting the throne, and precedents for queens ruling Egypt on a temporary (and in Hatchepsut's case not so temporary) basis on behalf of a young son or stepson. There are also precedents for kings taking co-rulers as a means of introducing the heir apparent to his future subjects and his future work. But, although many queens must have influenced the pattern of their husband's reigns, there is no precedent for a queen consort formally ruling alongside her husband as an equal. Nor is this a situation that will ever occur in later dynastic history. Akhenaten was not a man to be bound by pointless tradition, but there was always a purpose to his deviation from convention, and his innovative reforms were actually rooted in long-standing tradition. Why would he appoint Nefertiti as co-regent? There could be only one possible reason: he intended her to rule after him. This might, perhaps, make some sense if Akhenaten had no children. But the king had at least six daughters by the queen, plus an unspecified number of children, sons as well as daughters, by the other women in the royal harem. Any one of these would have made a more acceptable heir to the throne.

In the absence of any textual evidence to support the theory of Nefertiti as co-regent, hints as to her precise role have been sought in an examination of her appearance, her actions and her accessories as represented in reliefs and sculpture. The conclusions which can be drawn from such a survey are meagre and will always be open to doubt. Even though she is frequently depicted at the same scale as her husband, Nefertiti's size does not provide us with any clue to her status. The concept of the queen shown at the same scale as her husband had already been introduced with art of Amenhotep III and Tiy, and this naturally continues into the reign of their son. In fact Nefertiti's height differs from scene to scene; she variously appears at near-equal size to or much smaller than the king, and it seems that she was occasionally depicted at a smaller scale for artistic rather than political purposes, so that the descending line of king, queen and daughters would reflect the sloping rays of the Aten.[3]

Nefertiti's clothing is almost invariably feminine, and seems designed to stress her female form. Only in the handful of scenes where she is shown slaying the enemies of Egypt does the queen adopt the traditional king's smiting outfit of simple skirt and bare chest. As the smiting scene is very much a ritual one, it seems that Nefertiti needed to be dressed in the appropriate clothes for her task. Other images of Nefertiti, such as the Window of Appearance scene in the tomb of Ay, may well show her topless or naked, king-style, although, as Nefertiti's garments are frequently both clinging and transparent, and as the whole scene had yet to be painted, we cannot be sure that the artist did not intend to paint a dress over her outline.

Nefertiti's crowns and wigs tell a similarly vague story. We have already seen that during the early years at Thebes she favours the cow horns, disc and plumes introduced by her mother-in-law and associated with the cult of Hathor. By the time of the move to Amarna she is also wearing the tall, flat-topped crown that is likely to be her own version of Akhenaten's blue war crown. This new headdress carries its own overtones of fertility and rejuvenation and links the queen with the solar goddess Tefnut. The blue crown quickly becomes Nefertiti's favourite, worn with increasing frequency as the reign progresses, although occasionally she dons a close-fitting rounded cap which is sometimes mistaken for the true blue crown. The blue crown, which fits bonnet-style close to the head, is usually worn without a wig. Where her hair is shown, Nefertiti favours the true Nubian wig, a style originally reserved for men but which is now adopted by the most prominent of the royal women, Nefertiti and Kiya. Nefertiti also wears the *khat* head-cloth, a bag-like head cover usually worn by kings but also worn by Tiy, and by the female deities Isis and Nephthys.

Nefertiti never appropriates the king's blue crown, and even in the smiting scenes where we might expect to find her donning a more masculine headdress, she retains her own feminine crown. Only the unfinished stela of the soldier Pasi, recovered from Amarna and now housed in Berlin, appears to show a regally crowned Nefertiti as she sits alongside Akhenaten beneath the rays of the Aten.[4] The identification of these two figures of undetermined gender is, however, by no means certain and it is unfortunate that the cartouches that would have named the couple have been left blank. The 'male' figure on the right, which wears the double crown and what appears to be a pectoral, appears slightly larger that the 'female' figure on the left, which wears the blue crown and has more prominent breasts. The affection between the two is obvious. The left arm of the left-hand figure is placed protectively around her/his companion, while the right-hand figure turns towards his/her companion and raises his/her hand in a tender gesture. Are we looking at Akhenaten and Nefertiti? Or at Akhenaten and a young male co-regent, his son perhaps? Or are we looking at Akhenaten and his father, Amenhotep III?

Our only positive sighting of Nefertiti dressed in a kingly crown comes from the Amarna tomb of Panehesy (Fig 6.1), where we see the queen wearing a *khat* head-cloth topped by a highly ornate *atef* crown while directly in front of her stands the larger-scale Akhenaten sporting what appears to be a *nemes* head-cloth and an even more elaborate *atef* crown complete with two additional cobras and with three extra falcons perched on top.[5] The *atef*, a highly complicated headdress which, during the New Kingdom, incorporated ostrich feathers, ram and bull horns, a solar disc and numerous uraei, was invariably associated with kings and with the cult of Osiris; the only other woman known to have worn this crown was Hatchepsut in her role as female pharaoh. As Panehesy clearly shows Nefertiti in the *atef*, we can assume that she did wear this crown on at least one occasion, although we again run up against the problem that this is a stereotypical scene rather than a photograph – just how true-to-life should we expect such scenes to be? As he does not accord her kingly titles, it is tempting to speculate that the artist may well have confused his crowns. However, Nefertiti's crown is by no means identical to that worn by the king and need not signify either equality or kingship. Akhenaten's crown is larger, has more elements, and appears far more regal. Nefertiti's is a scaled-down, less elaborate version. We know that Nefertiti was by no means averse to appropriating 'male' wigs and headdresses, adapting them to her own use. The transfer of elements of kingly regalia and iconography to the queen has good precedent: the tall plumed crown, the uraeus, and even the cartouche had all originally been confined to the king.

Fig. 6.1   Nefertiti and Akhenaten wearing the *atef* crown

All this visual evidence combines to confirm what we might have expected from the complete evidence of textual references to Nefertiti as co-regent. While Nefertiti was undeniably a powerful woman, we have absolutely no proof that she was ever a queen regnant, sharing power with Akhenaten. The most compelling evidence that can be cited, the handful of striking scenes, the seat decorated with the Unity of the Two Lands and the occasional wearing of a scaled-down *atef* crown, is far outweighed by the many more scenes which show Nefertiti as an influential but relatively conventional consort taking second place to her husband. Her regalia, her association with the sphinx, and her appearance in the smiting scenes, seem to be very much a continuation of the elevation of the queenship which was started during the reign of Amenhotep III.

In fact we have no archaeological or historical evidence to indicate that Akhenaten ever regarded Nefertiti as anything approaching his equal. She is undeniably an active participant in all aspects of state ritual; in addition to the smiting scenes the Amarna tombs show her awarding gold to the élite, parading in a royal palanquin and even driving her own chariot. However, Nefertiti's prominence remains very much a function of her relationship to Akhenaten, and stems directly from him. She may act in parallel to the king but she never usurps his authority and wherever the two appear together Akhenaten remains the dominant figure, Nefertiti the dutiful wife.

If Nefertiti is not a king, is she a goddess? She is certainly able to function as a priestess. At Thebes we have seen Nefertiti worshipping the Aten in the role normally reserved for the king. Now, at Amarna, we see her worshipping alongside her husband and can presume that she continues to offer alone in the privacy of her sunshade. She is allowed to play a far more important, and far more public, role in state religion than her predecessors although, as both her elder daughters and Kiya are also occasionally allowed to put down their sistra and present offerings to the god, it may be prudent to interpret this as an increase in the religious status of all the Amarna royal women rather than a promotion specific to Nefertiti.

Nefertiti is now presented as the feminine element in the divine triad of Aten, Akhenaten and Nefertiti, where she plays the role of Tefnut to Akhenaten's Shu. She is also the mother-figure in the lesser triad formed by the king, queen and their children. Her sexuality, emphasized by her exaggerated body shape and her revealing garments, and her fecundity, stressed by the constant appearance of the royal princesses, indicate that she is to be regarded as a living fertility symbol. Again we have no means of telling whether Nefertiti herself is now divine, or whether she merely serves as a conduit to the king and his god. It would not have been unprecedented for a queen to be deified and indeed the earlier 18th Dynasty queen Ahmose Nefertari was worshipped as 'Mistress of the Sky' at Deir el-Medina for many years after her death; there is, however, no evidence to suggest that Ahmose Nefertari was worshipped in this way during her lifetime. Tiy, who had a temple dedicated to her at Sedeinga in Nubia was, in the colonies at least, acknowledged as semi-divine but never worshipped as a fully fledged goddess in Egypt proper. The fact that prayers were addressed to Nefertiti at Amarna cannot be taken as proof of her divine status, as we know that within the tomb of Huya prayers were also addressed to Queen Tiy.

The debate over Nefertiti's divinity has been fuelled by the evidence provided by Akhenaten's sarcophagus which was recovered in fragments from the Amarna royal tomb and subsequently reconstructed.[6] The sarcophagus was, as convention dictated, a carved stone-lidded box, made in this case from polished red Aswan granite. The four corners of the sarcophagus were embellished with representations of Nefertiti in raised relief, standing with her arms outstretched and palms flat along the sarcophagus sides as if to embrace and protect the dead king. The carving of the figures is somewhat clumsy, and does not bear much resemblance to other images of the queen, but she is clearly labelled and there can be little doubt over her identity. Nefertiti wears a fine pleated dress, a long curled wig, a double uraeus and a complicated and unusual crown incorporating a sun disc, cobra frieze, double uraeus and two tall feathers.

The kings of the post-Amarna period, Tutankhamen, Ay and Hor-emheb, also chose to embellish their sarcophagi with images of women. However, rather than their queens, they followed a precedent suggested by the canopic chest of Amenhotep II and selected the goddesses Isis, Nephthys, Neith and Selket. Under the old Osirid mythology these goddesses would protect the dead king, Isis and Nephthys being the two sisters who guarded the dead Osiris and Neith and Selket being added so that the four goddesses might complement the four sons of Horus who protected the canopic jars holding the intestines, stomach, liver and lungs of the deceased. Should we then have expected Akhenaten to employ a goddess to protect his remains? If so, is Nefertiti herself such a goddess?

This would almost certainly be too simplistic a conclusion. We have already noted how Akhenaten was happy to change the message of the old religion without necessarily changing its form, continuing to employ mummification, shabtis, canopic jars and scarabs even though their original meaning had gone. The idea of a woman to protect his body may have seemed appealing, but the traditional goddesses were now barred to him. What could be more natural than to replace them with a secular, and highly comforting, image of the wife who had supported him in life? Only if it could be proved that others, not intimately connected with the royal family, also included Nefertiti on their sarcophagus, could we start to assume that she was herself possessed of divine powers. Unfortunately, there is only one contemporary sarcophagus available for us to examine. The quartzite sarcophagus recovered from the tomb of Tutankhamen, Akhenaten's almost immediate successor, currently shows the four now-traditional goddesses with outstretched wings. However, it is clear that the sarcophagus has undergone extensive alteration, and that although the goddesses were carved according to the traditional proportions used in the pre- and post-Amarna era, they were provided originally with outstretched arms rather than wings. This strongly suggests that the figures were conceived as humans and converted to the divine following the change in official religious beliefs, an assumption which is reinforced by the observation that the goddess figures on Tutankhamen's canopic canopy also seem to have been made as Amarna queens, and later converted into goddesses. If it could be proved that these protective figures were intended to represent Nefertiti, we might by extension be able to prove that Nefertiti was herself a goddess. However, it is not possible to identify the lady or ladies, who may well have been Tutankhamen's wife, mother, sister or even a generalized female form.[7]

Although scholars have argued long and hard over the question of Nefertiti's divine status, it may well be that such arguments are essentially meaningless.[8] There is, to the modern western reader accustomed to the Judeo-Christian-Muslim tradition, a strong distinction between the divine and the mortal: the idea that one could be semi-divine seems very similar to the old joke of a naive girl claiming to be just a little bit pregnant. We should therefore be able to find a precise definition of Nefertiti's status. The Egyptians, however, did not draw such fine distinctions, and were capable of understanding a wide spectrum of divinity. Nefertiti was certainly presented in a way that associated her with the Aten cult and more specifically with fertility within the Aten cult. But her exact role was never made explicit, and it may be that many of those who worshipped before her image were themselves unsure of a distinction that even in our so-called sophisticated society many find hard to understand. Is the person who worships before a statue of the Virgin Mary worshipping the statue itself, or Mary herself, or God through the intervention of Mary? Presumably the answers to this question are as varied as the people who pray before the statue, although in ancient Egypt we do gain the impression that most of the people are in fact praying to the statue.

So, if the available evidence for Nefertiti as Akhenaten's consort ranges from the scanty to the non-existent depending on viewpoint, why has anyone suggested that Nefertiti advanced from co-regent to become sole king of Egypt? To understand the complexities of the Nefertiti-as-king argument, we need to understand the chain of events that saw the ending of the Amarna idyll.

7

Sunset

*Why should messengers be made to stay constantly out in the sun and
so die in the sun? . . . They are made to die in the sun.*[1]

Year 12 saw tremendous celebrations at Amarna, recorded in the tombs
of Huya and Meryre II, Steward of Nefertiti. The king, accompanied
by his queen and all six daughters (although only four appear in the
tomb of Huya), presents himself before a host of ambassadors and vassals
summoned from Nubia, Libya, the Mediterranean islands and the Near
East. There is feasting, merriment, and a great deal of standing about in
the hot Egyptian sun, a tedious feature of Amarna life for all except the
royal family who are prudently provided with sunshades. Best of all is
the reception of a huge amount of tribute including horses, chariots,
women and gold. No reason is given for the fantasia, but its purpose
seems clear. Akhenaten is celebrating his role as the head of a vast
empire, perhaps even as its living god, in his wonderful new city.

Meryre II (Fig. 7.1) shows us Akhenaten sitting on a throne with
Nefertiti beside him, although Nefertiti is represented only as an outline
drawn around the figure of her husband, a method of drawing which
may simply be a means of overcoming a lack of space, but which also
confirms the queen's unity with the king. Six small-scale daughters stand
in groups of three behind their parents. This is the last time that we see
the royal family together.

Suddenly the seemingly perfect life of the royal family was shattered
as Meketaten, who can have been no more than twelve years old, died.
The date of this tragedy goes unrecorded although, as we have seen
Meketaten participating in the Year 12 celebrations, we can tentatively
suggest that she passed away in Year 13 or 14. Akhenaten had already
started to carve a splendid royal tomb into the Amarna cliffs. This work
would never be completed, although the main corridors, principal burial

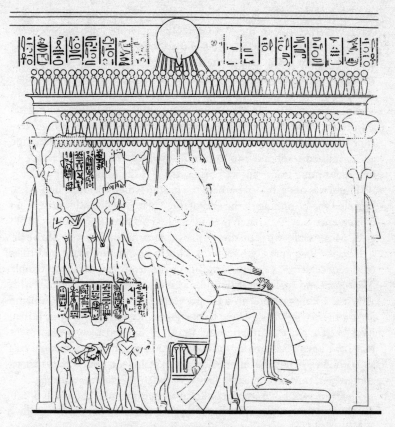

Fig. 7.1   Nefertiti, Akhenaten and family at the Year 12 celebrations

chamber and two subsidiary suites, one of which was intended for Nefertiti, had by now been cut. Meketaten was laid to rest within her father's tomb and it is here (Room Gamma, wall A), in some of the most simple and poignant illustrations of the entire dynastic period, that we see Nefertiti and Akhenaten grieving over their dead daughter.

The Amarna letters confirm that Meketaten died at a time when plague was rampant in the Near East. Perhaps, following the international festivities of Year 12, plague had arrived to threaten the security of life at Amarna. It may be no coincidence that other members of the

royal family disappear at this time, and Kiya, Tiy and the three younger
sisters Neferneferuaten-the-Younger, Neferneferure and baby Setepenre
all fade out of view. Indeed, the fact that Neferneferuaten was plastered
out of a family group within the royal tomb suggests that she, and her
youngest sister Setepenre who was never included in the scene, may
already have died. Both Neferneferure and Setepenre are excluded from
a scene of mourning for Meketaten, although the other three princesses
are present. The discovery of an amphora handle stamped with a reference to the 'robing room of Neferneferure' found within a dump outside
an unfinished tomb close to the royal tomb provides us with a clue to
her final resting place, but there is no trace of the tombs of the others.[2]

This series of deaths, or perhaps the plague which accompanied them,
signalled the beginning of the end of the Amarna idyll, and it may be no
coincidence that Akhenaten now intensified his campaign against the old
gods. Meanwhile, work on the non-royal Amarna tombs ground to a halt.

The royal sculptors set to work chiselling out the image and titles
of the deceased Kiya, removing her name from the sunshade temple
Maru-Aten and replacing it with the name of Meritaten. The ease with
which the king was prepared to substitute one beloved woman's name
for another is slightly shocking to over-sentimental modern eyes. It may
have been a practical response to a crisis – an immediate replacement
may have been necessary for the continuation of a female-orientated cult
at *Maru-Aten* – but the impression given, fairly or not, is that that to
Akhenaten, one royal woman was very much the same as another.

Nefertiti vanishes from the political scene soon after the death of her
daughter. The obvious inference is that she too is dead, possibly another
victim of the plague. If so, we might reasonably expect to find traces of
her interment within the royal tomb. Akhenaten's grief over the death
of his daughter had been expressed on the tomb walls with a sincere
dignity. How much more would he commemorate the loss of his
beloved wife, and how much more splendid would have been her
funeral? And yet, the royal tomb gives no evidence of any such burial
and there is no official pronouncement of the queen's passing. The only
evidence to suggest that she was interred at Amarna is provided by a
broken shabti figure whose separate pieces are now housed in the Louvre
and Brooklyn Museums, and whose inscription has been reconstructed
by Christian Loeben:

The Heiress, high and mighty in the palace, one trusted of the King of Upper and Lower Egypt Neferkheperure Waenre, the Son of Re [Akhenaten], Great in his lifetime, The Chief Wife of the King, Neferneferuaten-Nefertiti, Living for ever and ever.[3]

As the Egyptian royal family spent many years preparing their tomb equipment, there is no means of telling whether this figure was inscribed during Nefertiti's lifetime or after her death. Nor, of course, do we know that it was actually used in her burial.

Earlier twentieth-century historians noted the sudden, unexplained, disappearance of the queen. They linked this to the abrupt change of name at *Maru-Aten* but, erroneously, they believed that the obliterated name was that of Nefertiti rather than Kiya. This was a crucial mistake that led to a dramatic conclusion. Nefertiti had committed some heinous crime and had been banished. John Pendlebury envisaged a terrible family quarrel over Akhenaten's foreign policy which left Nefertiti, still the Aten's most faithful disciple, disgraced, divorced and confined to a northern palace named *Hwt Aten*, or the Mansion of the Aten.[4] Not everyone was convinced. It made little political sense that Nefertiti, now Akhenaten's implacable enemy, should have been allowed to establish a rival court at Amarna where she could cultivate her own pro-Aten supporters. Norman de Garis Davies, again basing his reasoning on the misinterpreted *Maru-Aten* inscriptions, proposed an alternative scenario where Nefertiti was not the defender of the new faith, but its first and greatest traitor:

One might even venture into the dangerous field of pure, or almost pure, conjecture and suppose that, when to shrewd sight the coming victory of Amun [sic] cast its shadow before it, the faithless Nefertiti allowed herself to be proclaimed by the faction as rival monarch at Thebes . . .[5]

He tentatively suggested that the underlying cause of Nefertiti's banishment was the fact that Akhenaten, anxious for a son and heir, had actually married his own daughter Meritaten. Davies was reluctant, however, to believe his own theory, and he added a footnote to his text that 'this would be a double blow to the idyll of El-Amarnah, and we may hope that evidence for it will fail'.

Davies was not the only egyptologist reluctant to abandon the ideal of the loving royal family. Many found it simply impossible to reconcile what they saw as Akhenaten's obvious affection for Nefertiti with such harsh treatment, and Baikie again spoke for many:

The Egypt Exploration Society's excavators have most unkindly and ungraciously tried to insinuate a serpent into this little Eden in the shape of a suggestion that the absence of the name of Queen Nefertiti from the fragmentary inscriptions which have been recovered from *Maru-Aten* points to domestic trouble in the royal family, and to the breaking up of that idyllic love and unity of which so may pictures have survived. Surely such a suggestion is an entirely unnecessary outrage upon our feelings, and upon the memory of a couple whose mutual affection must have been the only stay of their hearts in sore trouble. Akhenaten has had to bear enough blame, living and dead, without saddling him, almost gratuitously, with that of having quarrelled with his beautiful wife.[6]

Baikie may have been basing his argument on intuition rather than scientific evidence, and his blaming of the unfortunate excavators for their message is perhaps slightly unfair, but it would appear that he was substantially correct in his instincts. We now know that it was Kiya's name, not Nefertiti's, which was originally carved at *Maru-Aten*. If anyone was disgraced – and there is no need to assume that anyone was – that person was Kiya.

So what had happened to Nefertiti? In the 1970s John Harris used philology to develop an ingenious theory. Nefertiti had not died. She had remained at Amarna where, using an evolving succession of names, she had ruled as king first alongside and then as successor to Akhenaten.[7] Egyptologists already knew of one or maybe two potential co-regents/ successors to Akhenaten. The names Ankhkheperure Neferneferuaten and Ankhkheperure Smenkhkare had been discovered in sound archaeological contexts, but the names could refer to one individual or two. Harris convincingly demonstrated that it is possible to trace Nefertiti's name as it evolves from the simple Nefertiti to Neferneferuaten Nefertiti, then through the use of the double cartouche and the use of an enhanced form of the title King's Great Wife which occurred towards the end of Akhenaten's reign. Far more speculative is his proposed subsequent evolution, even later in the reign, to the use of a prenomen and nomen, until finally Nefertiti emerges as Akhenaten's co-ruler using the name

Ankhkheperure Neferneferuaten. Following the death of Akhenaten, the theory holds, Ankhkheperure Neferneferuaten (Nefertiti) ruled alone as Ankhkheperure Smenkhkare, before handing over the reins of power to the young Tutankhamen.

Ankhkheperure Smenkhkare, more usually known as Smenkhkare, was a real but shadowy figure, little more than a carved name. Like Beketaten before him, Smenkhkare seemed to spring from nowhere, exist for a short period as heir of Akhenaten, and then vanish. He had no known relationship to the royal family, no tomb, and no body. The attraction of the Nefertiti as Smenkhkare theory is obvious. By linking the sudden appearance of Smenkhkare with the sudden disappearance of Nefertiti, two archaeological mysteries could be cleared up with one elegant solution. However, recent research on human remains recovered from a small rock-cut tomb in the Valley of the Kings has highlighted a seemingly insurmountable flaw in this argument.

The modest entrance to Tomb KV 55 was discovered during the 1906–7 season of Theodore M. Davis's expedition to the Valley of the Kings, which was led by the English archaeologist Edward Ayrton.[8] The recording of the excavation and tomb clearance was lamentable. As Cyril Aldred has remarked, without exaggeration:

The evidence is all too clear that instead of proceeding with caution and skill, these men, two of them at least with specialist training and experience, some-how managed to carry out one of the worst pieces of excavation on record in the Valley [of the Kings].[9]

Hindsight and superior modern techniques of excavation make it all too easy to criticize the excavators of the past. But in this case Aldred is absolutely right to be critical. KV 55, definitely one of the most complex and potentially one of the most informative tombs in the Valley of the Kings, was swiftly stripped of its contents without any proper photo-graphic or written record, and with no real attempt at conservation. This failure to keep proper records has caused modern archaeologists to revisit the burial time and time again in an attempt to reconstruct its contents and make sense of its meaning.

The tomb itself was deceptively simple. The outer door, reached by a flight of steps, opened into a sloping rubble-filled corridor that led in

turn to the single burial chamber. This was a high, undecorated room
that was, when discovered, in a state of total disarray. Wooden panels,
boxes, mud bricks, stone chips, fallen plaster and tools dropped by the
ancient labourers were jumbled on the floor, and all were dusted with
a thin film of gold leaf which had flaked off the more fragile pieces. Mrs
Emma B. Andrews, who entered the tomb soon after its opening as the
guest of Mr Davis, made a note of her visit in her diary:

1907, Jan 19. At the Valley. Dr Wiedemann and wife and Mr Sayce were over
and lunched with us in the lunch tomb. I went down to the burial chamber
and it is now almost easy of access; and saw the poor Queen as she lies now
just a bit outside her magnificent coffin, with the vulture crown on her head.
All the woodwork of the shrine, doors &c. is heavily overlaid with gold foil
and I seemed to be walking on gold, and even the Arab working inside had
some of it sticking in his woolly hair.[10]

The vulture crown observed by Mrs Andrews was in fact a displaced
pectoral. There was no stone sarcophagus, perhaps a sign that the tomb
had been filled in a hurry, but four human-headed canopic jars stood in
a recess cut into the right-hand wall and there were magical bricks
intended to protect the deceased.

The elaborate inlaid anthropoid coffin had originally been placed on
a low wooden bed. But a narrow crack in the ceiling had proved
disastrous, allowing floodwater to drip into the tomb and rot the wood
beneath. When the bed collapsed the coffin was thrown to the ground
where it lay with its lid dislodged and the head of the mummy exposed.
The mummy, now lying in a pool of water, started to decompose.
Further damage to both mummy and coffin was caused when a rock fell
from the roof and split the coffin in two. By the time it was removed
from the tomb the coffin had disintegrated into hundreds of pieces; it
was later re-assembled in Cairo Museum where it is displayed today.

The coffin was made of wood, covered with gold leaf and decorated
with semi-precious stones. Its head was dressed with a wig rather than
a royal crown, but some time after its manufacture it had been fitted
with the beard and uraeus that would have made it suitable for the burial
of a royal male. Following the burial both the uraeus and the gold mask
that covered the face had been torn off, leaving the underlying wood

exposed.[11] A uraeus recovered by the excavators bore the name of the Aten, but it is by no means certain that this is the original uraeus from the coffin, as at least one other uraeus was recovered from the tomb.

The measurements and design of the reconstructed coffin show that it had originally been made for a woman. The twelve lines of text on the foot-end and the five bands of hieroglyphs that decorated the coffin agreed with this; they were words intended to be spoken by a woman, someone who could be described as the beloved of Waenre (Akhenaten). However, some time after the coffin had been completed, the inscriptions had been altered from feminine to masculine while the name of the original owner had been replaced by a royal name in a cartouche, which was itself later erased.

The confusion over the ownership of the coffin – a woman followed by a royal male whose name was later obliterated – merely added to the confusion over the ownership of the tomb. This was clearly an incomplete re-burial with a jumble of artifacts taken from different tombs; Davis found royal names ranging from Amenhotep II through Amenhotep III, Tiy and Akhenaten to Tutankhamen. Only one thing seemed clear. The discovery of Tutankhamen's sealings confirmed that KV 55 must have been closed some time after Tutankhamen had come to the throne, and as his was the last name in the tomb, it seemed safe to assume that he had been responsible for the re-burial.

The magical bricks bore the name of Akhenaten, and had presumably come from his burial equipment. The inscribed golden bands recovered within the mummy wrappings apparently also bore the name of Akhenaten, but these were stolen from Elliot Smith's laboratory before they could be properly recorded.

A series of large gilded wooden panels recovered from both the corridor and the burial chamber were the constituent parts of a shrine made by Akhenaten for inclusion with Tiy's burial equipment where it would have been erected around her coffin. The shrine's inscriptions made its ownership clear: 'The King of Upper and Lower Egypt, living on truth [Akhenaten]; what he made for the King's Mother, the Great King's Wife Tiy'. Akhenaten's image had been erased from the panels, but Tiy remained to worship beneath the Aten's rays. Unfortunately the panels were in a highly fragile state, and disintegrated, again before they could be properly recorded.

The four alabaster canopic jars were equally perplexing. They had originally been carved with the name of their owner but this too had been erased, leaving the jars anonymous. We now know that they probably belonged to Kiya.[12] The lids of these jars do not display the traditional four sons of Horus but four delicately carved heads wearing Nubian-style wigs. These beautiful lids are remarkably ill-fitting, so much so that it is generally accepted that they may not be the original stoppers. Various identifications of the heads have been attempted; on the basis of the wigs and the features of the faces, it would appear that the heads most probably represent either Kiya or Meritaten. Of the three jars which have been subjected to analysis two were found to contain a 'hard, compact, black, pitch-like mass surrounding a well-defined centrally situated zone of different material, which was of a brown colour and friable nature', while the third yielded the same compact black mass, but the inner material had been removed some time after its discovery.[13] This friable brown substance was almost certainly the remains of the original viscera, and it would seem that the jars when discovered held their original contents. These three jars are now in the collections of Cairo Museum. The fourth jar was given to Davis and is now in the Metropolitan Museum, New York.

The golden shrine clearly belonged to Queen Tiy, and on this basis it was first assumed that both the coffin and the body were those of Tiy. Following the analysis of the coffin this theory had to be amended, so that the coffin became that of Tiy, usurped by Akhenaten. Sir Alan Gardiner proposed a different owner.[14] Pointing out that the inscription on the foot-end, quoted as the introduction to Chapter 6, did not indicate a female occupant of the coffin, merely a female speaker, and comparing KV 55 with more traditional royal burials where the foot-end of the coffin was the position held by Isis, he tentatively suggested that the speaker might be Nefertiti, taking over the role of Isis in the funerary ritual. This would imply that the coffin was originally intended for Akhenaten, but that the text had been attacked and defaced during the post-Amarna period when the mummy of Akhenaten may even have been removed from the tomb and that of Smenkhkare put in its place. This argument, however, ignored the fact that the coffin was originally built for a woman. More recently the textual evidence has been reviewed and it is now generally accepted that the coffin, like the canopic jars, had initially been prepared for Kiya. The inscription which decorated the three bands on the exterior of the coffin had originally read:

[Wife and greatly beloved of] the King of Upper and Lower Egypt, living in order, Lord of the Two Lands [Neferkheperure Waenre], the perfect little one of the living disk, who shall be alive continuously for ever, [Kiya, justified].[15]

The body within the tomb seemed, superficially at least, relatively well preserved. Davis was present as it was removed from its coffin:

Presently, we cleared the mummy from the coffin, and found that it was a smallish person, with a delicate head and hands. The mouth was partly open, showing a perfect set of upper and lower teeth. The body was enclosed in mummy-cloth of fine texture, but all of the cloth covering the body was of a very dark colour. Naturally it ought to be a much brighter colour. Rather suspecting injury from the evident dampness, I gently touched one of the front teeth (3,000 years old) and alas! it fell into dust, thereby showing that the mummy could not be preserved. We then cleared the entire mummy . . .[16]

Ayrton adds to this description, telling us that the left arm was bent with the hand on the breast and the right arm was straight with the hand on the thigh, while Walter Tyndale records a 'dried-up face, sunken cheeks, and thin leathery-looking lips, exposing a few teeth'.[17] Unfortunately, the unwrapping of the mummy was never properly recorded, and no photographs were taken. Once it was agreed that the body was damaged beyond salvation, little care was taken as the rotten bandages were stripped away to expose the bare bones.

   From almost the moment of its discovery there was controversy over the identity of the body. Theodore Davis never wavered in his belief that he had discovered Queen Tiy, and sought to prove his case by calling on the services of a local doctor, Dr Pollock, and an American obstetrician who was fortunately spending the winter in Luxor. These two examined the body, or rather the 'disconnected bones with a few shreds of dried skin and flesh adhering to or hanging from them' which were all that remained of the unfortunate corpse, and pronounced the remains to be female on the basis of the wide pelvis. It was as the tomb of Queen Tiy that Davis published his record of the discovery, and as Arthur Weigall, no great admirer of Mr Davis, observed:

. . . Owing to some curious idiosyncrasy of old age Mr Davis entertained a most violent and obstinate objection to the suggestion that he had discovered the body of Akhenaten. He had hoped that he had found Queen Taia [sic], and when he was at last forced to abandon this fallacy, he seemed to act almost as though desiring to obscure the identification of the body. He was still in a passionate state of mind in this regard when, a few years later, his brain gave way, and a tragic oblivion descended upon him.[18]

Elliot Smith, however, begged to differ. Examining the bones in the Cairo Museum he found them to be the remains of a young man about twenty-five years old. This was what many had been waiting to hear; virtual confirmation that the body was that of Akhenaten himself. Admittedly, Akhenaten was generally supposed to have lived for longer than twenty-five years, but Smith, when pressed, cheerfully amended his diagnosis to admit that 'the skeleton is that of a man of twenty-five or twenty-six years of age, without excluding the possibility that he may have been several years older'.[19] He himself had always been convinced that the bones were those of Akhenaten:

I do not suppose that any unprejudiced scholar who studies the archaeological evidence alone would harbour any doubt of the identity of this mummy, if it were not for the fact that it is difficult from the anatomical evidence to assign an age to this skeleton sufficiently great to satisfy the demands of most historians, who want at least 30 years into which to crowd the events of Khouniatonou's eventful reign.[20]

Weigall, perhaps Akhenaten's greatest admirer, was delighted to think that he had gazed on the misshapen skull of 'the first of the wise men of history'. He had already made his own rather belated attempt to preserve the remains:

I may mention, in order to debar any possible suggestion of confusion or mistake in regard to the body, that I soaked the bones in paraffin wax so as to preserve them, and that the bones examined by Elliot Smith were thus distinguished.[21]

Weigall's attempt at conservation archaeology was far too little, far too late; the skull was already broken, possibly as a result of the rock fall within the tomb. By the time Professor Douglas Derry examined the remains in the late 1920s the skull was in fragments. 'Fortunately the majority of the most important parts of the face were found in the box containing the skeleton, as well as the missing parts from the side of the cranium, and with a little trouble these were replaced and the face restored.'[22] Professor Derry disputed the identification as Akhenaten, feeling that the unfused epiphyses and an unerupted right upper third molar indicated that their owner could have been no more than twenty-five years old at death, whereas Akhenaten is likely to have been in his forties when he died.

Professor Harrison, re-examining the bones in 1963, similarly concluded that they were the remains of a male less than twenty-five years old who had shared the same relatively rare blood group (A2 and MN) as Tutankhamen and Thuyu, a blood group which seems to have run through the Amarna royal family.[23] Later, X-ray and skull-shape analysis allowed Dr James Harris to conclude that there is a high degree of probability that the bones from KV 55 are those of a slight-framed male whose cranio-facial morphology bore a striking resemblance to the skulls of both Tutankhamen and Tuthmosis IV.[24] The most recent analysis of the KV 55 bones was conducted in 2000 by egyptologist and physical anthropologist Joyce Filer. Her analysis coincides exactly with the diagnosis of Professors Derry and Harrison: 'The human remains from Tomb 55, as presented to me, are those of a young man who had no apparent abnormalities and was no older than his early twenties at death and probably a few years younger.'[25]

So, the bones in KV 55 represent a young man closely related to Tutankhamen: either his son, his brother or his father. Tutankhamen does not give details of his parentage in his tomb, but a block recovered from Hermopolis Magna, originally from Amarna, describes him as 'the bodily son of the King, his beloved'.[26] Curiously, on the Prudhoe lions recovered from Soleb and now housed in the British Museum, he claims to be the son of Amenhotep III, 'he who renewed the monument for his father, the King of Upper and Lower Egypt, Lord of the Two Lands, Nebmaatre, image of Re, Son of Re, Amenhotep Ruler of Thebes'. However, this text was inscribed relatively late in Tutankhamen's reign, at a time when he may well have felt it prudent to associate himself with the orthodox Amenhotep III rather than the heretic Akhenaten. The word used for 'father' is in any case a word that may with equal validity be taken as meaning grandfather or even forefather. The most likely king to have fathered Tutankhamen is Akhenaten – we would have to accept a very long Amenhotep III–Akhenaten co-regency for Amenhotep to have fathered Tutankhamen. As the KV 55 mummy died in his late teens/early twenties, he is unlikely to be Akhenaten who ruled for seventeen years, and he is even less likely to be the aged Amenhotep III. The body cannot be Tutankhamen's son, as Tutankhamen himself died in his late teens or early twenties, too young to have buried a twenty-year-old son. The KV 55 body must therefore be Tutankhamen's brother. The person who best fits this description is the ephemeral Smenkhkare, the ruler who enjoyed a brief reign between Akhenaten and Tutankhamen.

If Smenkhkare and Tutankhamen are brothers, both sons of Akhenaten and therefore both heirs to the throne, who was their mother? There is a possibility that Nefertiti bore sons as well as daughters, although it is curious that we have not one mention of sons in the nuclear royal family. A stronger contender for the role of mother is Kiya. We know that she was Akhenaten's favourite during the middle years of his reign, when we may assume that the boys were born, and the fact that she was able to provide the king with a son may well have accounted for her position of unusual honour at Amarna. This would explain the exclusion of the boys from formal depictions of the royal family, and their sudden appearance as from nowhere towards the end of their father's reign.

Indirect evidence as to Tutankhamen's parentage is provided by a more detailed consideration of the reliefs within the royal tomb at Amarna. Two scenes, carved on wall F of room Alpha, lie one above the other (Fig. 7.2). In the first scene, which is set at the palace, we see Akhenaten and Nefertiti with their right arms raised to their heads in grief as they stand before something or someone who has unfortunately been lost to us. Outside the room a woman cradles a tiny baby in her arms, while an attendant holds an open fan, symbol of royalty, over the baby. Behind them female attendants grieve, and a group of male dignitaries raise their arms in sorrow. In the scene below we see the stiff body of a young woman lying on a bier. Akhenaten and Nefertiti are again shown in an attitude of mourning, and Akhenaten reaches out to grasp his wife's arm in a poignant gesture of comfort and solidarity.

Fig. 7.2   The death of Kiya

There is no sign of the baby, but female attendants again weep and one, overcome by sorrow, is supported by two men.

The story behind the tragedy seems clear and simple. A mother has died giving birth to a royal child. The presence of the queen in her distinctive flat-topped crown rules Nefertiti out as the mother. It is possible that the dead mother is one of the royal daughters, but this seems unlikely given that Meketaten's death is depicted elsewhere in the tomb, while Meritaten and Ankhesenpaaten, the only other daughters old enough to themselves bear children, outlived their parents. Instead, Geoffrey Martin has suggested that the lady on the bier might be Kiya, dying as she gave birth to Tutankhamen.[27]

If the KV 55 body is Smenkhkare, it follows that Nefertiti and Smenkhkare cannot be the same person. It does not exclude the possibility that Nefertiti (or someone else, perhaps a missing royal brother?) took the throne as Ankhkheperure Neferneferuaten before power passed to Ankhkheperure Smenkhkare, and this might well explain why their shared name is occasionally found written in a feminine form.[28] This reasoning has led to the development of two conflicting scenarios,

outlined briefly below. Argument for and against both the original
and the revised theory has raged long and fierce, with all sides being
handicapped by a lack of direct evidence with which either to prove
their case or disprove their rivals.

In the first scenario, Akhenaten and Ankhkheperure Neferneferuaten
ruled together until Akhenaten died, when Ankhkheperure Neferneferuaten retired and Ankhkheperure Smenkhkare took the throne. To
explain the fact that neither Nefertiti nor Ankhkheperure Neferneferuaten are mentioned in the contemporary diplomatic correspondence,
James P. Allen has gone further in suggesting that the co-regency may
have been an actual rather than a theoretical division of the king's role,
with 'Akhenaten as pharaoh in Amarna and in foreign affairs (which
would explain the co-regent's absence – if not accidental – from the
Amarna letters) and Neferneferuaten ruling the rest of Egypt'.[29] If this is
the case Nefertiti may well have lived through the reign of Smenkhkare
and into the reign of Tutankhamen.

In the second version, Akhenaten's intended successor Ankhkheperure Smenkhkare was married to Princess Meritaten and made co-
regent but died either before or soon after Akhenaten. The next in line
for the throne, Smenkhkare's brother Tutankhamen, was too young to
rule unaided and Nefertiti rather than Meritaten was called upon to act
as regent under the name Ankhkheperure Neferneferuaten. This would
fit quite well with the tradition that a widowed queen might rule on
behalf of her son, although Nefertiti is likely to have been Tutankhamen's stepmother rather than birth-mother, but it does not explain why
a queen regent would feel it necessary to take her own throne name.
Are we to imagine that Nefertiti was making the preliminary moves
towards annexing the kingship?

In considering Nefertiti's fate we have wandered far into the dangerous realm of speculation. The only type of evidence that we have not
so far considered is that provided by Amarna's sculptors. Here we are
able to witness an interesting progression. Mid-way through Akhenaten's reign Nefertiti has evolved from a queen who very much mirrors
her husband's exaggerated, ugly look into a woman whom we today
recognize as beautiful. The best-known representation of the new-style
Nefertiti is provided by the world-famous Berlin bust (cover illustration
and Plate 19). A yellow quartzite head also recovered from the Amarna

workshop of Tuthmosis (Plate 14) shows a woman of equal beauty. To Dorothea Arnold:

The serene expression on the lean, austere face speaks of strength, equanimity, and that unwavering sense of justice that the ancient Egyptians understood to be the quintessential quality of a pharaoh. This is a queen who looks as if she is entirely capable of joining the king, at the great Year 12 festivities, on his 'carrying chair of electrum in order to receive the products of Kharu [lands in the Near East] and Kush [Nubia], the west and the east . . . while granting that the breath of life is made to them' . . .[30]

The last sculpture recovered from the workshop of Tuthmosis (Plate 17) tells a different story. This broken and probably unfinished limestone statuette shows Nefertiti as a middle-aged woman. She stands erect, with her hands by her side, wearing a dress so clinging that all the features of her body are revealed and we can clearly see her drooping breasts and rounded tummy. On her bald head she wears the cap crown, and she has sandals on her feet. The face of the figure is that of a woman well past her prime; the cheeks are plumper than usual making the eyes appear small, the skin sags and the mouth is dragged downwards giving an expression of sadness tinged with resignation. We are here being presented with the Amarna equivalent of Tiy's wrinkled and elderly Gurob head.

It may be that this sad and somehow lonely figure, carved after the deaths of the royal children, is intended to show a mother aged by grief. However, this would be unusual as Egyptian art tended to ignore unflattering signs of female aging. Could Tiy have died, allowing her daughter-in-law to advance from the role of fertility symbol to family 'wise woman'? If so, would this be a promotion, allowing Nefertiti to become Akhenaten's near equal and even co-regent, or, as we might expect from a consideration of Tiy's peripheral role within the Amarna family, a demotion into semi-retirement? Are we looking at a woman whose influence has started to wain as she loses her fertility? Setepenre was born sometime before Year 10, and Nefertiti's last recorded appearance is at the funeral of Meketaten, some four or five years later. We have already noted how Nefertiti's influence increased with the birth of the first three children; could it have started to decline as it became evident that she was never going to produce a son?

Now, as so many female members of the royal family disappear, Meritaten attains new importance, until eventually she is recognized as a royal wife. But wife to whom? For a long time egyptologists toyed with the idea that Meritaten may have married her father. But now we have Smenkhkare as a living, flesh-and-blood heir to the throne, it makes far more sense to suggest that she married Smenkhkare, co-regent to Akhenaten. We might go further. We know that Ankhesenpaaten was later to marry Tutankhamen her half-brother and full brother to Smenkhkare. Could the middle sister, Meketaten, have married a third half-brother, perhaps even the ephemeral Ankhkheperure Neferne-feruaten?

Although Meketaten died at a time when plague was sweeping across the Near East, she did not necessarily die from plague. Within the Amarna royal tomb the scene of Nefertiti and Akhenaten mourning over their daughter's bier is depicted on Room Gamma wall A, while Room Alpha wall F shows the death of Kiya in childbirth. In Room Gamma we are presented with a tableau highly reminiscent of that in Room Alpha, although here there has been extensive damage to the wall so that the body and most of the grieving parents are missing (Fig. 7.3). An inscription carved above the dead princess is now largely obscured but, as it was recorded by Bouriant at the turn of the century, we know that it originally read 'King's Daughter of his body, his beloved, Meketaten, born of the Great Royal Wife Nefertiti, may she live for ever and eternally'. The identity of the deceased is therefore not in doubt.

Once again the royal couple are facing a bier and, although only their feet remain, we can imagine Akhenaten again reaching out to comfort his wife in her distress as she views her dead daughter. Outside the chamber there are three registers of figures. The bottom row is taken up by a row of tables prepared for a feast. Above this we see a nurse, standing before a group of mourners and holding a child in her arms. The nurse is followed by two female attendants who carry the fans customarily used to signal royalty. The upper register shows a distressed female figure being restrained and groups of frenzied mourners including a dignitary who may have been summoned to witness an imminent royal birth. It is the greatest misfortune that the inscription which would have named the baby is now lost. Although some have sought to identify

Fig. 7.3   The death of Meketaten

the infant as either Setepenre or a subsequent child of Nefertiti, or even a baby born to Kiya, the otherwise unexplained presence of an infant at a death scene leads to the inevitable conclusion that twelve-year-old Meketaten has died in labour.

A subsequent scene in the royal tomb, recorded on Room Gamma wall B (Fig. 7.4), shows the dead Meketaten, or perhaps her statue, standing within a garden bower or pavilion whose papyrus columns are entwined with convolvulus and lotus blossom. Meketaten, again specifically named, wears a long transparent robe, a short wig and a perfume cone. She stands to face her grieving parents and three of her sisters who raise their arms to their heads in an attitude of extreme mourning. Neferneferure and Setepenre are missing from the family group, and may already be dead. Beneath the mourners are shown tables laden with food, drink and flowers. Meketaten's bower is strongly reminiscent of the birth bowers used by pregnant women in labour, and adds weight to the suggestion that she has died giving birth. However, bowers or temporary booths holding food and drink were a part of the Memphite, but not Theban, funeral ritual, and so the connection with childbirth may be a more subtle one, with Meketaten's symbolic bower intended to signify the wish for her re-birth rather than the cause of her own death.[31]

There is no record of any Meketaten-the-Younger at Amarna, although it is of course possible that the baby was male, died in infancy, or was given a more original name. But there are two unexplained princesses. Meritaten-the-Younger and Ankhesenpaaten-the-Younger, who may well be children born to Meritaten and/or Meketaten and/or Ankhesenpaaten.[32] Their titles rank them as the daughters of an unnamed king, who for a long time was assumed to be Akhenaten, but who might more realistically be his co-regent Smenkhkare and/or his lost brother. Alternatively, the two princesses may be the daughters of Kiya and Akhenaten, who may well have chosen to name their daughters after their illustrious half-sisters. The ultimate fate of these two princesses is as unclear as their origins. Like so many Amarna characters they are ephemeral, appearing for a brief time only to fade into obscurity.

So, what really happened at the end of the Amarna Age? During Year 14 or 15 of her father's reign, Meritaten married her half-brother and heir to the throne, Smenkhkare. Smenkhkare then assumed the role of

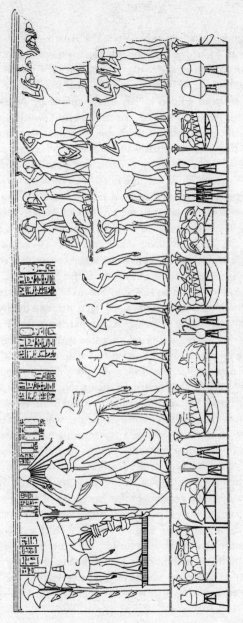

Fig. 7.4 Meketaten in her bower

co-regent alongside his father Akhenaten. The Amarna tomb of Meryre II provides us with a glimpse of changes in the royal family at this time.[33] Here, on the south wall of the main chamber, we see the royal family in a conventional scene. Akhenaten and Nefertiti stand at the Window of Appearance to hand golden collars to the miniature Meryre. Only five princesses are present; they are unnamed, but it would appear that it is Setepenre who is missing, possibly because she was too young to take part in the ritual. On the east wall of the same chamber we see the royal family, now with all six princesses, enjoying the international celebrations of Year 12. However, the north wall shows a very different scene. The picture is unfinished and has suffered damage, but it shows a king and queen standing beneath the rays of the Aten to reward their faithful servant. The figures of the royal couple are sketched in typical Amarna style, and could well be Akhenaten and Nefertiti. But the cartouches which accompanied them were, when the tomb was recorded during the late nineteenth century, those of the 'King of Upper and Lower Egypt, Ankhkeprure son of Re, Smenkhkare' and the 'King's Great Wife Meritaten'. The wall has since been attacked by thieves, and only the queen's cartouche remains. A comparison with the Theban tomb of Ramose would suggest that Akhenaten had died while Meryre's tomb was being prepared, and the artists had adapted the decoration to incorporate the new monarch and his wife, possibly altering a scene of Akhenaten and Nefertiti and re-writing the cartouches to convert them into Smenkhkare and Meritaten. No official record of Akhenaten's death has survived, but we know from a wine jar sealing, whose date of Year 17 is crossed out and rewritten as Year 1 (of an unnamed successor), that Akhenaten died during his seventeenth year on the throne. Given that it was Akhenaten's express wish that he be buried at Amarna, we may assume that the unfinished royal tomb was hastily made ready for its king.

Smenkhkare enjoyed a very brief reign, most, if not all, of which was spent ruling alongside his father. Barely had Smenkhkare interred his predecessor in the royal tomb, when he himself died and was in turn buried, presumably at Amarna. As he left no male heir, Smenkhkare was succeeded by his young brother Tutankhaten and his sister-queen, Ankhesenpaaten. It was now Meritaten's turn to vanish; her body has never been traced and we know neither when she died or where she was buried.

By this time Nefertiti has completely disappeared. The last delivery of wine from her estate, the 'House of Neferuaten' is dated to Year 11 and, although wine from the 'House of the King's Wife' is known to have been delivered to Amarna in Years 14, 15 and 17, it is by no means certain Nefertiti is the king's wife of the label. We must assume, for the want of any evidence to the contrary, that she too is dead and buried, most probably within the Amarna royal tomb. It is unsatisfying to have to end a biography by admitting that we have no details of the subject's ultimate fate, but such discomfort can never be an excuse for shirking unwelcome archaeological conclusions.

Tutankhaten and Ankhesenpaaten ruled from Amarna for three or four years. Then, with a seemingly sudden rejection of Akhenaten's beliefs, they moved the royal court to Thebes. At the same time they altered their given names to remove the reference to the Aten, becoming Tutankhamen and Ankhesenamen. From this point onwards Tutankhamen showed a determined devotion to Amen, and regarded Thebes rather than Amarna or Memphis as his capital.[34] Here the old temples were officially re-opened, the old priesthoods re-established, and at Amen's home, the Karnak Temple, Tutankhamen erected a large stela which was to proclaim his devotion to the traditional deities of Egypt. This 'restoration stela' explains how it has fallen to the new king to restore the gods to their rightful place:

When his majesty arose as king, the temples of the gods and goddesses, beginning from Elephantine down to the marshes of the Delta, had fallen into decay, their shrines had fallen into desolation and become ruins overgrown with weeds, their chapels as though they had never been and their halls serving as footpaths. The land was topsy-turvy and the gods turned their backs on the land.[35]

The restoration of the old temples was the best move that a new king could make to appease the old gods who might reasonably have been expected to feel angry over the Amarna heresy. Tutankhamen's proclamation is intended to restore confidence in the monarchy by appealing to the Egyptians' innate conservatism; a traditional pharaoh has returned to the throne, chaos will soon be banished and *maat* will be restored throughout the land. In spite of his youth and his unconventional

Amarna upbringing, Tutankhamen (or his advisors) was very aware of
the duties expected of a conventional New Kingdom monarch. During
his reign we see him performing all the approved kingly deeds. There
is a spate of building work at Karnak, extensive restoration of the
monuments of his forebears, and even the re-emergence of the huntin',
shootin' and fighting pharaoh with the king practising his archery and
the army employed in military action in Syria.

Ankhesenamen, following the precedent set by her mother and
paternal grandmother, retains a high queenly profile. With her once
egg-shaped head restored to normal proportions she appears on many of
Tutankhamen's public monuments and on more private items recovered
from his tomb. Here, on the king's golden shrine which is decorated in
the Amarna style, we are treated to what Howard Carter identified as
simple domestic scenes:

... depicting, in delightfully naive fashion a number of episodes in the daily
life of king and queen. In all these scenes the dominant note is that of friendly
relationship between the husband and wife, the unselfconscious friendliness
that marks the Tell el Amarna school.[36]

In fact the queen is now assuming a priestly role before her husband.
Ankhesenamen pours liquid into a ceremonial goblet held by her seated
husband just as, years before, her mother had poured wine for Akhenaten. In other images she mirrors the traditional postures of Maat,
companion to the king, as she squats at her husband's feet to receive the
water which Tutankhamen pours into her cupped hands, or hands him
an arrow to shoot in the marshes, while in the more formal scenes on
Tutankhamen's shrine she takes the role of Weret Hekau, Mistress of
the Palace.[37]

The collapse of Akhenaten's religion seems to have been greeted with
a general feeling of quiet relief, and those who had formerly expressed
their public devotion to the Aten were quickly re-converted back to
the old ways. The changeover appears to have been relatively low-key
and painless. There was no sudden attack on the memories of Nefertiti
and Akhenaten, and no attempt was made to remove the Aten from the
pantheon. However, the cult of the Aten now became a very minor
part of the pantheistic state religion. With the re-opening of the temple

of Amen, and the restoration of its offerings, the Aten temples at Karnak quickly fell into decay.

No real reason is given for Tutankhamen's return to the old gods. But Akhenaten's insistence on centring the cult of the Aten on his own immediate family can have done little to ensure its long-term survival. Aten worship had always been Akhenaten's austere and demanding individual dream, offering little to others, even to members of his own family. The death of its only prophet naturally brought the experiment to a close. Beyond the isolation of Amarna twenty centuries of tradition had not been wiped out by a mere seventeen years of idiosyncratic monotheism. The relative ease with which the country was able to return to pre-Amarna theology following the death of the king must serve as proof that the religious 'revolution' was due very much to the efforts of Akhenaten alone. We may hazard a guess that outside Amarna the old ways had never been fully abandoned. Once the decision had been taken to discontinue Akhenaten's religious programme it became possible, and indeed sensible, to leave Amarna in favour of a more convenient bureaucratic base.

Amarna was not abandoned immediately. The wealthier members of society merely boarded up their houses and waited to see what would happen. Eventually, however, as it became clear that the court would not be returning, some of the more valuable parts of the houses, the wooden and stone elements, were salvaged, while the mud-brick walls were left to decay. There was still a significant population at Amarna during the reign of Tutankhamen, but slowly the numbers dwindled until the town was deserted. In contrast, the workmen's village, which had been abandoned as the court moved away, was reoccupied and even underwent a phase of expansion during Tutankhamen's reign, before being finally abandoned during the reign of Horemheb.

The transfer of the court away from Amarna forced the abandonment of the royal tomb. Whether this was left sealed, under guard, or whether it was immediately opened and the bodies moved, is not clear. The Egyptians were certainly not shy of transplanting their forebears, and an unpopulated and therefore largely unsupervised Amarna may not have been considered a suitable, or more particularly a secure, resting place. Tutankhamen may well have reasoned that he, rather than the thieves, should rescue the Amarna royal gold. Several of the items included in

Tutankhamen's own burial, including one of his golden coffins, were made for Smenkhkare and other members of the Amarna family. Can we assume that Tutankhamen opened the tomb, took the best for himself, and gave his beloved elder brother a semblance of a royal burial, complete with valueless but still effective funerary artifacts, at Thebes? If we can make this assumption, we have to ask what happened to the other Amarna bodies. Had they already been destroyed by robbers? Or were they, too, taken back to Thebes? Are they still buried at Thebes, or are they included in one of the known royal caches?

The first Amarna queen to have been 'identified' at Thebes is Tiy. We know that Tiy lived long into her son's reign; the shrine that Akhenaten prepared for her bore the later form of the Aten's name, only used after Year 9, while a single wine docket shows that wine from her estate was still being delivered to Amarna during Year 14. Although it has been suggested that Tiy and Sitamen were interred in the Valley of the Kings tomb of Amenhotep III, it seems highly unlikely that Akhenaten would have buried his mother anywhere other than at Amarna, and indeed fragments of Tiy's sarcophagus were found inside the Amarna royal tomb. However, the presence of Tiy's shrine in KV 55 shows that at least part of her burial was transported to Thebes. Are we to imagine that Tiy was first interred at Amarna, then transferred with Smenkhkare to KV 55 during the reign of Tutankhamen, and finally moved again to a mummy cache, possibly via a sojourn in the tomb of Amenhotep III where fragments of Tiy's shabti figures have been found?

We have several anonymous New Kingdom female mummies recovered from the Valley of the Kings. And there are many missing New Kingdom royal women, including Tiy, Kiya, Nefertiti, and all her daughters. It is natural, but frustrating, to try to match up the two. For a long time Amarna scholars have focused their attention on a trio of mummies recovered from the tomb of Amenhotep II (KV 35). Here, in 1898, Victor Loret discovered seventeen royal mummies of the 18th, 19th and 20th Dynasties, stripped of their riches and stored in the tomb by the Third Intermediate Period necropolis officials. Amenhotep II still lay in his open sarcophagus, and a large walled-up room held nine coffins housing, amongst others, Tuthmosis IV, Seti II, Ramesses IV–VI and 'Amenhotep III' who may have been mislabelled. Another mummy was found in the tomb corridor. Meanwhile a small side room held three naked, coffinless and unlabelled mummies, each showing damage to the head and abdomen. Loret first identified these as an older woman, a little prince and a young man. Soon after the 'man' was reclassified, and the trio became widely known as the Elder Lady, the Younger Lady (the man) and a prince.

For a long time it was accepted that the Elder Lady might be Tiy. This mummy, described by Elliot Smith as 'a middle-aged woman with long, brown wavy, lustrous hair',[38] had been recovered in a quasi-regal pose with her left arm bent in front of her chest and her left hand clenched as if to hold a symbol of rank. Subsequent examination proved her to be a woman in her forties, highly similar in cranio-facial morphology to Thuyu, mother of Tiy.[39] This estimate of the lady's age made her perhaps slightly younger than might have been expected, but when a strand of hair taken from the mummy was matched to a lock of hair found within a miniature coffin labelled with Tiy's name and included amongst Tutankhamen's grave goods, the identification seemed complete. However, it sometimes seems that nothing in egyptology is ever simple – how can we know that the hair in the tomb of Tutankhamen actually came from Tiy? Meanwhile, more recent research suggests that the mummy may not be as 'elderly' as was first supposed and, unless we are again to accept a long co-regency between Amenhotep III and Akhenaten, Tiy must have been relatively old when she died. Although mummy ages obtained by X-ray analysis need to be treated with some caution, this leaves us with a tantalizing question. If not Tiy, who could this lady be?

Lately attention has turned to the second 'Lady', originally identified by Loret as a man of somewhat unusual appearance:

The last corpse nearest the wall seemed to be that of a man. His head was shaved but a wig lay on the ground not far from him. The face of this person displayed something horrible and something droll at the same time. The mouth, running obliquely from one side nearly to the middle of the cheek, bit a pad of linen whose two ends hung from the corner of the lips. The half-closed eyes had a strange expression; he could have died choking on a gag but he looked like a young, playful cat with a piece of cloth. Death, which had respected the severe beauty of the woman and the impish grace of the boy, had turned in derision and amused itself with the countenance of the man.[40]

Marianne Luban was the first to propose, on the grounds of skull shape, bone structure, the shaven head and evidence of ear-piercing, that this mummy may be Nefertiti.[41] Such identification is hard to sustain, however, without any positive proof. Certainly superficial appearance can be no guide to the identity of a mummy. Leaving aside the tendency for all female mummies to look pretty much the same, and Nefertiti's tendency to have a startlingly different appearance from year to year, styles in hairstyles, wigs and ear-piercings lingered for decades, and we might reasonably expect Nefertiti, Kiya and her daughters to have adopted the same fashions.

More recently a team from York University, led by Dr Joann Fletcher, has had the opportunity of carrying out a non-invasive examination of the mummy, and they too have suggested that she might be Nefertiti – a suggestion that the *Sunday Times* took to extremes by proclaiming on its cover 'This is Nefertiti, the fabled queen of Egypt. Before Cleopatra, the Queen of Sheba and even Helen of Troy she was the most powerful and famous woman in the world. *The Sunday Times Magazine* was there when she was discovered.'[42] Unfortunately the situation is not as clear-cut as the *Sunday Times* would suggest, and the age of the mummy indicates that she may simply be too young to be Nefertiti. If she has to be an Amarna mummy, she is more likely to be one of the royal daughters. But there is no real reason to assume that she is an Amarna mummy; the fact that she was found without a coffin suggests that she, and her two companions, may be original occupants of the tomb, perhaps relations of Amenhotep II whose coffins had been destroyed long ago by thieves. How else would the Third Intermediate Period restorers have transferred three coffinless mummies to their last resting place?

The final word – for the moment – on the identification of the mummy must rest with the Egyptian Supreme Council of Antiquities, headed by Dr Zahi Hawass, who have recently released a report indicating that DNA testing shows the 'Younger Lady' to be male.

Chief amongst the prominent converts to the restored religion was God's Father Ay, who served as vizier under the young Tutankhamen. Throughout this tale of Amarna Nefertiti's putative father has been a constant background figure, his career stretching from the end of the reign of Amenhotep III through that of Akhenaten, Smenkhkare and now Tutankhamen. A tiny piece of gold foil, recovered from tomb KV 58, gives an indication of Ay's exalted status during his step-grandson's reign. Here we see Tutankhamen slaying an enemy, with Ankhesenamen standing in the approved wifely position behind him. To the left of the royal couple, dressed as a fan-bearer, stands Ay. Traditionally, such smiting scenes were performed in the presence of the god, not the vizier. The inclusion of a private individual in such a ritual is unprecedented, and surely indicates that Ay, Tutankhamen's mentor, has become a force to be reckoned with. In fact, Ay is described as the 'eldest king's son', an obviously honorary title which nevertheless implies that the elderly Ay is recognized as the young Tutankhamen's heir. The adoption of a successor, no matter how elderly, must have seemed a prudent measure. Already two still-born daughters had been born to Ankhesenpaaten; their tiny bodies, carefully mummified and each encased in a double anthropoid coffin, were found stored in a box within Tutankhamen's tomb. Professor Douglas Derry conducted an autopsy on the babies in 1932, finding that one had been born after approximately five months gestation, the other after seven or eight. More recent re-examination led by Professor Harrison has suggested that the older child may have suffered from a condition known as Sprengel's deformity, which would have led to spina bifida and scoliosis.[43]

It fell to Ay to inter Tutankhamen in a private tomb hastily adapted to accommodate its royal occupant. This tomb (KV 62), possibly the tomb which Ay was preparing for himself, is now perhaps the best-known tomb in the world. Tutankhamen's own tomb was unfinished at his premature death; its completion may well have been handicapped by the need to re-establish the Deir el-Medina workmen's village following the return from Amarna. Ay's burial of Tutankhamen was a highly significant act, as it was by burying his predecessor that the king of Egypt confirmed his right to rule. However, there is no evidence to prove that Ay killed Tutankhamen in order to seize the throne.

Copies of a cuneiform text dating to this period have survived to tell a remarkable tale. A widowed queen of Egypt, without a son, took the highly unusual step of writing to Suppiluliumas, king of the Hittites, asking that a prince be sent as a husband and future pharaoh:

My husband has died. I do not have a son. But, they say, many are your sons.

If you would give me one of your sons he would become my husband. I shall
never pick out a servant of mine and make him my husband.[44]

Suppiluliumas was both surprised and suspicious. Everyone knew that
the Egyptian princesses did not marry foreigners, while a promise of
inheriting the throne of Egypt seemed too good to be true. An ambassa-
dor was sent to investigate, and eventually a prince, Zannanza, was
dispatched. The unfortunate bridegroom was ambushed and killed on
his way to meet his bride, and relations between Egypt and the Hittites
plunged to a new low.

The name of the letter-writer has not been preserved in a recognizable
form; she is referred to as Dahamunzu, a phonetic version of the queen's
standard title *ta hemet nesu* or 'king's wife'. However, there are only
three queens who could possibly have written such a letter and as two
of these, Nefertiti and Meritaten, were, if not already dead, certainly
one step removed from the problem as dowagers rather than queens,
Ankhesenamen is generally accepted as the author. If the whole letter-
writing episode is not itself to be regarded as a cunning diplomatic trick,
we must assume that Tutankhamen's successor did not take kindly to
the queen's actions. We do not see Ankhesenamen again and her ultimate
fate, like that of her sisters, is unknown.

Ay, adopted heir to Tutankhamen, took the throne as 'God's Father
Ay, Divine ruler of Thebes, beloved of Amen' with his wife Tey as
queen.[45] He could never have been anything other than a stop-gap king
as, by the time he became pharaoh, he would have been an old man
even by modern standards. After a reign of only four years Ay too died
and was buried in a relatively simple unfinished tomb in the Western
Valley (WV 23), close by the tomb of Amenhotep III and possibly the
tomb which Tutankhamen had intended for himself. The excavation of
this tomb has yielded fragments of coffin, statues, and pieces of uraeus
but no mummy. However scattered fragments of human skeletal material
recovered from the vicinity of the tomb and believed by the excavator
to be female, may well represent the last remains of Nefertiti's nurse
Tey.[46]

Ay was followed on the throne by General Horemheb, a soldier of
obscure origins who had served under both Tutankhamen and Ay.
Horemheb was not himself of royal birth, but his second wife was a lady

with close links to the royal family. Queen Mutnodjmet, 'God's Wife of Amen', is now widely recognized as the younger sister of Nefertiti whom we last saw in the Amarna tomb of Ay and Tey. She is therefore the last known surviving member of Nefertiti's family.[47] Like her sister before her, Mutnodjmet proved to be a strong queen; we see her seated beside her husband, at equal scale, on his coronation statue, and a scene on the side of the royal throne shows her in the guise of a winged sphinx wearing the flat-topped crown associated with Tefnut. Mutnodjmet died aged thirty-five to forty during Year 14 or 15 of her husband's rule, and was buried in the tomb that Horemheb had prepared for himself at Memphis. Included in her grave was the tiny skeleton of a baby or foetus, suggesting that Mutnodjmet had died in childbirth.

Horemheb developed into a solid, old-fashioned Egyptian pharaoh, ruling Egypt for over twenty years. He did not share Tutankhamen's devotion to Amen. As an experienced politician he may, with good reason, have been wary of allowing the re-established priesthood too much power too soon and so we find, throughout his reign, the other major gods of the pantheon allowed an increased prominence. Traditionally the persecution of the memory of Akhenaten and Nefertiti has been assigned to the personal spite and excessive religious zeal of Horemheb. While Horemheb was certainly responsible for the closing, demolition and re-use of much of Akhenaten's Karnak temples, there is increasing evidence to show that some buildings had already been dismantled during the reign of Tutankhamen and, indeed the persecution of Akhenaten's memory lasted well into the reign of Ramesses II when much of the stone was taken from Amarna for re-use in the pylons of Hermopolis.

The removal of the name and image of a dead person, occasionally called a *damnatio memoriae*, served two distinct purposes. Firstly, it permitted a valid re-writing of history, allowing Akhenaten's successors to convince themselves that his reign had never occured. Secondly, it provided a means of attacking the spirit of the deceased. Traditional theology dictated that, in order for the spirit or soul to live for ever, the body, the image or at least the name of the deceased must survive; it was this need to preserve the dead body which led to the development of mummification, a practice which Akhenaten continued even if he did not subscribe to all its theological implications. If all memory of a dead person was lost or destroyed the spirit too would perish, and then would come the dreaded 'Second Death'; total obliteration from which there could be no return. We have already seen how Tutankhamen, as his reign progressed, stressed his role as a traditional New Kingdom monarch, preferring to be associated with Amenhotep III rather than Akhenaten. It is therefore unfortunate that, as far as Egypt's official historians were concerned, Akhenaten and his descendants were all tarred with the same heretical brush. Akhenaten, Nefertiti, Smenkhkare, Tutankhamen and Ay were all omitted from the official King Lists, which jumped from Amenhotep III to Horemheb. Nefertiti's name was rapidly lost in the mists of time while Akhenaten himself was dismissed as the 'criminal of Akhetaten'.

Epilogue
The Beautiful Woman Returns

Tell el-Amarna is not usually included in the itinerary of a visitor to Egypt. This is partially due to the not undeserved reputation for wickedness on the part of the inhabitants.[1]

Amarna, once proud capital of a mighty empire, rapidly deteriorated into a ghost town, surviving only as a useful quarry for the stone which was needed in the extensive building works at nearby Hermopolis. Once the supply was exhausted the city was quickly forgotten and, over the centuries, the mud-brick walls gradually collapsed to be buried beneath a blanket of wind-borne sand, leaving a low, bumpy landscape punctuated by occasional mud-brick ruins. Amarna remained an obvious archaeological site, but one of little interest to anyone. Its geographical limitations ensured the preservation of its secrets. No other pharaoh was tempted to establish a city on the Amarna plain and no substantial modern town ever developed, although the site is sprinkled with evidence of late Roman/Christian occupation and a handful of modern villages have caused the riverside sections of the Great Palace to disappear under cultivated fields. As the desert sands blew over their city, and the temple scribes adjusted their country's official history to exclude the heretic kings, the names of Akhenaten and Nefertiti vanished from Egypt.[2]

Our first modern reference to the as yet unnamed archaeological site comes from the writings of Edme Jomard, a Frenchman who visited Amarna during the 1798–9 Napoleonic invasion and who made a plan of his discovery, noting 'a great mass of ruins . . . [which] does not feature on any map'.[3] Twenty-five years later John Gardner Wilkinson, under the mistaken impression that he was exploring Alabastronopolis, became the first egyptologist to visit the tombs of the Amarna nobles. Sketches of some of the scenes within Meryre's tomb, together with a hastily drawn map of the city, were later to appear in his great work

Manners and Customs of the Ancient Egyptians.[4] Other antiquarians followed over the years but, although the tombs were recorded by Robert
Hay, Nestor L'Hote and A. Prisse d'Avennes, their work remained
unpublished and the city site generally unknown. It was only in 1842
with the arrival of Richard Lepsius, leader of the Prussian epigraphic
expedition, that a thorough record was made of the then known monuments and tomb scenes.

The brief Prussian expedition, two seasons totalling a mere twelve
days of what must have been extremely hard labour, was followed by a
far longer French mission which again concentrated on the cliffs. The
French held the concession to work at Amarna between 1883 and 1902,
during which time they uncovered more of the southern tombs of the
nobles and fitted protective iron gates to prevent the theft of engraved
scenes which enterprising tomb robbers were eager to saw off the walls
and sell to western collectors. This precaution almost certainly came
too late. Amarna had already become the focus of gangs of unofficial
excavators, local people employed by black-market traders to dig for
treasures which could be sold on the increasingly rapacious antiquities
market. Their furtive digging disrupted the stratigraphy, robbed the site
of its valuables and threw up vast piles of ancient potsherds, which may
still be seen on the surface today.

The 'accidental' discovery, in 1887, of the Amarna letters by a local
woman reportedly digging for *sebakh*, sparked a renewed interest in the
site, which was gradually establishing itself on the tourist map. Already
in 1873 Amelia B. Edwards, author of the first travellers' guide to
Egypt, *A Thousand Miles up the Nile*, had included Amarna in her list of
important Middle Egyptian sites, although due to bad weather conditions
she herself was thwarted in her intention to visit the tombs.[5] Miss
Edwards, like many other European visitors accustomed to the
westernized luxury of Cairo, was shocked by the levels of poverty and
disease to be seen in Middle Egypt:

It may be that ophthalmia especially prevailed in this part of the country, or
that being brought unexpectedly into the midst of a large crowd, one observed
the people more narrowly, but I certainly never saw so many one-eyed human
beings as that morning at Minieh . . . I believe it is no exaggeration to say that
at least every twentieth person, down to little toddling children of three and

four years of age, was blind of an eye. Not being a particularly well-favoured race, this defect added the last touch of repulsiveness to faces already sullen, ignorant and unfriendly.[6]

So affected was Miss Edwards by the sight of the native Egyptians that she found herself unable to visit modern towns. She was not alone in her shock. Almost half a century later Mary Chubb, who accompanied the Egypt Exploration Society's expedition to Amarna at a time when the western archaeologists were expected to treat the illnesses of the local people, was similarly struck by the high level of 'pink eye', 'eyelids badly swollen and red, the eye closed and discharging, and the eyeball, if you could manage to see it at all, very bloodshot', which fortunately responded well to an application of warm boracic water.[7]

Amarna never ranked highly as a casual tourist attraction. Sadly deficient in spectacular temples and awe-inspiring pyramids, the nearby modern towns were not geared up to the tourist trade and, lacking the sophistication of Cairo and the romance of Thebes, had very little to offer the visitor with a limited interest in egyptological research. Access to the site could be a problem for those who did not enjoy the luxury of their own boat; in John Pendlebury's 1930 account of Amarna he stressed how difficult it was to actually reach the antiquities. The intrepid traveller was instructed to drive out from Malawi in a hired car and cross the river by boat having first arranged for donkeys on the opposite bank. Failure to arrange for the donkeys in advance would mean 'the complete absence of transport at the proper price of five piastres the donkey and three the boy, and also of the guards who are supposed to keep the keys of the tombs'.[8] The local people enjoyed a bad reputation for theft and general unspecified wickedness, and as Norman de Garis Davies noted, 'the evil reputation of the inhabitants of El Amarna seems to have deterred early visitors from penetrating inland'.[9] This local churlishness and lack of respect for their own womenfolk was something that the western archaeologists could turn to their own advantage:

The introduction of girls [into the workforce], never used by us at Abydos, is explained by the fact that in the district round Tell el-Amarna women hold a distinctly lower position in the eyes of their men-folk than in the villages further south, and consequently do much more of the hard work.[10]

Flinders Petrie, who worked at Amarna for a 1891–2 season, brought
the first scientific excavation to the city site, although his technique of
what was essentially rapid random sampling combined with occasional
conservation now seems very dated in comparison with modern archaeological practice. He was followed, in 1902, by Norman de Garis Davies
who, working under the aegis of the Egypt Exploration Society founded
by Miss Edwards, commenced a detailed epigraphic study of the tombs
of the nobles. The tombs were dirty, dark and bat-infested; their walls
had suffered from ancient and modern vandalism and much of the plaster
which held the reliefs had started to crumble from the walls. The
American egyptologist James Breasted, visiting Amarna while on honey-
moon in 1895 and taking the opportunity to copy some of the tomb
scenes, had been shocked by what he found:

Unfortunately, and to the shame and disgrace of the French administration, I
find the finest inscriptions in Amarna so mutilated by the fellahin that I
can hardly use them. I told Brugsch of it at the museum today – he was
greatly surprised, having known nothing of it. I am so filled with indignation
against the French and their empty, blatant boasting, 'la gloire de la France',
that I can hardly contain myself. I could have wept my eyes out in Amarna.
Scarcely less indignant must one feel against the English who are here only
for the commerce and the politics of it, and who might reform matters if they
would. A combination of French rascality, of English philistine indifference &
of German lack of money is gradually allowing Egypt to be pillaged and
plundered from end to end. In another generation there will be nothing to be
had or saved.[11]

Davies, working under the most trying of conditions, recorded the
tombs and boundary stelae from 1902 to 1905, eventually publishing his
Rock Tombs of el-Amarna in six volumes,[12] a magnificent achievement
and one which, as the walls of the tombs have continued to deteriorate
over the years, is of ever increasing value to egyptologists.

   The royal tomb, which had been discovered by locals in the early
1880s, had been thoroughly stripped of all valuables by the time the
secret of its entrance was revealed to the French mission. A. H. Sayce,
writing from Luxor on 26 February 1890, was able to give details of the
'new' tomb:

THE BEAUTIFUL WOMAN RETURNS

The tomb and mummy of Amenophis IV, the 'Heretic King' of Egyptian history, have been found at Tel el-Amarna . . . The tomb has proved a second pit of Der el-Bahari to the antiquity dealers of Ekhmim, by whom it has been worked. Now that it has been despoiled of the precious objects it once contained, they have condescended to inform us of its exact position . . . The mummy of the king has, unfortunately, been torn to pieces . . . The beautiful objects of ivory and alabaster which have lately been on the market of 'antikas', the bronze rings and enamelled porcelain [faience] which bear the cartouches of Amenophis IV and the solar disc, the delicate glass and bracelets of solid gold which have been offered for sale to travellers, have all come from the desecrated sepulchre.[13]

Despite Sayce's fear that the inscriptions within the tomb must be hopelessly ruined, those scenes which had escaped the New Kingdom vandalism inflicted by those determined to eradicate all memory of Akhenaten's reign were at this time substantially complete. It is therefore the greatest misfortune that the photographic record of the French mission has been lost, while the surviving line drawings are both incomplete and inaccurate. Since the official discovery of the tomb the walls have suffered greatly, particularly during 1934 when a feud between rival groups of guards resulted in the deliberate mutilation of rooms Alpha and Gamma. Work on the clearance and recording of the tomb had started in the 1930s but was interrupted by the war, so that the first publication of the tomb was eventually made a century after its discovery.[14]

In 1907 the Amarna concession was awarded to a team of archaeologists from the German Oriental Society working under the direction of Ludwig Borchardt. Their initial work, a survey of the whole city site and an exploratory series of trial trenches, was followed by an excavation proper. Working in the eastern section of the city they made their way down what was known as 'High Priest Street', digging a small strip trench along the road. It was during this expedition that the now world-famous bust of Nefertiti was recovered from the workshop of the sculptor Tuthmosis. The advent of the First World War put an end to the German excavations, and the furore which followed the unveiling of the Nefertiti head in Berlin ensured that their concession was never renewed. Instead, in 1921 the Egypt Exploration Society started work at Amarna where they have continued intermittently ever since under a

series of highly distinguished directors including T. Eric Peet, Leonard
Woolley, Francis Newton (who was taken ill during the 1924 season at
Amarna and sadly died at Asyut), F. Ll. Griffiths, Henry Frankfort and
John Pendlebury. The present phase of work, which started in 1979, is
under the direction of Barry Kemp of Cambridge University. His team
has so far produced a detailed survey of the site, and has conducted a
series of excavations focusing primarily on the workmen's village.

The decoding of hieroglyphics at the beginning of the nineteenth
century had allowed egyptologists to read the inscriptions carved into
the great Amarna boundary stelae. Once again the names of Akhenaten
and Nefertiti could be spoken at Amarna. However, far from casting
light on the hitherto little-known late 18th Dynasty, the readings at first
caused intense confusion. Who was this new pharaoh? None of the
rediscovered names could be tied in to the King Lists which formed the
backbone of Egyptian history. It took several years for the fragmented
evidence for Akhenaten's unconventional reign to be pieced together,
and for the reasons behind his subsequent obliteration to be understood.
Although Nefertiti was now recognized as Akhenaten's consort, and her
name was matched to her image on the boundary stelae, little was known
of her role within the royal family. The stelae made it obvious that
Akhenaten held his wife and daughters in great affection, but it was
Queen Tiy, whose monuments had not been erased during the purges
which followed the Amarna period, who was cast as the influential
female figure in Akhenaten's life. Nefertiti attracted little attention, and
it was only with the discovery, or more particularly the display, of the
Berlin bust, that the general public became Nefertiti-conscious.
Instantly, Nefertiti became the most recognized female figure from
ancient Egypt, famous not for her achievements, which were still largely
unknown, but for her beauty. Many scholars of the Amarna period have
seen the recovery of the bust as the true start of Nefertiti's tale, and have
begun their accounts of her life accordingly.

The studio of 'the Chief of Works, the Sculptor', Tuthmosis, lay in
the southern suburb, home to several workshops producing goods for
the temples and palaces of the central city.[15] Tuthmosis is one of the few
Amarna period sculptors whom we know by name, the others being
Bak, son of Men, whose works had held pride of place at Thebes, and
Iuty (or Auta), chief sculptor of Queen Tiy, who is shown in the tomb

Fig. 8.1   The workshop of the sculptor Iuty

of Huya working on a statue of the ephemeral Princess Beketaten. As
Chief of Works Tuthmosis was as much a civil servant as an artist,
administering a large factory-like workshop whose sculptors and appren-
tices would have been dedicated to producing endless portraits of the
royal family.

Excavation of his studio, and the attached house where Tuthmosis
lived with his family, at first suggested that the workshop must have had
two separate production lines: the carving of heads and limbs for
inclusion in composite stone statues, and the production of gypsum

plaster casts of both royal and non-royal heads. In fact these plaster heads, some so realistic that they were originally identified as 'death masks', played an important part in the production of the stone sculptures.[16] It would have been unthinkable for the royal family to spend endless hours sitting before a sculptor as he laboriously chipped away at a stone block. Instead, the stone sculpture was preceded by a clay or wax model of the subject, plaster casts of the model being submitted to the commissioning official for approval at various stages in its development. When all were agreed that the model conformed to accepted artistic standards, and was as good a likeness as required, it was copied in stone. At this stage the plaster casts would have become redundant and, being of no further use, were presumably thrown away. Twenty-three plaster heads and faces were recovered from Tuthmosis's workshop, and we must assume that these represent either busts which were in the process of being carved when Amarna was abandoned, or plaster casts which Tuthmosis had kept for some reason, possibly as a form of reference library. Two of the female heads have been identified on stylistic grounds as depictions of Nefertiti, and it seems highly likely that Kiya is represented among the anonymous non-royal women.

Tuthmosis was forced to relocate his studio when the court moved from Amarna. We may assume that he removed everything which he considered to be of value, leaving only the unwanted and broken fruits of his labours. Model heads, unfinished statues and miscellaneous limbs of the Amarna royal family, now dead and not particularly revered, were not worth transporting to Thebes, and Tuthmosis packed over fifty examples of his work into a small storeroom which he sealed before departing. The now world-famous limestone bust of Nefertiti was left sitting on a shelf, but eventually, as the shelf collapsed, toppled forward to be buried knee-deep in rubble.

The discovery of the head, and the story of its export – or its smuggling – to Germany, is an archaeological tale which has grown in the telling, entering the realms of mythology with accounts of Borchardt concealing the bust among a bushel of vegetables or encasing it in plaster so that it resembled a plain block of stone.[17] We know that the bust was discovered by a local workman on the afternoon of 6 December 1912. The rules by which concessions were then granted dictated that all finds should be split 50:50 between the museum service, then run by the French, and the excavator, who would normally distribute his share of the booty among his sponsors. This 'division' occurred at the end of the digging season, and the authorities always had first pick of the finds. Instead of the bust of Nefertiti, Inspector Lefebvre accepted on behalf of the museum service a painted relief of the royal family. Borchardt's role in this choice is unclear. Did he deliberately conceal the true nature of the head by displaying it to the inspector coated in grime? Was the inspector merely shown a bad photograph, or even a crude copy of the bust? Did Borchardt argue that Berlin already had a relief of the royal family, while Cairo had other statue heads of the royal family? Now, having seen the bust cleaned and displayed in its full glory in Berlin, Lefebvre's choice seems inexplicable. To the inspector, however, faced with the task of dividing up the spoils of an entire season, and perhaps confronted with a dirty bust in a dark Egyptian room, the true value of the head may not have seemed obvious.

When, in November 1913, the Amarna finds were exhibited in Berlin, the head was excluded from the display. It had been given to James Simon, the backer of Borchardt's expedition, and it was not until 1920 that the bust was donated to the New Museum, Berlin. In 1924 Nefertiti also went on display. Public reaction was immediate and enthusiastic. Egyptology was all the rage in post-war Europe and the well-publicized discovery of the tomb of Tutankhamen some two years earlier had already sparked a wave of interest in Egyptian-style jewellery, clothing and interior design.[18] Nefertiti with her clean-cut, almost contemporary good looks fitted well into the current craze and soon became the museum's star exhibit. Predictably, the Egyptian government responded to the publicity by demanding the immediate return of their 'stolen' treasure, and all German excavations in Egypt were stopped. The Germans, however, would not consider losing Nefertiti without some compensation. The return of an archaeological artefact apparently obtained by legitimate means would set a dangerous precedent and, in any case, Nefertiti had acquired a symbolic value beyond her artistic or historical importance and she continued to draw large crowds to the museum.

Eventually a swap was negotiated. In return for the head, Berlin would receive two famous statues, each of great artistic merit: a standing statue of Ranefer and a seated statue of Amenhotep son of Hapu. From an egyptological point of view, this was an eminently sensible exchange. However, public opinion was very much against the deal, and it was eventually called off. Another move was made to return Nefertiti to mark the accession of King Fuad in 1933, but Hitler, who is rumoured to have included the bust among his favourite pieces of art, ensured that the head remained in Berlin. During the Second World War the bust was hidden for safety in a salt mine whence it was recovered by American troops and eventually donated to the Egyptian Museum, (West) Berlin. Today Nefertiti's head, accession number 21300, remains in the reunited Berlin Museum. Whether it is right that it should do so is very much a matter of opinion. While most archaeologists would agree that a collection of artefacts should not be broken up without good reason, Cairo Museum is undoubtedly a very crowded place suffering from a permanent shortage of funds and a chronic lack of space. In Berlin Nefertiti receives the care and attention fitting to a star exhibit. She stands as a symbol of Egypt, a useful ambassadress who introduces visitors to the history of her homeland. Whether she would ever have attracted this kind of attention as just one among the many exhibits of Cairo is a moot point.

The bust is carved from a brittle limestone coated with a layer of gypsum plaster moulded to even out faults in the symmetry of the piece. Forty-eight centimetres high, it shows Nefertiti's head, her long neck and her collar region but is deliberately cut off before her shoulders. Nefertiti wears her unique flat-topped blue crown decorated with golden streamers whose red, blue and green inlays reflect the colours in her broad beaded necklace. Her whole head, with the exception of the eye sockets, is painted in natural colours; Nefertiti has a delicate pink-brown skin, deeper red-brown lips, a straight nose and delicately arched black eyebrows. There is no hair visible under her heavy crown. She has suffered remarkably little damage, although the tips of the ears and the top edge of the crown have been slightly chipped, but the left eye is missing from its socket. The right eye, which glances slightly downwards, is inlaid with rock crystal, ringed with a black kohl line and has a black pupil. Despite an intensive search Borchardt was unable to find the missing left eye and, as the socket shows no trace of any adhesive, it is generally accepted that this was not in place when the head was stored away.

Various explanations have been put forward to explain the missing eye, some more fanciful than others. Several authorities have, for example, suggested that Nefertiti must have suffered from a serious eye complaint; either cataracts, which would cause the eye to appear opaque, or an ancient equivalent of the eye diseases observed at Amarna thousands of years later by Amelia Edwards and Mary Chubb. None of her other images, however, confirms this diagnosis and all show two matching, apparently healthy eyes. At least one writer of romantic biography has suggested that the eye was deliberately omitted by Tuthmosis as a means of gaining revenge on the promiscuous queen who had spurned him as a lover.[19] It is unlikely that the bust is simply unfinished, as its style would indicate that it is a relatively early piece falling somewhere between the exaggerated Theban depictions of the queen and her later, more realistic images. Nor is it likely that a single eye would be gouged out as a means of attacking the memory of the dead queen. More reasonable is the theory that the piece was intended to serve as an artist's model and teaching aid, the eye socket being deliberately left empty to allow pupils to study inlay techniques.

Nefertiti, on the strength of this one piece, is now widely recognized as an international, timeless beauty:

The portraits of other queens of romance, such as Cleopatra and Mary of Scotland, are apt to leave one wondering where the charm came in about which all men raved, but no one could question for a moment the beauty of Nefertiti. Features of exquisite modelling and delicacy, the long graceful neck of an Italian princess of the Renaissance, and an expression of gentleness not untouched with melancholy, make up the presentation of a royal lady about whom we should like to know a great deal and actually know almost nothing.[20]

Everyone accepts that beauty is a highly subjective concept, and that features which appear beautiful to one race or generation may not have any appeal to others. Undoubtedly, the fact that this image of Nefertiti fits well into a westernized ideal of beauty, her pale skin, slender neck and delicate bone structure occasionally leading to comparisons with the late, and undeniably beautiful, Audrey Hepburn, has added to her public appeal. Several writers have attempted to explain the impact of the bust on those seeing it for the first time. Julia Samson, for example, has described watching visitors approach Nefertiti:

All are held in wonderment, spellbound by its appearance; some immobilized longer than others; some returning not once, but again and again, almost unbelievingly.[21]

Personal experience suggests that others, less well informed, may be faintly disappointed as they view the queen for the first time. They do not expect to find the left eye missing; most modern reproductions either make good the defect, or show the queen in profile. Nor do they quite expect the stark symmetry of the queen's face. Few of us are blessed with absolutely symmetrical features but Nefertiti, in the form of her bust, has been, and this contributes to her perfect but remote and faintly inhuman appearance.[22] To Borchardt this symmetry endows Nefertiti with an aura of peace, making her 'the epitome of tranquillity and harmony'.[23] To Camille Paglia, who uses Nefertiti's name and image in the title of her exploration of the continuity of western culture through art, Nefertiti in the form of her bust appears beautiful but streamlined, severe and untouchable:

As we have it the bust of Nefertiti is artistically and ritualistically complete, exalted, harsh and alien . . . This is the least consoling of great art works. Its popularity is based on misunderstanding and suppression of its unique features. The proper response to the Nefertiti bust is fear.[24]

Nefertiti herself would probably have approved.

Historical Events

	LOCAL CHRONOLOGY	EGYPT
3000	Archaic Period (Dynasties 1–2)	Unification of Egypt
2500	Old Kingdom (Dynasties 3–6)	Djoser step-pyramid at Sakkara Great Pyramid of Khufu at Giza
2000	First Intermediate Period (Dynasties 7–11)	
	Middle Kingdom (Dynasties 11–13)	Theban kings re-unify Egypt
1500	Second Intermediate Period (Dynasties 14–17)	Hyksos kings in Northern Egypt
	New Kingdom (Dynasties 18–20)	Amarna Period Ramesses II
1000	Third Intermediate Period (Dynasties 21–25)	Kings at Tanis Nubian kings
500	Late Period (Dynasties 26–31)	
	Ptolemaic Period	Egypt part of Roman Empire

A.D. 1

Notes

Introduction

1 Description of Nefertiti from the tomb of Apy; Davies, N. de G. (1906), *The Rock Tombs of el-Amarna*, vol. 4, London: 19–20.

2 Breasted, J. H. (1924), Ikhnaton, The Religious Revolutionary, *The Cambridge Ancient History*, vol. 2, Cambridge: 109.

3 The modern myths and legends surrounding Akhenaten are fully explored in Monserrat, D. (2000), *Akhenaten; history, fantasy and ancient Egypt*, London.

4 Desroches-Noblecourt, C. (1963), *Tutankhamen: life and death of a pharaoh*, London: 75.

5 Velikovsky, I. (1960), *Oedipus and Akhnaton*, New York: 201.

6 Weigall, A. (1922), *The Life and Times of Akhenaton*, London: 44.

7 Buttles, J. (1908), *The Queens of Egypt*, London: 131–6.

Chapter 1   The Imperial Family

1 From the legend of the divine birth of Amenhotep III as recorded on the walls of the Luxor Temple. For a full translation of this text consult Davies, B. G. (1992), *Egyptian Historical Records of the Later Eighteenth Dynasty*, fascicule 4, Warminster: 28–31.

2 The conception of Amenhotep III. See Davies, *Egyptian Historical Records of the Later Eighteenth Dynasty*, fascicule 4: 28–31.

3 During the 18th Dynasty it was believed that the sphinx was a representation of the sun god Re-Harakhty.

4 Smith, G. E. (1912), *The Royal Mummies*, Catalogue Général des Antiquités Egyptiennes du Musée du Caire, Cairo: 42–6.

5 Amarna Letter 19. For a full translation and commentary on this and all other Amarna letters consult Moran, W. L. (1992), *The Amarna Letters*, Baltimore and London.

6   Mortuary temple stela of Amenhotep III. Translated in Davies, *Egyptian Historical Records of the Later Eighteenth Dynasty*, fascicule 4: 1–5.

7   We know that the marriage was celebrated before Year 2 as one of Amenhotep's hunting scarabs, dated to that year, includes the name of the queen. It is highly unlikely that Tiy was younger than ten years of age as Egyptian girls were not usually married before they reached puberty.

8   For a full translation of this and other Amenhotep III scarabs consult Blankenberg-van Delden, C. (1969), *The Large Commemorative Scarabs of Amenhotep III*, Leiden.

9   As suggested by Maspero in Davis, T. M. *et al.* (1910), *The Tomb of Queen Tiyi*, London: xv. A parallel may perhaps be drawn with the marriage of Prince Charles and Lady Diana Spencer in 1981; the future Princess of Wales may have been technically a commoner, but she was certainly not of 'mediocre extraction'.

10   Aldred, C. (1957), The end of the el-Amarna period, *Journal of Egyptian Archaeology* 43: 30–41: 35.

11   It is now recognized that the name Yuya does not bear any resemblance to known Asiatic names of the period.

12   The opinions of Petrie and Budge are quoted and discussed in Davis, T. M. (1907), *The Tomb of Iouiya and Touiyou*, London: xviii–xxi.

13   Simon, V. S. (1984), Tiye: Nubian queen of Egypt, in I. van Sertima (ed.), *Black Women in Antiquity, Journal of African Civilizations* 6:1: 56–63.

14   For a discussion of 'race' in ancient Egypt consult Baird, K. A. (1996), Ancient Egyptians and the issue of race, in Lefkowitz, M. R. and Rogers, G. M. (eds), *Black Athena Revisited*, Chapel Hill and London: 103–11.

15   Davis, *The Tomb of Iouiya and Touiyou*: xxviii. See the commentary on Davis's text given by Dennis Forbes in Forbes, D. C. (1991), Finding pharaoh's in-laws, *Amarna Letters* 1, 4–14.

16   Osiris beds were a physical manifestation of the re-creative powers of Osiris, god of the underworld. A seed bed in the shape of the god was planted so that it would sprout with life in the same way that the god himself was reborn after death.

17   Discussed in Troy, L. (1986), *Patterns of Queenship in Ancient Egyptian Myth and History*, Uppsala: 86.

18   The Epigraphic Survey (1980), *The Tomb of Kheruef*, Chicago: 42.

19   Buttles, J. (1908), *The Queens of Egypt*, London.

20   Aldred, C. (1980), *Egyptian Art*, London: 170.

21   Scott, N. (1957), Amun-Hotpe the magnificent, *Bulletin of the Metropolitan Museum of Art*, 15.6: 149.

22   Amarna Letter EA 4.

23   Amarna Letter EA 1.

24   See Blankenberg-van Delden, *The Large Commemorative Scarabs of Amen-hotep III*, 18, 129–33. Schulman discusses this scarab together with all the evidence for Amenhotep's diplomatic marriages in Schulman, A. R. (1979), Diplomatic marriage in the Egyptian New Kingdom, *Journal of Near Eastern Studies* 38: 177–93.

25   Amarna Letter EA 29.

26   Amarna Letter EA 22.

27   Amarna Letter EA 17.

28   Davis, *The Tomb of Iouiya and Touiyou*: 37–41.

29   The Epigraphic Survey, *The Tomb of Kheruef*: 43. For a description of Amenhotep's festivals consult Kemp, B. J. (1989), *Ancient Egypt: anatomy of a civilization*, London: 213–17.

30   Davies, *Egyptian Historical Records of the Later Eighteenth Dynasty*, fascicule 4: 36.

31   For a description of the site, its history and its inscribed material see Hayes, W. C. (1951), Inscriptions from the Palace of Amenhotep III, *Journal of Near Eastern Studies* 10: 35–40, 82–104, 156–83, 231–42.

32   For a comprehensive review of the later sculpture of Amenhotep III consult Johnson, W. R. (1996), Amenhotep III and Amarna: some new considerations, *Journal of Egyptian Archaeology* 82: 65–82.

33   Steindorff, G. and Seele, K. C. (1957), *When Egypt Ruled the East*, Chicago: 79; for the publication of this stela see Griffiths, F. Ll (1926), Stela in honour of Amenhotep III and Taya from Tell el-Amarnah, *Journal of Egyptian Archaeology* 12: 1–2.

34   Baikie, J. (1926), *The Amarna Age: a study of the crisis of the ancient world*, London.

35   Some believe that the fact that both kings were depicted in this kind of garment is intended to convey a specific meaning; consult Sourouzian, H. (1994), Inventaire iconographique des statues en manteau jubilaire de l'époque thinite jusqu'à leur disparition sous Amenhotep III, in C. Berger *et al.*, *Hommages à Jean Leclant I*, Paris.

36   Velikovsky, I. (1960), *Oedipus and Akhnaton*, New York: 48–9. Velikovsky is the strongest proponent of the idea that Amenhotep was now a bisexual cross-dresser, as this fits well with his theory linking Amenhotep IV with the legend of Oedipus.

37   Baikie, *The Amarna Age*: 236.

38   Amarna Letter EA 23. W. L. Moran, *The Amarna Letters*: 61–2, believes that the statue of the goddess was sent to Egypt not to cure the ailing king

but so that she could be present as a religious symbol at his marriage to
Tadukhepa.

39   Amarna Letter EA 59. Tunip was never an official vassal of Egypt and
     could more properly have expected to receive protection from Mitanni.

40   For a full description of the mummified remains of 'Amenhotep III' see
     Smith, G. E. (1912), *The Royal Mummies*, Catalogue Général des Antiquités
     Egyptiennes du Musée du Caire, Cairo: 46–51.

41   See Wente, E. F. and Harris, J. E. (1992), Royal Mummies of the 18th
     Dynasty, in Reeves, C. N. (ed.), *After Tutankhamun: research and excavation
     in the royal necropolis at Thebes*, London and New York: 2–20.

Chapter 2   A Beautiful Woman Has Come

1   Text taken from the colonnade of the 'Mansion of the *Benben*-Stone',
     Karnak. Translated in Redford, D. B. (1984), *Akhenaten: the heretic king*,
     Princeton: 77.

2   See for example Redford, *Akhenaten: the heretic king*: 57: 'It may well be
     that he [Amenhotep] was kept in the background because of a congenital
     ailment which made him hideous to behold.'

3   Dodson, A. (1990), Crown Prince Djhutmose and the royal sons of the Eight-
     eenth Dynasty, *Journal of Egyptian Archaeology* 76: 87–96. See also Dodson, A.
     (1991), Two who might have been king, *Amarna Letters* 1: 26–30.

4   Davis, T. M. (1907), *The Tomb of Iouiya and Touiyou*, London.

5   See for example Petrie, W. M. F. (1894), *Tell el Amarna*, London: 38ff.

6   Redford has given a detailed account of all the evidence presented in
     favour of a joint reign. Consult Redford, D. B. (1967), Amenhotep III
     and Akhenaten, *History and Chronology of the Eighteenth Dynasty of Egypt:
     seven studies*, Toronto: 88–169.

7   Amarna Letter EA 26.

8   The question of Nefertiti's parentage is discussed in Seele, K. C. (1955),
     King Ay and the close of the Amarna Age, *Journal of Near Eastern Studies*
     14: 168–80, and in Aldred, C. (1957), The end of the el-Amarna period,
     Journal of Egyptian Archaeology 43: 30–41. These two experts employ the
     same evidence but draw different conclusions.

9   The suggestion that the two women could be Tey and Nefertiti was first
     made by Christiane Desroches-Noblecourt and accepted by Julia Samson:
     see Desroches-Noblecourt, C. (1978), Une exceptionnelle décoration
     pour 'la nourrice qui devint reine', *La Revue du Louvre et des Musées de*

France 28: 20–27; Samson, J. (1985, revised 1990), *Nefertiti and Cleopatra: queen-monarchs of ancient Egypt*, London: 57–8. The equally plausible suggestion that they may in fact be Nefertiti and Meritaten is made by Dorothea Arnold in Arnold, D. (ed.) (1996), *The Royal Women of Amarna: images of beauty from ancient Egypt*, New York: 91–3.

10 The suggestion that 'God's Father' should be translated as 'King's father-in-law' was first made by L. Borchardt (1905), Der Ägyptische Titel 'Vater des Gottes' als Bezeichnung für 'Vater oder Schwiegervater des Königs', *Berichte über die Verhandlungen*, Leipzig: 254.

11 For a review of all the evidence for Mutnodjmet at Amarna consult Hari, R. (1964), *Horemheb et la Reine Moutnedjemet*, Geneva.

12 As suggested by Aldred, The end of the el-Amarna period, *JEA* 43: 30–41, 39.

13 Davies, N. de G. (1908), *The Rock Tombs of el-Amarna*, vol. 6: *Tombs of Parennefer, Tutu and Ay*, London: 21.

14 Now housed in the Petrie Museum, London.

15 Davies, N. de G. (1923), Akhenaten at Thebes, *Journal of Egyptian Archaeology* 9: 136–45.

16 For the history of the Nubian-style wig, consult Aldred, C. (1957), Hair styles and history, *Bulletin of the Metropolitan Museum of Art*, 15.6: 141–8; Eaton-Krauss, M. (1981), Miscellanea Amarnensia, *Chronique d'Egypte* 56: 245–64.

17 Petrie, W. M. F. (1931), *Seventy Years in Archaeology*, London: 138–9.

18 Extract from the second Amarna boundary stela, translation adapted from Davies, B. G. (1995), *Egyptian Historical Records of the Later Eighteenth Dynasty*, fascicule 6, Warminster: 12.

19 See Ray, J. D. (1985), Review article of Redford's Akhenaten, *Göttinger Miszellen* 86: 81–93. Ray suggests that Akhenaten may have been celebrating his thirtieth birthday. This would, however, make the king older at the time of his accession than is generally supposed.

20 The origins of the word *talatat* in this context are obscure, although it may be derived from the Arabic word for three, referring to the fact that the blocks are three hand-spans long.

21 The work of the Akhenaten Temple Project is described in detail in Smith, R. W. and Redford, D. B. (1976), *The Akhenaten Temple Project*, Warminster. See also Smith, R. W. (1970), Computer helps scholars re-create an Egyptian temple, *National Geographic* 138: 5: 634–55. Younger readers will be amused to find that Smith's 'space-age' computer employed punch cards and magnetic tape.

22 Figures taken from Smith and Redford, *The Akhenaten Temple Project*: 78.

NEFERTITI

200

23 Ibid. 34.

24 See Cooney, J. D. (1965), *Amarna Reliefs from Hermopolis in American Collections*, Brooklyn.

25 Consult Hall, E. S. (1986), *The Pharaoh Smites His Enemies*, Berlin: 4.

26 For a discussion of this crown consult Samson, J. (1973), Amarna crowns and wigs, *Journal of Egyptian Archaeology* 59: 47–59; Green, L. (1992), Queen as Goddess, the religious role of royal women in the late-eighteenth dynasty, *Amarna Letters 2*: 28–41.

27 Discussed with references in Arnold, *The Royal Women of Amarna*: 107–8.

28 Some *Hwt-Benben* blocks display the shorter form of her name carved deeply and on a large scale beside the longer name which, scratched lightly and at a smaller scale, appears to have been added as an afterthought by the mason. For a discussion of the development of Nefertiti's name, see Samson, J. (1976), Royal Names in Amarna, *Chronique d'Egypte* 51: 30–38.

Chapter 3   The Aten Dazzles

1 From the Great Hymn to the Aten, preserved in the tomb of Ay at Amarna. For a full translation see chapter text.

2 Johnson, W. R. (1993), The Deified Amenhotep III as the living Re-Herakhty; stylistic and iconographic considerations, *Sesto Congresso Internazionale de Egittologia*, vol. 2, Turin: 231–6.

3 Discussed in Johnson, W. R. (1996), Amenhotep III and Amarna: some new considerations, *Journal of Egyptian Archaeology* 82: 65–82.

4 From the divine conception of Hatchepsut carved on the wall of the Deir el-Bahri mortuary temple. Consult Sethe, K. and Helck, W. (1906–58), *Urkunden des 18. Dynastie*, Leipzig and Berlin, 4.219, 13–220, 6; Breasted, J. H. (1988), *Ancient Records of Egypt*, 2nd edition, vol. 2, part 2, Chicago: 187–212.

5 Redford, D. B. (1981), *Bulletin of the Egyptological Seminar of New York* 3: 87ff.

6 Amarna boundary stela. For a full translation of this text consult Davies, B. G. (1995), *Egyptian Historical Records of the Later Eighteenth Dynasty*, fascicule 6, Warminster: 9.

7 Androgyny and creation is discussed in detail in Troy, L. (1986), *Patterns of Queenship in Ancient Egyptian Myth and History*, Uppsala: 1.2.

8 Even Hatchepsut, whose lack of a husband and son allowed her to step

outside the traditional queen's role, acted as she did in order to preserve her dynasty. Consult Tyldesley, J. A. (1996), *Hatchepsut: the female pharaoh*, London.

9   Inscription from the Amarna tomb of Panehesy. For a full publication of this tomb consult Davies, N. de G. (1905), *The Rock Tombs of el-Amarna*, vol. 2, London. Davies's footnote to the quoted text (p. 31) reads: 'It will be noticed that these court favours, although in the gift of the king, would largely depend upon the goodwill of the queen.'

10 Davies, N. de G. (1905), *The Rock Tombs of el-Amarna*, vol. 3, London: 18.

11 Consult Ikram, S. (1989), Domestic shrines and the cult of the royal family, *Journal of Egyptian Archaeology* 75: 89–101.

12 As discussed in Arnold, D. (ed.) (1996), *The Royal Women of Amarna: images of beauty from ancient Egypt*, New York: 100. The garden shrines associated with the private houses were believed by their original excavators to be birth bowers.

13 See Silverman, D. P. (1982), Wit and Humour, *Egypt's Golden Age*, Boston Museum, Boston: 277–81.

14 Woolley, C. L. (1922), Excavations at Tell el-Amarna, *Journal of Egyptian Archaeology* 8: 48–81.

15 Kemp, B. J. (1979), Wall paintings from the workmen's village at el-Amarna, *Journal of Egyptian Archaeology* 65: 47–53.

16 For a discussion of the role of Bes at Amarna consult Bosse-Griffiths, K. (1977), A Beset Amulet from the Amarna Period, *Journal of Egyptian Archaeology* 63: 98–106.

17 Weigall, A. (1922), *The Life and Times of Akhenaton*, revised edition, London: 136.

18 Aldred, C. (1968), *Akhenaten, Pharaoh of Egypt: A New Study*, London: 189.

19 This interpretation of the Great Hymn to the Aten is based on a translation suggested by Steven Snape. Many versions of this hymn have been published, some literal, others more lyrical. See, for example, Gardiner, A. (1961), *Egypt of the Pharaohs*, Oxford: 225–7; Lichtheim, M. (1976), *Ancient Egyptian Literature II: the New Kingdom*, Los Angeles: 96–100; Simpson, W. K. (ed.) (1973), *The Literature of Ancient Egypt*, New Haven and London: 289–95.

20 Translation given in Martin, G. T. (1986), Shabtis of private persons in the Amarna Period, *Mitteilungen der Deutschen Archäologischen Instituts Abteilung Kairo* 42: 109–29.

21 Weigall, *The Life and Times of Akhenaton*: 166.

22 Samson, J. (1985, revised 1990), *Nefertiti and Cleopatra: queen-monarchs of ancient Egypt*, London: 27.

23 Redford, D. B. (1984), *Akhenaten: the heretic king*, Princeton: 235.

24 Davies, N. de G. (1923), Akhenaten at Thebes, *Journal of Egyptian Archaeology* 23: 132–52: 150.

Chapter 4   Images of Amarna

1   Extract from the rock stela of father and son sculptors Men and Bak, at Aswan. For a full translation of this stela consult Davies, B. G. (1994), *Egyptian Historical Records of the Later Eighteenth Dynasty*, fascicule 5, Warminster: 71.

2   Weigall, A. (1922), *The Life and Times of Akhenaton*, London: 51–2.

3   Gardiner, A. (1961), *Egypt of the Pharaohs*, Oxford: 214.

4   Grimal, N., *A History of Egypt*, translated by I. Shaw (1992), Oxford: 233.

5   Aldred, C. (1973), *Akhenaten and Nefertiti*, London: 11.

6   The more louche of Amenhotep's representations may well have been carved some time after his death.

7   Petrie, W. M. F. (1894), *Tell el Amarna*, London: 38.

8   Ibid.: 39.

9   This is the solution considered by Aldred in Aldred, C. (1968), *Akhenaten: Pharaoh of Egypt: A New Study*, London: 133–9.

10 Samson, J. (1985, revised 1990), *Nefertiti and Cleopatra: queen-monarchs of ancient Egypt*, London: 22.

11 See, for example, Samson, J. (1972), *Amarna, City of Akhenaten and Nefertiti*, London: 23. The fact that Mrs Samson has had the courage to reconsider her published opinion does not, of course, make her revised views invalid, and she is certainly not the only egyptologist to interpret the piece as Nefertiti. See, for example, Reeves, C. N. (1990), *The Complete Tutankhamun: the king, the tomb, the royal treasure*, London: 19.

12 The role of 'God's Wife' and 'God's Hand' is briefly discussed in Robins, G. (1993), *Women in Ancient Egypt*, London: 152ff.

13 See, for example, Aldred, C. (1980), *Egyptian Art*, London: 182: 'She [Nefertiti] is shown in relief and in the round as a woman of great allure, according to the Oriental ideal of voluptuousness . . .'

14 The changes in Nefertiti's appearance are discussed in Arnold, D. (ed.) (1996), *The Royal Women of Amarna: images of beauty from ancient Egypt*, New York: 38ff.

15 For a simple description of the revised canon of proportions during this
     reign consult Robins, G. (1986), *Egyptian Painting and Relief*, Princes
     Risborough: 43–52.
16 Arnold, *The Royal Women of Amarna*: 56.

Chapter 5   Horizon of the Aten

1   This extract, and all subsequent extracts from the Amarna boundary stelae,
     is based on the translation given in Davies, N. de G. (1908a), *The Rock
     Tombs of el-Amarna*, vol. 5, London: 28–34. For a more modern translation
     consult Davies, B. G. (1995), *Egyptian Historical Records of the Later Eigh-
     teenth Dynasty*, fascicule 5, Warminster: 5–13.
2   As suggested by Cyril Aldred, in Aldred, C. (1976), The Horizon of the
     Aten, *Journal of Egyptian Archaeology* 62: 184.
3   Davies, *The Rock Tombs of el-Amarna*, vol. 5: 30.
4   I am here making the assumption that the Middle Kingdom capital,
     Itj-Tawi, was a suburb of Memphis.
5   Estimate given by Barry Kemp; see Kemp, B. J. (1989), *Ancient Egypt:
     anatomy of a civilization*, London: 269. Estimates of the population of the
     city vary between 20,000 and 50,000.
6   Davies, *The Rock Tombs of el-Amarna*, vol. 5: 26.
7   Discussed in Redford, D. B. (1984), *Akhenaten: the heretic king*, Princeton:
     142.
8   Petrie, W. M. F. (1894), *Tell el Amarna*, London: 1.
9   See, for example, M. Mallinson's comments on the replacement of brick
     by stone at the Small Temple of Aten, in Kemp, B. J. (ed.) (1989), *Amarna
     Reports 5*, London, 115–42; 138.
10 Discussed in Kemp, B. J. (1977), The city of Amarna as a source for the
     study of urban society in ancient Egypt, *World Archaeology* 9:2: 123–39.
11 Riefstahl, E. (1964), *Thebes in the time of Amunhotep III*, Oklahoma: 189.
12 Davies, N. de G. (1906), *The Rock Tombs of el-Amarna*, vol. 4, London:
     16. Davies's interpretation of the scene differs slightly from my own: 'The
     queen, regardless of the situation, seems to pester the king with talk,
     though his whole thought is given to the management of his steeds.'
13 Whittemore, T. (1926), The Excavations at El-Amarnah, Season 1924–
     5, *Journal of Egyptian Archaeology* 12: 3–12.
14 Ibid.: 6.
15 As we have good reason to believe that the Window of Appearance may

have been a part of the King's House, rather than the Great Palace, the women's quarters here depicted may well have been a part of the House. However, it is apparent that the ancient artists were not averse to combining elements of separate buildings for greater artistic effect. For the mention of eunuchs see Davies, N. de G. (1908b), *The Rock Tombs of el-Amarna*, vol. 6, London: 20.

16 Discussed in Tyldesley, J. A. (1994), *Daughters of Isis: women of ancient Egypt*, London: 130.

17 See, for example, Manniche, L. (1991), Music at the court of the Aten, *Amarna Letters* 1, 62–5: 65: 'It is possible that invisible essence (sound) emanating from the tangible object (the musician or his instrument) was interpreted as symbolic of the immaterial substance transferred to the deity [the Aten] from the actual food offerings presented in the temple or palace.'

18 Sandman, M. (1938), *Texts from the time of Akhenaten*, Brussels: 13:II.9–13.

19 See Kemp, B. J. (1976), The Window of Appearance at el-Amarna and the basic structure of this city, *Journal of Egyptian Archaeology* 62: 81–99.

20 Petrie, W. M. F. (1931), *Seventy Years in Archaeology*, London: 138.

21 This is discussed with references to the various accounts in Kemp, B. J. and Garfi, S. (1993), *A Survey of the Ancient City of El-Amarna*, London: 58.

22 For a reference to the Heliopolis *benben* consult Habachi, L. (1971), *Beitrage zur Ägyptischen Bauforschung und Altertumskunde* 12, 42: fig. 20. Davies illustrates and describes the Panehesy stone in Davies, N. de G. (1905), *The Rock Tombs of el-Amarna*, vol. 2, London: 24, Plate XIX.

23 Petrie, *Tell el Amarna*: 18.

24 Discussed and reproduced in Shaw, I. (1994), Balustrades, stairs and altars in the cult of the Aten at al-Amarna, *Journal of Egyptian Archaeology* 80: 109–27: 119. Shaw gives earlier references to this piece.

25 The history of this building is discussed in Badawy, A. (1956), Maru-Aten: pleasure resort or temple?, *Journal of Egyptian Archaeology* 42: 58–64.

26 For references to Kiya consult Harris, J. R. (1974), Kiya, *Chronique d'Egypte* 49: 25–30; Eaton-Krauss, M. (1981), Miscellanea Amarnensia, *Chronique d'Egypte* 56: 245–64: 2; Reeves, C. N. (1988), New Light on Kiya from texts in the British Museum, *Journal of Egyptian Archaeology* 74: 91–101.

27 Suggestion put forward in Redford, D. B. (1984), *Akhenaten: the heretic king*, Princeton: 150.

28 Suggestion made in Manniche, L. (1975), The wife of Bata, *Göttinger Miszellen* 18: 33–8. For a translation of this story consult Lichtheim, M.

(1976), *Ancient Egyptian Literature 2: The New Kingdom*, Los Angeles: 203–11.

29 A relief in the Ny Carlsberg Glyptotek, Copenhagen, shows Kiya apparently standing before an offering table, a role usually taken by a priest.

30 There is no absolute proof that this village was the home of the labourers who worked on the Amarna tombs, although a comparison with the Theban workmen's village of Deir el-Medina makes this seem very likely. There is, however, an unexcavated village further to the east which may have housed the workers involved on the royal tomb. For a discussion of all aspects of the excavation of the workmen's village see Kemp, B. J. (ed.) (1984, 1985, 1986, 1987), *Amarna Reports 1–4*, London: 1.

31 'This material, as well as paintings of Bes and Thoeris [Taweret] in other houses in the village, point to the importance placed on womanhood and childbirth in New Kingdom society, including that of the Amarna workmen's village.' Kemp, B. J. (ed.) (1986), *Amarna Reports 3*, London: 25.

32 For the history of and further references to the Amarna chapels consult Bomann, A. P. (1991), *The Private Chapel in Ancient Egypt*, London.

33 Gardiner, A. (1961), *Egypt of the Pharaohs*, Oxford: 223.

34 Davies, *The Rock Tombs of el-Amarna*, vol. 5: 4.

35 Davies, N. de G. (1908b), *The Rock Tombs of el-Amarna*, vol. 6, London: 10.

36 Ibid.: Plate IV.

37 Discussed in Arnold, D. (ed.) (1996), *The Royal Women of Amarna: images of beauty from ancient Egypt*, New York: 28.

38 Beketaten and the Huya scenes, and their importance with regard to a proposed Amenhotep III–Akhenaten co-regency, are discussed in Redford, D. B. (1967), *History and Chronology of the Eighteenth Dynasty of Egypt: seven studies*, Toronto: 105–9.

39 Discussed in Gabolde, M. (1992), Baketaten fille de Kiya?, *Bulletin de la Société d'Egyptologie Genève* 16: 27–40.

40 Velikovsky, I. (1960), *Oedipus and Akhnaton*, New York: 101. Velikovsky, wishing to promote the equation of Akhenaten with Oedipus, had to make Tiy into a knowing Jocasta. Believing Tiy to be of foreign extraction, he speculates that 'the kings of Mitanni, being worshippers of the Indo-Iranian gods, must have regarded incest between mother and son as not only a pardonable relation but a holy union.'

Chapter 6   Queen, King or Goddess?

1 Inscription engraved on the foot-end of the coffin recovered from tomb
KV 55. Translation based on that of Sir Alan Gardiner, cited in Gardiner,
A. (1957), The so-called tomb of Queen Tiye, *Journal of Egyptian Archaeology* 43: 10–25: 19.

2 Maspero, G. (1912), in Gauthier, H. (ed.) *Livre des Rois II*, Cairo: 344:2.
The quotation is taken from Samson, J. (1985 revised 1990), *Nefertiti and
Cleopatra*, London: 22.

3 Robins, G. (1986), *Egyptian Paintings and Reliefs*, Princes Risborough: 50.

4 Discussed in detail in Harris, J. R. (1973), Nefertiti Redivia, *Acta Orientalia*
35: 5–13. See also Tawfik, S. (1975), Aten studies, *Mitteilungen des
Deutschen Archäologischen Instituts Abteilung Kairo* 31: 159–168.

5 It is just possible that we have a second representation of Nefertiti wearing
this crown in the tomb of Ay. Both scenes are illustrated and discussed in
Ertman, E. L. (1992), Is there visual evidence for a 'king' Nefertiti?,
Amarna Letters 2; 50–55.

6 Described in Martin, G. T. *The Royal Tomb at el-Amarna I: the objects*,
London: section A.

7 For a discussion of Tutankhamen's sarcophagus consult Eaton-Krauss, M.
(1993), *The Sarcophagus in the Tomb of Tutankhamen*, Oxford. The canopic
canopy is discussed in Robins, G. (1984), Isis, Nephthys, Selket and Neith
represented on the sarcophagus of Tutankhamun and in four free-standing
statues found in KV 62, *Göttinger Miszellen* 72: 21–5.

8 See, for example, Green, L. (1992), Queen as Goddess: the religious role
of royal women in the late-eighteenth dynasty, *Amarna Letters I*: 28–41.

Chapter 7   Sunset

1 Amarna Letter EA 16, written by the king of Assyria. For a full translation
of this and other letters consult Moran, W. L. (1992), *The Amarna Letters*,
Baltimore: 38–41.

2 See El-Khouly, A. and Martin, G. T (1984), *Excavations in the Royal
Necropolis at El-Amarna*, Cairo: 8, 16.

3 Loeben, C. E. (1986), Eine Bestrattung der grossen Königlichen Gemahlin
Nofretete in Amarna, *Mitteilungen des Deutschen Archäologischen Instituts*

Abteilung Kairo 42: 99–107. Aldred suggests that the shabti would have been inscribed during the embalming period; if he is correct, it would indicate that Nefertiti had indeed died at Amarna. See Aldred, C. (1988), *Akhenaten King of Egypt*, London: 229.

4   Pendlebury, J. (1935), *Tell el-Amarna*, London: 28–9. For other references to Nefertiti's 'disgrace' see Seele, K. C. (1955), King Ay and the close of the Amarna Age, *Journal of Near Eastern Studies* 14: 168–180.

5   Davies, N. de G. (1923), Akhenaten at Thebes, *Journal of Egyptian Archaeology* 9: 132–152: 133.

6   Baikie, J. (1926), *The Amarna Age; a study of the crisis of the ancient world*, London: 281.

7   Consult Harris, J. (1973), Nefernefruaten, *Göttinger Miszellen* 4: 15–17; (1973), Nefertiti Rediviva, *Acta Orientalia* 35: 5–13; (1974), Nefernefruaten Regnans, *Acta Orientalia* 36: 11–21. See also the work of Perepelkin, Y. Y. (1967), *Perevorot Amen-Hotpa IV*, i, Moscow: sect 87; idem (1968), *Taina Zolotogo groba*, translated as *The Secret of the Golden Coffin*, 120.

8   For a modern description of the opening of this tomb see Romer, J. (1981), *Valley of the Kings*, London: 211–220. See also Reeves' introduction to the re-publication of Davis' 1910 report, in Davis, T. M. *et al* (1990), *The Tomb of Queen Tiyi*, San Francisco. For further references to the opening of the tomb see Gardiner, A. (1957), The so-called tomb of Queen Tiye, *Journal of Egyptian Archaeology* 43:10–25.

9   Aldred, C. (1988), *Akhenaten, king of Egypt*, London: 195.

10 Quoted in Gardiner, A. (1957), *op. cit.*: 25.

11 Most experts are agreed that the gold mask had been torn off the coffin in antiquity, but see the comment in el Mahdy, C. (1999), *Tutankhamen; life and death of a boy king*, London: 45, that 'the few surviving photographs of the coffin within the tomb show that at the time of discovery the face was made of gold . . . later when the coffin lid arrived in Cairo, the golden face was missing . . .' This would not be the only gold from KV 55 to go missing post-discovery, but the photograph published by Davis of the coffin lying in situ (*op. cit* Plate XXX) shows a mummy whose face has been ripped away. Davis's text (2), tells us that 'on the floor . . . lay the coffin made of wood, but entirely covered with gold foil and inlaid with semi-precious stones . . .'. In contrast, the catalogue of finds compiled by George Daressy and published in the same volume mentions (16) 'The face was covered by a gold mask . . . Of this the lower part is missing from below the eyes.'

12 Krauss, R. (1986), Kija – ursprüngliche Besitzerin der Kanopen aus KV 55, *Mitteilungen des Deutschen Archäologischen Instituts Abteilung Kairo* 42: 67–80.

13   Lucas, A. (1931), The canopic vases from the 'tomb of Queen Tiyi',
     Annales du Services des Antiquités: 120–122.

14   Gardiner, A. (1957), *op. cit.*

15   Translation given in Allen, J. P. (1988), Two altered inscriptions of the
     Late Amarna Period, *Journal of the American Research Center in Egypt* 25:
     117–126.

16   Davis, T. M. *et al.* (1910), *The Tomb of Queen Tiyi*, London: 2.

17   Tyndale, W. (1907), *Below the Cataracts*, London.

18   Weigall, A. (1922), The Mummy of Akhenaton, *Journal of Egyptian Archae-
     ology* 8: 193–200: 194.

19   G. Elliot Smith, writing in Davis, T. M. *et al.* (1910), *op. cit.*: xxiv.

20   Smith, G. E. (1912), *The Royal Mummies*, Cairo: 51–56.

21   Weigall, A. (1922), *The Life and Times of Akhnaton: pharaoh of Egypt* (revised
     edition), London: xxii.

22   Derry, D. E. in Engelbach, R. (1931), The so-called coffin of Akhenaten,
     Annales du Service des Antiquités 31: 98–114, 116.

23   Harrison, R. G. (1966), An anatomical examination of the pharaonic
     remains purported to be Akhenaten, *Journal of Egyptian Archaeology* 52: 95–
     119. Connoley, R. C., Harrison R. G. & Ahmed, S. (1976), Serological
     evidence for the parentage of Tutankhamun and Smenkhkare, *Journal of
     Egyptian Archaeology* 62: 184–6. See also Costa, P. (1978), The frontal
     sinuses of the remains purported to be Akhenaten, *Journal of Egyptian
     Archaeology* 64: 76–9.

24   Wente, E. F. and Harris, J. E. (1992), Royal Mummies of the Eighteenth
     Dynasty, in C. N. Reeves (ed.) *After Tutankhamun: research and excavation
     in the royal necropolis at Thebes*, London and New York, 2–20.

25   Filer, J. M. (2002), Anatomy of a Mummy, *Archaeology* March/April 2002,
     26–9. See also the discussion of this analysis in J. Tyldesley (2000), *Private
     Lives of the Pharaohs*, London, Study 2.

26   Discussed in Ray, J. (1975), The parentage of Tutankhamun, *Antiquity*
     49: 45–7.

27   Martin, G. T. (1989), *The Royal Tomb at El-Amarna II*, London: 37–48.

28   Or could the feminine form have been deliberately adopted by Smenkh-
     kare's wife, as suggested in Krauss, R. (1978), *Das Ende de Amarnazeit*,
     Hildesheim?

29   Allen, J. P. (1994), Nefertiti and Smenkh-ka-re, *Göttinger Miszellen* 141:
     7–17: 13. Allen provides a detailed summary of the evidence for and
     against a joint reign.

30   Arnold, D. (1996), *The Royal Women of Amarna: images of beauty from
     ancient Egypt*, New York: 74. Arnold is writing about a brown quartzite

head of Nefertiti, recovered from Memphis but almost certainly created by an artist of the Amarna school.

31 Discussed in Arnold, D. (1996) *op. cit.*: 115.

32 Discussed in Redford, D. B. (1975), Studies on Akhenaten at Thebes II, *Journal of the American Research Center in Egypt* 12, 9–14; Robins, G. (1981), Hmt nsw wrt Meritaten, *Göttinger Miszellen* 52: 75–81.

33 Davies, N. de G. (1905), *The Rock Tombs of el-Amarna* 2, London: 36–45.

34 See discussion in van Dijk, J. and Eaton-Krauss, M. (1986), Tutankhamun and Memphis, *Mitteillungen des Deutschen Archäologischen Instituts Abteilung Kairo* 42: 35–41.

35 Gardiner, A. (1961), *Egypt of the Pharaohs*, Oxford: 236–7.

36 Carter, H. and Mace, A. C. (1923), *The Tomb of Tut-ankh-Amen*, London: 119.

37 These scenes are discussed with further references in Troy, L (1986), *Patterns of Queenship in Ancient Egyptian Myth and History*, Uppsala: 100ff. See also Bosse-Griffiths, K. (1973), The Little Golden Shrine of Tutankhamen, *Journal of Egyptian Archaeology* 59: 100–108.

38 Elliot Smith, G. (1912), *The Royal Mummies*, Cairo: 38.

39 Harris, J. E. *et al.* (1978), Mummy of the 'elder lady' in the tomb of Amunhotep II, *Science* 200:9: 1149–1151.

40 Quoted in Luban, M. (1999), *Do We Have The Mummy of Nefertiti?*, www.geocities.com.

41 Luban, M. (1999) *op. cit.*

42 Fletcher, J. (2004), *The Search for Nefertiti; the true story of a remarkable discovery*, London. The quotation is taken from the cover of the *Sunday Times Magazine* 8th June 2003.

43 See Harrison R. G. *et al* (1979), A Mummified Foetus from the tomb of Tutankhamun, *Antiquity* 53: 19–21.

44 Translation after H. G. Guterbock, as quoted in Schulman, A. R. (1978), Ankhesenamun, Nofretity and the Amka Affair, *Journal of the American Research Center in Egypt* 15: 43–8.

45 Suggestions that Ay had consolidated his claim to the throne by marrying his widowed granddaughter Ankhesenamen are now known to be based on a single piece of doubtful evidence.

46 See Schaden, O. J. (1992), The God's Father Ay, *Amarna Letters* 2, 92–115: 108. Schaden gives a full discussion of Ay's known career.

47 See Hari, R (1965), *Horemheb et la Reine Moutnedjemet*, Geneva.; Hari, R. (1976), La reine d'Horemheb était-elle la soeur de Nefertiti?, *Chronique d'Egypte* 51: 39–46.

Epilogue   The Beautiful Woman Returns

1   Pendlebury, J. D. S. (1935), *Tell el-Amarna*, London: ix.
2   Accounts of the history of the archaeology of Amarna are given in Aldred, C. (1988), *Akhenaten, King of Egypt*, London; Kemp, B. J. and Garfi, S. (1993), *A Survey of the Ancient City of el-Amarna*, London.
3   Jomard, E. (1818), Antiquités de l'Heptanomide, *Déscription de l'Egypte, Antiquités, Déscriptions*, vol. 2, Paris: XVI: 13.
4   Wilkinson, J. G. (1837), *Manners and Customs of the Ancient Egyptians*, London: Plate VI.
5   Edwards, A. B. (1877, revised 1888), *A Thousand Miles up the Nile*, London: 69.
6   Ibid.: 85.
7   Chubb, M. (1954), *Nefertiti Lived Here*, London: 75.
8   Pendlebury, *Tell el-Amarna*: x.
9   Davies, N. de G. (1903), *The Rock Tombs of el-Amarna*, vol. 1, London: 3.
10 Peet, T. E. (1921), Excavations at Tell el-Amarna: a preliminary report, *Journal of Egyptian Archaeology* 7: 169.
11 Letter written by Breasted from Cairo, dated 24 January 1895. Quoted in Larson, J. A. (1992), Other Amarna Letters, *Amarna Letters* 2: 116–25: 124.
12 Published by the Egypt Exploration Society, London.
13 Sayce, A. H. (1990), [Letter from Egypt] Luxor: Feb. 26, 1890, *The Academy* 933: 195. This letter and its subsequent postscript is quoted in full in Martin, G. T. (1989), *The Royal Tomb at El-Amarna 2: the reliefs, inscriptions and architecture*, London: 1.
14 Martin, *The Royal Tomb at El-Amarna 2*.
15 For a full description of this workshop and its contents consult Arnold, D. (ed.) (1996), *The Royal Women of Amarna: images of beauty from ancient Egypt*, New York: 41–83. See also Phillips, J. (1991), Sculpture Ateliers of Akhetaten, *Amarna Letters* 1: 31–40. A second sculptor's workshop, specializing in inlay work and tentatively attributed to 'Ipu' was also excavated by Borchardt.
16 Roeder, G. (1941), Lebensgrosse Tonmodelle aus einer altägyptischen Bildhauerwerkstatt, *Jahrbuch der preussischen Kunstsammlungen* 62:4: 145–70: 154–60.
17 The history of the discovery of the bust is briefly discussed by Wiedemann, H. G. and Bayer, G. (1982), The Bust of Nefertiti, *Analytical Chemistry*

54:4: 619–28. It was also the subject of a television programme presented by Nicholas Ward Jackson for Channel 4, produced by Brian Lapping Associates.

18 For a review of the influence of the Tutankhamen discovery on contemporary society see Frayling, C. F. (1992), *The Face of Tutankhamun*, London.

19 Vandenberg, P. (1978), *Nefertiti: an archaeological biography*, translated by R. Hein, London.

20 Baikie, J. (1926), *The Amarna Age: a study of the crisis of the ancient world*, London: 242–3.

21 Samson, J. (1985, revised 1990), *Nefertiti and Cleopatra: queen-monarchs of ancient Egypt*, London: 7.

22 Discussed in Krauss, R. (1991), Nefertiti – a drawing-board beauty, *Amarna Letters 1*, 47–9.

23 Borchardt, L. (1923), *Porträts der Königin Nofret-ete*, Leipzig: 33.

24 Paglia, C. (1990), *Sexual Personae; art and decadence from Nefertiti to Emily Dickinson*, Yale and London: 68.

Further Reading

Literally hundreds of books and articles of varying degrees of specialization and complexity have been published on the Amarna period. The references listed below include the more basic and accessible publications with preference given to those written in English. All the works listed include bibliographies that will be of interest to those seeking more detailed references on specific subjects. Those seeking further references should also consult the notes on each chapter, and Martin, G. T. (1991), *A Bibliography of the Amarna Period and its Aftermath*, London.

Aldred, C. (1973), *Akhenaten and Nefertiti*, Brooklyn.

Aldred, C. (1988), *Akhenaten, King of Egypt*, London.

Arnold, D. (1996), *The Royal Women of Amarna: Images of Beauty from Ancient Egypt*, New York.

Desroches-Noblecourt, C. (1963), *Tutankhamen: Life and Death of a Pharaoh*, London.

El Mahdy, C. (1999), *Tutankhamen: the Life and Death of a Boy King*, London.

Filer, J. M. (2004), *Health in Ancient Egypt and Nubia: Sources and Issues*, London.

Freed, R. E. et al. (1999), *Pharaohs of the Sun: Akhenaten, Nefertiti, Tutankhamen*, London and Boston.

Kemp. B. J. (1989), *Ancient Egypt: Anatomy of a Civilization*, London.

Kemp, B. J. and Garfi, S. (1993), *A Survey of the Ancient City of El-Amarna*, London.

Monserrat, D. (2000), *Akhenaten: History, Fantasy and Ancient Egypt*, London and New York.

Pendlebury, J. D. S. (1935), *Tell el-Amarna*, London.

Redford, D. B. (1984), *Akhenaten: the Heretic King*, Princeton.

Reeves, C. N. (2001), *Akhenaten, Egypt's False Prophet*, London.

Reeves, C. N. (1990), *The Complete Tutankhamun: the King, the Tomb, the Royal Treasure*, London.

Romer, J. (1981), *Valley of the Kings: Exploring the Tombs of the Pharaohs*, New York.

Samson, J. (1978), *Amarna, city of Akhenaten and Nefertiti: Nefertiti as Pharaoh*, Warminster.

Samson, J. (1985 revised 1990), *Nefertiti and Cleopatra, queen-monarchs of ancient Egypt*, London.

Smith, W. S., revised by W. K. Simpson (1981), *The Art and Architecture of Ancient Egypt*, London.

Thomas, A. P. (1988), *Akhenaten's Egypt*, Aylesbury.

Troy, L. (1986), *Patterns of Queenship in Ancient Egyptian Myth and History*, Uppsala.

Index

(Figures in italics refer to illustrations.)